Building Credible
Multicultural Teams

Cover design by Dan Battermann.

Scripture quotations are from the New Revised Standard Version of the Bible, copyright 1989 by the Division of Christian Education of the National Council of the Churches of Christ in the USA. Used by permission. All rights reserved.

Library of Congress Cataloging-in-Publication Data

Roembke, Lianne.
   [Multikulturelle teams: Risken und Chancen. English]
   Building credible multicultural teams / Lianne Roembke.—1st U.S. ed. p. cm.
   Includes bibliographical references and index.
   ISBN 0-87808-340-5 (pbk. : alk. paper)
      1. Missions. 2. Intercultural communications—Religious aspects—Christianity. 3. Christianity and culture. I. Title.

BV2063 .R5513 2000
266—dc21   00-058607

6 5 4 3 2 1
04 03 02 01 00

Printed in the United States of America

Building Credible Multicultural Teams

Lianne Roembke

William Carey Library
Pasadena, California

What people are saying about *Building Credible Multicultural Teams*:

Thank you so much for your book. I dipped in at once and was fascinated! I want to order several copies, one for each of our WEC home-bases. Our people need this book!

—Dr. Helen Roseveare,
WEC International

I read your book last week with great interest and much profit. Thank you for this enrichment to the worldwide mission movement. I was particularly impressed with your emphaiss on the orientation of the multicultural team to the host country. My compliments for such open, honest words. Thanks for all your hard work.

—Dr. Detlef Blöcher,
Director of the German Missionary Society

I have enjoyed reading your book. Excellent work. As a twenty-two year veteran in Southeast Asia, I can appreciate your great insights.

—Dr. Michael P. McCarty,
Southeast Asia Field Director,
Church of the Nazarene

William Carey Library
P.O. Box 40129
Pasadena, California 91114
inquiries@wclbooks.com
www.wclbooks.com
(626) 798-0819

Contents

List of Illustrations

Preface

Multicultural mission teams have been of particular interest to me even before my first term as a foreign missionary began in 1975. Working in the area of Staff Development and Training for Campus Crusade for Christ, Europe (now *Agape-Europe*) brought me into close contact with many such teams (also many from other mission agencies) in Western Europe as well as in Africa, Asia, the Middle East and Eastern Europe over the years. Experience has shown that there are indeed unique advantages to having a team composed of missionaries from more than one culture and that there are unique problems as well. The issue of how missionaries from various cultures relate together in a team as well as their image in the host culture is not a tangential issue but rather one of profound theological consequence bearing on spiritual vitality and affecting the receptivity of the gospel.

In the eleven years that have gone into this research I have found little written material on the topic of multicultural teams as such; most material has been drawn from the related topics of culture, missions, contextualization, indigenization, teams, personal identity and cultural adaptation. On the contrary, a wealth of information and insights came from the many national and expatriate missionaries from various mission agencies who were eager to answer my questions in personal interviews and written surveys. To them I am indebted and hope this work will lighten their load, enrich their team lives and contribute to removing more of the barriers to a credible communication of the gospel.

My appreciation goes to Professors Klaus Fiedler and Karl Rennstich for their expertise, critique and encouragement in the process of writing the dissertation, which is the basis for this book, to Professor Jan Milic Lochman for getting me started, Professor William Wagner for paving the way in transition to the *Evangelische Theologische Faculteit*.

The leadership of Campus Crusade for Christ, International and Europe are to be thanked for their support and encouragement of this project. I hope it will benefit the ministry for years to come. I owe a great deal to friends and family who supported and encouraged me in many ways through their prayers, words, gifts and advice: to my parents who gave me their blessing to serve the Lord away from the homeland, to my sisters and brother and their families who have encouraged me each step of the way as well as my friends and supporters. A special thanks is due Linda Brown and Christine Goodman-Callison, who corrected drafts of the first manuscript at a time when I was working almost entirely in German. Thanks to David Denyer, Justus Piater, Jürgen Hoffmann-Boesler, and Paul Miller, who helped me understand my computer. The cooperation with Dr. Ralph Winter of William Carey Library was a pleasure.

I would like to dedicate this work to my two friends and cultural guides who kept me going during the eleven years, Christiane Posselt, who, although she did not live to see this work finished, contributed much in reflection on these issues, and Doris Döring, a continual encouragement in word and deed.

To God be the glory.

Introduction

Why is this topic of multicultural mission teams not a peripheral issue in theology? According to Martin Kähler (1908), "Mission is the mother of theology." Theology began "not as a luxury of the world-dominating church" but as "an accompanying manifestation of the Christian mission."[1] Mission is on the heart of God. From the very beginning of God's interaction with the world a definite outward-, other-orientation was conceived in His plan. This relationship with Him was not to be private and exclusive, but to be offered to all who were willing to obey God's commands.

It is to be deplored that still in many theological institutions missiology and missions courses are not taken seriously by students of theology. They are viewed as secondary and purely for the specialist. But nothing is more central to the heart of God than His mission. Without the sending aspect of God's character, He remains aloof and distant. Without the Sent One, Jesus Christ, Christology becomes merely anthropocentric. Without the gifts of the Spirit of God, sending and teaching, the continuing work of Christ through the Church in the parenthesis between His ascension and return would be without concrete meaning. And without the outward orientation of missions, the Church becomes ingrown, complacent and ethnocentric. The history of the expanding Church is the history of missions. "The church has a history only because God has granted it the privilege of participating in the *missio Dei*."[2] Missiology in

---

[1] Martin Kähler, *Schriften zur Christologie und Mission* (Munich: Kaiser, 1971), 189-90.

[2] David J. Bosch, *Transforming Mission: Paradigm Shifts in Theology of Mission* (Maryknoll: Orbis, 1991), 495. Karl Hartenstein was first to use the term *missio Dei*. "Mission is . . . participation in the sending of the Son, the *Missio Dei*." Walter Freytag, ed., *Theologische Besinnung: Mission zwischen Gestern und Morgen* (Stuttgart: Evangelischer Missionsverlag, 1952), 54.

its *dimensional* aspect is to permeate all disciplines. Yet it is justified as a separate discipline in order to challenge and be challenged by them.[3]

Karl Rennstich rightfully notes the all-encompassing nature of mission in the New Testament in his study of over 100 related words.[4] The central point of missions in theology is not to be considered as one among many options of involvement to be included or not in the curriculum of church life. If the church is not integrally involved in sending, in training and motivating the children and youth as well as adults through exposure to missions, in giving, praying and sending, then its purpose statement is too narrow and the church is predestined to self-impoverishment.

> *Nothing is more central to the heart of God than His mission.*

Dr. Bill Bright, Campus Crusade for Christ's founder and president and recipient of the 1996 Templeton Prize for Progress in Religion, when working with producer John Heyman on the Jesus film,[5] became aware that the scriptwriters had initially omitted the Lord's Great Commission and His Ascension. The script was changed to include the rest of Luke's account, rightfully integrating missiology with Christology.

Purpose and Structure

The purpose of this book is to identify and clarify credibility factors as well as problem areas of multicultural mission teams. Further, based on widely gathered information and my own twenty-five years of experience working in multicultural teams, I wish to offer concrete points of action for mission executives, team leaders and missionaries in multicultural teams. These are aimed both at training missionaries initially and correcting harmful patterns which teams and individuals may have al-

---

[3] David J. Bosch, ibid., 494-95. Newbigin and Gensichen, who describe missiology in free partnership with and penetrating other disciplines of theology, use the term *dimensional* for this aspect of missiology. Hans-Werner Gensichen, *Glaube für die Welt: Theologische Aspekte der Mission* (Gütersloh: Gerd Mohn, 1971), 80-95; 251f.

[4] Karl Rennstich, "Mission nach dem Neuen Testament," unpublished.

[5] The film *Jesus* produced by Campus Crusade for Christ's "Here's Life" is an account of the life of Christ based on the Gospel of Luke. As of December 1997, it had been translated into more than 500 languages in 223 countries, the most languages of any film in history (with 199 translations in process). It had been viewed by more than 2 billion people.

ready formed. These points are integral to the biblical and cross-cultural aspects of missionary training.

Subsequent to introducing the subject of multicultural mission teams and establishing the parameters of the theological framework (chapters 1 and 2), the process of missionary adjustment to a new host culture is discussed (chapter 3). Chapter 4 gives the analyses of surveys and interviews, draws conclusions and offers suggestions in the following areas: cultural norms in team life, language learning, team concept and functions, communication, decision-making, authority, leadership styles, finances, lifestyle, trust factors, meeting personal needs, women and non-Western missionaries in multicultural teams. In chapter 5 the issues of selection, training and team formation are discussed as they relate to multicultural teams. Guidelines for discussions in the teams themselves, soliciting and giving feedback, as well as guidelines for conducting multinational conferences for missionary teams are included in chapter 6. Summary and conclusions form the basis of chapter 7. The surveys and statistics as well as other important tools available to help multicultural teams are in the appendices.

With missions being a central theme in theology, it follows that the credibility of the missionary message and *praxis* in a cross-cultural context is a key issue in the theology of missions. While it is difficult to measure quantitatively the negative effects on the reception of the gospel because of a lack of credibility in the transmission or a negative reflection on the gospel by the messengers themselves, it is nevertheless a matter of integrity. The Apostle Paul himself went to great measures to insure the credibility of the message and himself, the messenger, on the part of his hearers. To him credibility included not just a culturally untainted message but also a messenger who was culturally relevant and personally disciplined.[6] Admittedly, a portion of this may be a *perceived* lack of credibility, but it is nevertheless responsible for indifference towards or rejection of the message along with the messenger.

Multicultural teams are, strictly speaking, a group of missionaries from different cultural backgrounds working together in one location. The optimal size of such teams will be discussed later. To heighten personal awareness of potential or actual explosive situations, one could analyze the dynamics of the following multicultural team. The story is fictitious; I know of no one team which has this whole set of problems

---

[6] 1 Corinthians 9:19-27. Scripture quotations are from the New Revised Standard Version of the Bible, copyright 1989 by the Division of Christian Education of the National Council of the Churches of Christ in the USA. Used by permission. All rights reserved.

and tensions, nevertheless these areas of conflict between missionaries in teams of different cultural backgrounds have been observed.

> *Several years ago Stephanie and Daniel Kaufmann were sent from their home church in a Central European country to Africa. They had been well prepared in their professions and through their missions course, or so they thought. They had sent their household goods, including a refrigerator, on ahead and arrived a month later after getting their vaccinations and securing adequate financial support. But Africa and the Africans were not the greatest surprise that awaited them, rather it was their coworkers.*
>
> *The team consisted of missionaries from different countries of Europe, America and Africa. Those from the Western countries lived in the diplomatic quarter of the city in contrast to their African colleagues who lived in more modest surroundings. Servants and modern appliances made life easier for the Western missionaries, who, nevertheless, had little time to learn the language of the people. It was automatically assumed that the language of the majority, in this case English, would be the means of communication among team members as well as in the ministry. Although the national missionaries had been in the ministry for a long time, the leadership of the team was still in Western hands. The leadership style was definitely "American" and foreign to European and African alike, but discussions about change only led to misunderstandings and revealed prejudices.*
>
> *There was never enough money for the full salaries of the national missionaries but the other missionaries had their cars and regular furloughs. When the Africans suggested a more spontaneous form for worship services they were judged as "unspiritual." Although the Africans were attentive to the speakers during the Bible conferences, they didn't take notes and they missed the way their old preachers told Bible stories.*
>
> *The national missionaries were disappointed that their coworkers didn't drop in on them at home and eventually they stopped inviting their foreign colleagues to their feasts or to their homes. The expatriates felt more comfortable relaxing with each other playing Scrabble, telling jokes and watching videos of the latest football games.*
>
> *There was often disagreement over methodology during the development of Bible studies and curricula for use in the country. The Europeans were embarrassed when their American team leader expressed what they had told him in confidence as a prayer*

request for the team. Once a European corrected an American child in front of his parents and since that time one could feel the increasing coolness between the families. The topic of child-rearing was a sensitive one that was avoided from then on.

With such different cultures represented on the team there were often big misunderstandings in non-verbal communication. Was it more appropriate to shake hands, kiss, hug or just say "Hi!" when greeting? Every visitor from afar was asked to bring favorite items from home, which the missionaries could not live without. And for the Christmas holidays, the desire of some expatriates for their traditional Christmas tree could not be repressed, no matter what the cost.

A degree of mutual understanding in these - and other - areas, sets the pace for good relations in a multicultural team: standard of living, use of money, leadership style, common language, methods of teaching, systems of logic, meaning of "confidentiality," trust, eating habits, celebrations, use of leisure time, child rearing, and worship practices.

In addition to the feelings - ranging from uneasiness to rage - that these differences create in the team, they also project a distinct impression to those in the host culture, to the very ones missionaries want to influence in a positive way with the gospel. How important is it, for example, to learn the local language, in order for the people to hear the good news in their heart language? What kind of impression does it make when missionaries really enjoy the food and customs of the people? Or when they understand their history and political situation? Or when they have the goal of training national missionaries to take the positions of leadership?

The history of the early church is replete with incidences of wrestling with incarnating the gospel in cultures. The first church council in Jerusalem (Acts 15) took up the then crucial issue of requiring the Jewish rite of circumcision for all male converts, Jewish or not. In the letter to the Romans, Paul discusses other cultural issues, such as the eating of meat offered to idols. Paul was amazingly liberal in allowing women to participate in church life and mission despite the confining cultural practices in his day. Peter, among others, fought the idea of changing his Jewish dietary practices for the sake of the new Gentile believers. It took God's direct revelation to him to convince him to distinguish between "pure gospel" and culture, the negotiables and the non-negotiables of the Christian life. The Apostle

> *The history of the early church is replete with incidences of wrestling with incarnating the gospel in cultures.*

Paul and his multicultural mission teams demonstrated how willing they were to sacrifice their own personal cultural values to yield to a higher value, that of communicating the message of Christ in terms understandable to the recipients. Paul himself, a product of Jewish and Hellenistic education, seems to have moved with ease in pluralistic societies and different cultures. Paul recommends a method of mission that he exemplified; he says, I became *"all* things to *all* people, that I might by *all* means save some."[7] He did not ignore the culture of the recipients of the gospel; he sought ways to win people to Christ using their culture as a vehicle.

Since the 1970s much has been written in mission's circles about culture shock and the dynamics of a cultural change.[8] The extreme of adapting too far, "going native,"[9] and its distortion of the truth of the message, as well as the opposite extreme, an unwillingness to adjust at all, forcing the recipients of the good news to make a cultural transition to understand the message, are now more well-known and, hopefully, avoided. But how does the modern mission team cope with the increasing complexity of the variety of cultures within one team while trying to adjust to the host culture?

> *How does the modern mission team cope with the increasing complexity and variety of cultures within one team while trying to adjust to the host culture?*

Will they always be concentrating their energies on adapting to one another, just getting along, so they're not a bad reflection on the gospel of love they proclaim? What elements of their relationships together add credibility to the message? What problems or blind spots detract or even discredit the gospel in the eyes of the recipients?

An encouraging sign of growth in any church is that it becomes a sending church. More countries that formerly received missionaries are now sending them internationally. Lawrence E. Keyes says that from 1972 to 1982 the number of Third World agencies grew 81 percent, and that they continue to increase rapidly. Countries such as Nigeria, Brazil,

---

[7] 1 Corinthians 9:22 [italics my emphasis].

[8] Cf Charles Kraft, *Christianity and Culture* (Maryknoll: Orbis Books, 1979); Louis Luzbetak, *The Church and Cultures* (Maryknoll: Orbis, 1988); Marvin Mayers, *Christianity Confronts Culture* (Grand Rapids: Zondervan, 1974); Eugene A. Nida, *Message and Mission* (Pasadena: William Carey Library, 1960).

[9] A definition of "going native" can be found in the discussion of the adjustment process.

Korea, Japan and Singapore, which were once primarily receiving missionaries are now sending them as well.[10]

Special problems result in the consequent increase in the number of missionary teams that are culturally mixed. Such issues as communication, language, leadership styles, use of finances, lifestyles, decision making, authority, roles of women and men, expressing trust and love, and relaxation are all key to team life and very culturally determined and can create problems. Though these areas are not unique to multicultural teams, in a team that is culturally mixed, the problems are certainly magnified and more complex. What are the Achilles heels of multicultural mission teams? How can they be dealt with so as to lend credibility to the message rather than erecting barriers?

> *How can the Achilles heels of multicultural teams be dealt with so as to lend credibility to the message rather than erecting barriers?*

And what are the implications for the selection and training of missionaries for cross-cultural service? Are some people, due to personality, strong national characteristics or lack of maturity, unable to adjust and become useful? Will their self-concept be hurt in such a way in the process of adaptation that they feel they will lose their personal identity and no longer be able to function? Can seeming inabilities be changed? What can training do? What can it not do?

More than twenty-five years of personal experience in multicultural teams, living in another country, training others for cross-cultural ministry, and discussing these issues with national and expatriate missionaries "on location" have motivated me to pursue this topic. In 1975, when I first arrived in Germany[11] from the United States to assume responsibilities as Assistant Coordinator of Staff Development and Training for

---

[10] Larry Keyes, *The Last Age of Missions* (Pasadena: William Carey Library, 1978), xi. Although some think that Keyes compares "apples with oranges" in his definition of "missionary," in his statistics, an upward trend of missionaries from former receiving countries is nonetheless undisputed. cf Klaus Fiedler, "Wo sind die 20 000? - Eine kritische Analyse von Lawrence E. Keyes' Konzept der 'transkulturellen Drittweltmissionare' und der ihm zugrundeliegenden Daten." *Evangelikale Missiologie* 3/1989.

[11] I hesitate to mention the country to which I was sent for fear of misunderstanding. Some may assess such a move from a Western to a Western country as demanding little adjustment apart from perhaps learning the language. I maintain, however, such moves without some of the more obvious physical adaptations are often the hardest because of the subtleties involved. The psychological elements are indeed the most difficult to adapt to in any culture. There is much under the surface that demands the same kind of analysis and change as a so-called E-3 or M-3 (culturally distant) move.

Western Europe for our mission, Campus Crusade for Christ, International, I had strong convictions about approach to ministry and culture in my new country. My job description required that I take certain initiatives and there were expectations from the European leadership to bring form and substance to a staff development program in Europe, similar to what I had developed for staff in the USA. The national ministries,[12] some brand new, none older than eight years at the time, were pleading for help in the training of new national staff. In the first eighteen months

> *The decision was made to learn the language so as to be able to communicate the gospel in a culturally relevant way as accent-free as possible.*

of residence in Germany, I managed to squeeze in four months of language courses and three additional months of private tutoring using the LAMP method[13] with trips to the ministries in fourteen countries of Europe and the U.S. and, after a year, assuming the job as Coordinator of Staff Development and Training. Both of my directors (the leadership changed hands from an American to a Finn) were also convinced of the importance of learning German well, though regrettably they themselves had had to make concessions to their jobs which compromised their language learning. I, too, had to resist the pressures of the job and the tensions of meeting real needs of other expatriate missionaries around me, pulling me away from language study and preparations to live in a new country long-term. This is mentioned at the outset lest one think my decisions were made in a sterile, theoretical world. The decision was made to learn the language so as to be able to communicate the gospel in a culturally relevant way as accent-free as possible. This decision meant months of not understanding what was spoken nor being able to make myself understood, which meant I felt like an outsider most of the time.

For want of a better comparison it could be explained this way: I left the mission's headquarters to live in Berlin with native German-speakers (missionaries who worked full time with university students) who sent me off to my "special school" (language school) each morning where I performed reasonably well and made progress daily. In the afternoons I hired a tutor, a student, for a nominal fee, who answered questions, corrected pronunciation and made tapes of words and phrases for me to

---

[12] The structure in Campus Crusade for Christ, International is arranged by continents (now divided into subcontinents as a result of growth in numbers of fulltime missionaries or staff). Under these continental divisions (called Areas of Affairs) are the countries or national ministries.

[13] E. T. and E. S. Brewster, *Language Acquisition Made Practical* (Colorado Springs: Lingua House, 1976). Cf. section under language in chapter 4.

mimic in his absence. But, for the longest time, whenever I stepped back into the "real world" I would be hopelessly frustrated by high-speed German (German spoken at the normal Berlin rate), failing to comprehend the simplest things. The day of total comprehension seemed an eternity away and full expression in German nearly impossible. But somehow, through the patience and tolerance of many who endured my "baby Deutsch," that day neared, to the point where I could make basic needs known, gather necessary information for living and even one day give my first speech in my new language. It didn't happen overnight, nor without discipline, isolating myself from English speakers and the fellow countrymen with whom it would have been comfortable to spend time, avoiding reading English books to which I longed to escape, even refusing to draw spiritual nutrition primarily from English sources. I began a program of "Reading through the Bible in a Year" in German and was eventually finished in two years. I asked question after question to try to understand the reasoning behind ways foreign to me. Parts of the puzzle began to fit together intellectually but my emotional reactions were still tied to my cultural conditioning, which tended to make me judgmental towards new ways. "It's not wrong, it's just different," we expatriates reminded ourselves day in and day out. To speak of something becoming second nature seemed far-fetched indeed. Would one ever feel really comfortable here? Certainly, I felt accepted, graciously so with all my ways that were surely strange to them, but would I ever feel at ease, at home? Would I always have to be overly conscious of what I was doing and the way I was expressing things? How long would their patience last?

During my stay in Berlin I was in an obvious minority as one of two Americans among many Germans on the team. But back at the European Headquarters in Müllheim, Baden in southern Germany I was a member of a plurality culture; during the first years the Americans outnumbered Finns, Dutch, Germans and Swiss on the team. The office language was *It's not wrong, it's just different!* English (because the ministry was Europe-wide). But the missionaries needed German for buying groceries, registering with the proper officials, renting an apartment, being involved in the local church, securing things necessary for living and chatting with the neighbors, to say nothing of communicating what was really on their hearts: they were in love with Jesus and wanted others to share that joy, too. As a single person, I didn't have to deal directly with some other complicated issues, like the schooling of children, although I weighed the pros and cons of national schooling versus missionary schooling[14] with every incoming family who asked my advice.

Some of the seemingly insignificant things in my multicultural team became sources of contention, some even threatening to divide the team or causing all to wonder if the tensions of such a cultural mix were really worthwhile. When we finally did agree on time available up-front for learning language before newcomers were swallowed up in job responsibilities, the financial issues stretched our agape love to its limits. Financial policies, even if equitable on paper, could not adequately take into account all the varieties of tax laws from the countries they represented nor the degrees of hardship encountered in raising our own support. Our mission policy is that each full-time staff member is responsible for securing enough personal financial support from churches and friends to cover a modest salary and ministry expenses, including, of course, health insurance and taxes. This is psychologically healthy as well as financially sound but not all countries have equal financial capability. Nor do they have the large pool of Christians to draw from or the mentality of giving to missions.

And, where one might least expect tensions, to our dismay, they appeared. One example was during a weekend retreat, designed to deepen fellowship among our co-laborers, give them a chance to relax and enjoy activities together away from job and home responsibilities. To begin with, the preschool children from the different countries couldn't even talk to one another, so the childcare program was difficult for them and their parents. Songs had to be carefully chosen so that no one's language was forgotten (or at least the two official languages were included) and the words had to be available for all to see. Spontaneous singing, which normally would have lent a spirit of unity to the team, tended to slow things down and make those who didn't know the songs feel excluded. Even limiting the interaction to the two official languages created problems for newcomers (and the team was always about 30 percent new at any given time). Translation needed to be provided for those who hadn't adequately mastered English or German.

If any kind of sports were involved, other subtle, sometimes private issues came to light, for example, body hair. For women to shave hair on their legs and underarms is a high cultural value for North Americans, as is covering certain kinds of body smells. Some of the European women, knowing this but not feeling the necessity of change (rightly so), were nevertheless embarrassed. Unless the issues were talked about, the wedge of differences was driven even further to split the team.

---

[14] This was before the advent of home schooling; see "home schooling."

One might think that with these things taken care of everyone would feel at home. Not so. They all had been trained to think and come to conclusions in life in very particular patterns and that affected the way they preferred to have their spiritual nutrition. One would hear varying comments after a Bible teaching session such as: "That really ministered to my heart," or "that left me cold," and wonder if any one speaker could ever meet the needs of such a diverse group. The truth is, it would be very difficult to do so. Not only were the needs diverse but the avenues to the heart, or patterns of logic, are so different that no *one* person could possibly be on target for all of the people all of the time. Frustration ensued particularly for those of minority cultures in the team whose needs consistently were left unmet. And if the retreats were expensive and those particular staff accounts were low, that only added to the frustration and feelings of ostracism.

> *Frustration ensued for those of minority cultures in the team whose needs consistently were left unmet.*

The pinnacle of frustration occurred most often, however, when we were supposed to be having fun. I never realized how culturally conditioned fun was until I saw the dismay of the staff who planned what was to be a fun skit night that flopped. Some types of fun were so connected to language ability that invariably some were excluded. Other types of entertainment were viewed by some as far too superficial to really be enjoyed. And yet to others, "planned fun" seemed far too competitive. So this "fun-filled, relaxing weekend away" more often than not left many from the minority cultures so stressed out they didn't care when the next retreat came. How could this compilation of people ever become a real multicultural team?

> *The pinnacle of frustration occurred most often when we were supposed to be having fun.*

In this work I am operating under several presuppositions important to note here. It is not the scope of this book to give the rationale behind these presuppositions, important as they are. Suffice it to mention them: the Bible is God's Word to all peoples, not a document from a Western culture to be imposed upon other cultures; it is, in fact, very non-Western. Its principles are valid and can be applied in any given context. Jesus Christ is fully God and fully human in His incarnation. His life, substitutional death and resurrection are central to the message. His great commission is as valid for His followers today as when it was given, which is the mandate to take His message to the whole world, which, without Him, is lost. God's Holy Spirit is responsible to apply the message individually to the hearts of the people; every follower of Christ is responsible to take the message as Christ brought us the message. All believers are equal before God (priesthood of all believers) without distinction of race, gender or nationality. All believers have the opportunity, and the responsibility, to mature in their faith and entrust it to others, who will in turn do the same. No person, or people, has more ownership of this message than another.

This book deals with only one point in the vast issue of "gospel and culture;"[15] it deals with the concerns of a multicultural mission team living together in such a way as to attract others to the person of Christ. The concentration is on communication between members of this team and the outworkings beyond the team in the host culture. The communication, whether verbal or non-verbal, should be credible to the observers or participants outside the team. This means it should be plausible, in the logic of the recipients; tenable, something they would be positively inclined to grasp; believable and trustworthy. It should not be unreliable or subject to doubt. Basically it means the lives of the messengers are transparent and full of integrity, supporting the message they communicate. Furthermore, the message and the messenger are perceived as congruent by the recipients of the message. In the process of adaptation, however, the identity of the missionaries is retained, actually enhanced in a way not thought possible. The purpose of the book is to help missionaries avoid ungodly suffering in their adjustment process.

---

[15] This subject can hardly be exhausted and there are many new books currently being released. Some sources to be recommended are: Lesslie Newbigin, *The Gospel in a Pluralist Society* (Grand Rapids: Eerdmans, 1989) and *A Word in Season: Perspectives on Christian World Mission* (Grand Rapids: Eerdmans, 1994); Marvin Mayers, *Christianity Confronts Culture* (Grand Rapids: Zondervan, 1974); Louis Luzbetak, *The Church and Cultures* (Maryknoll: Orbis, 1988); Sherwood Lingenfelter, *Transforming Culture: A Challenge for Christian Mission,* (Grand Rapids: Baker, 1992); Charles Kraft, *Christianity in Culture* (Maryknoll: Orbis, 1979); John Stott, *Christian Mission in the Modern World* (London: Falcon, 1975); H. Richard Niebuhr, *Christ and Culture* (New York: Harper and Row, 1951).

1

THEOLOGICAL AND ANTHROPOLOGICAL

CONSIDERATIONS RELATING TO

MULTICULTURAL TEAMS

Culture

In the anthropological sense, culture has less to do with the degree of "higher civilization," with its sophistication in forms of art, music and literature. Etymologically the term culture has its roots in the Latin *colere*, meaning to care for, or design in nature. The persons doing this are involved physically and mentally in changing their environment, and are thereby developing themselves. Wherever there are people, there is culture because people are cultural beings.[16] Every culture is in a process of change, which seems to have been accelerated by the advent of the age of technology. To rank cultures as higher or lower is senseless because each culture has its own values, no culture being the ultimate against which all others are to be compared. It is nevertheless the natural, universal tendency to perceive one's own culture as superior and compare all others to it. Culture is the way life is organized to give meaning to a particular group of people in their environment. Culture is used to form the person and the group. It is "a kind of road map . . . designed to get people where they need to go,"[17] which is why many of the older generation get so upset when cultural values are meddled with (e.g., Western dress for Middle Eastern young women). The fear is very real that the misunderstandings will be great. Culture is then not a superficial element in the missionary outreach but rather a deep context into which the gospel must work. Culture is a person's second nature. Sensitivity to another's culture is, then, at least a matter of respect for the person and therefore incum-

---

[16] E. Nunnenmacher, "Kultur." Karl Müller und Theo Sundermeier, *Lexikon missionstheologischer Grundbegriffe* (Berlin: Dietrich Reimer, 1987), 235.
[17] Charles Kraft, *Christianity in Culture*, 113.

bent on the Christian missionary. It follows then that as soon as people from various cultures confront each other conflicts are bound to arise.

The early church had to deal with the issue of culture from the very outset of her existence. Paul's own mission teams were culturally mixed (Timothy and Titus) and his missionary thrust was beyond the Jews to the Romans and Greeks. His letter to the Galatians was to a Gallic church, yet another culture. The question of imposing one culture (in this case the Jewish culture) on another was a matter of great importance in the communication of the gospel. Paul confronted the issue with clear principles: no culture had a right to exert power of conformity over another; all cultures are to conform to the values of the supreme God manifest in Christ Jesus. Paul even rebuked Peter for his double standard, first eating with the Gentiles and then pulling back and associating only with the Jews.[18] Either the Gentiles were full members of the body of Christ without fulfilling Jewish customs or Peter was acting hypocritically. This was to be condemned. So from the beginning of the early church in the early days of its expansion there was freedom to allow the gospel to work in the culture of the recipients, a freedom which Paul staunchly protected.

Niebuhr in his book *Christ and Culture*, outlines and illustrates three possibilities for Christ to relate to culture: 1) Christ against culture (an "anti" stance against the inherent evils of culture based on such passages as 1 John 2:15-16; 5:19 resulting in an escapism), 2) Christ of culture (producing a dualism, man having a double loyalty, to both church and state, the two remaining separate), and 3) Christ above culture.[19] The latter can be subdivided into three classes: "a) the synthesists, who look upon Christianity as the fulfillment and restorer of human values, b) the dualists, who contend that man is subject to two moralities and must live in this tension, and c) the conversionists, who believe that God comes to man within his culture in order to transform man and through him the culture."[20] Because Niebuhr's discussion predated much of the recent discussion regarding culture, Charles Kraft has added a fourth - "Christ above-but-through culture."[21] He views culture as essentially neutral, though "warped by the pervasive influence of human sinfulness."[22] "Given these two complex realities - Christ and culture - an infinite

---

[18] In Galatians 2:11-14 Paul confronted Peter on his hypocrisy openly because he mislead others, including Barnabas, to dissociate from the Gentiles. Paul allowed no racism or nationalism to encroach on the unity of the body of Christ.

[19] H. Richard Niebuhr, *Christ and Culture*.

[20] Summarized in Eugene A. Nida, *Message and Mission*, 208.

[21] Kraft, *Christianity and Culture*, 113.

[22] Kraft, ibid.

dialogue must develop in the Christian conscience and the Christian community."[23]

One of the areas in which cultural anthropologists[24] criticized missionaries the most was in their relationship to the culture. Missionaries were criticized for destroying cultural practices in remote tribes. Conversely, anthropologists were criticized for being academic in their studies without having the good of the people as their ultimate goal. This led them to take an observer's stance rather than being involved in changing harmful practices. Slavery, for example, was an area of critical dispute. There was,

> Blumhardt saw missionary activity as paying retribution for the ills that colonists had brought.

however, a difference of opinion on how to protect the rights of the Africans to their culture, land and resources. At one point, one faction, supported by most of the missionaries, wanted to give the Africans the full privileges of Western society immediately. Johannes Zimmerman of the *Basler Mission*, who was married to a former-slave-now-missionary, wanted to free the slaves in a seven year progressive program, as in the Old Testament. In their 1862 General Conference the *Basler Mission* strongly urged the immediate abolition of slavery as it was unreconcilable with the Gospel.[25] Christian Gottlieb Blumhardt saw missionary activity actually as paying retribution for the ills that colonialists had brought. Missionaries should never forget what the whites had done to the blacks in Africa and should treat them with the utmost of patience

> It was primarily the missionaries who saw colonialism as incompatible with their mission and protested to their governments.

and love in order to heal the wounds of the terrible deeds of the Europeans.[26] And he was not alone. Former slave trader John Newton renounced his profession and worked to free slaves. His song "Amazing Grace, how sweet the sound, that saved a wretch like me . . ."

---

[23] Niebuhr, *Christ and Culture*, 39.

[24] Cultural anthropology came into its own following the abolition of slavery in England in the early nineteenth century. One of the spearheads of modern anthropology was Margaret Mead, *Anthropology: A Human Science* (Princeton: Van Nostrand, 1964). Today missions and cultural anthropology are viewed by missiologists as disciplines to be integrated. Cf. Paul Hiebert, *Cultural Anthropology* (Philadelphia: J.B. Lippincott, 1976); Eugene Nida, *Customs and Cultures* (New York: Harper and Row, 1954).

[25] Karl Rennstich, *Handwerker-Theologen und Industrie-Brüder als Botschafter des Friedens* (Stuttgart: Evangelischer Missionsverlag, 1985), 58-60.

[26] Rennstich, ibid., 193.

was his own testimony to his genuine repentance and God's forgiveness. However, those who criticize all missionaries for being the major carriers of colonialism simply do not know the facts. On the contrary, it was primarily the missionaries who saw colonialism as incompatible with their mission and protested to their governments.[27]

The area of slavery is but one example in which many missionaries felt compelled to challenge the practices of culture, giving the gospel credibility in the eyes of the recipients. "Unfortunately, thereafter the missionaries and reformers too often pursued programs of planned change without perceiving the cultural contexts in which the change took place, while the anthropologists too often proceeded to study the people with little thought to how this knowledge could benefit the people."[28] Every new generation of missionaries must guard itself against stereotyping and judging former generations. Even many early missionaries were deeply sensitive to the cultures of the people with whom they worked.[29]

Increased interaction between anthropologists and missionaries came after World War II. Some Christian colleges, notably Wheaton College (Wheaton, IL), had included anthropology courses in the curriculum prior to this. Journals such as the Catholic *Anthropological Quarterly*, the primarily Protestant *International Review of Missions* and later *Practical Anthropology* dealt with these topics. In this century the work of Eugene Nida and the members of the American Bible Society translation teams brought real impetus of anthropological awareness to missions.[30] On the other side, "the younger generation of anthropologists seems to have grown beyond the acerbic reactions towards missions that characterized earlier scholars like Malinowski or the blindness to church life shown by people like Margaret Mead."[31]

---

[27] Rennstich, ibid., 194-95 and Bosch, *Transforming Mission*, 311-312.

[28] Paul G. Hiebert, "Introduction: Mission and Anthropology," William Smalley ed., *Readings in Missionary Anthropology II* (Pasadena: William Carey Library, 1978), xxiii.

[29] Hiebert, ibid. More specific examples can be found in the Chapter "Adjustment of the Missionaries to one another."

[30] Larry Keyes and Larry Pate, "Two-thirds world missions: The next 100 years," *Missiology*, Vol. 21, xxiv. Nida wrote *Customs and Cultures* in 1954 and *Message and Mission* in 1960.

[31] Charles W. Forman, "The Study of Pacific Island Christianity," *International Bulletin of Missionary Research*. Vol 18, No. 3 (July 1994), 103.

Cultural Values and Norms

Cultural values, in this context, refer to any pattern or aspect of life that a given culture or subculture shares and is, therefore, of consequent worth to the people of that society and contributes to their identity and self-perception. A normative cultural value (or cultural norm) is, then, the value which characterizes and is accepted by the majority, if not all people, in a given culture or subculture. For example, in strict Muslim cultures it is normative for women to cover their bodies almost entirely in public. Or a norm can be as simple to observe as: most Germans have German as their mother tongue. Mayers calls a norm, "that which is the foundation for expectation within society."[32] Any deviation from expected or normative behavior is considered abnormal to a greater or lesser degree. "The norm of any social group equals the sum total of its values, norms, expectations, rules, and aspirations."[33] In this sense, says Mayers, norm is synonymous with culture. It is that which comes automatically to persons of a common culture. It is exactly this "automaticness" of norms which conserves energy to expend creatively; one doesn't have to consciously think through every process; one reacts predictably. Conversely, it is because it's not automatic for the foreigner and because no area of life is culture-free, that the compound effects are energy-consuming or stressful until the missionary adapts to the norms/values.

The only absolute cultural values to which every culture must bow are the eternal biblical values, to which Jesus held. These are the values above time and above culture, not bound by culture, but which should penetrate and reform culture. All cultures, the host culture, even supposed Christian cultures, must be held up to the eternal light of Christ and His Word. The Apostle Paul contrasts the values of the Roman culture with imitable

> *The only absolute cultural values to which every culture must bow are the eternal values, to which Jesus held.*

spiritual values.[34] Values which are not to be imitated, such as envy, anger, jealousy and drunkenness, are juxtaposed against the fruit of the

---

[32] Marvin Mayers, *Christianity Confronts Culture*, 82. One of the best discussions of values is found in this book especially in chapter 11, "The Group: Value."

[33] Mayers, ibid.

[34] Karl Rennstich in "Missionarische Ethik" (unpublished, 1996) studies the prevalent Roman values and the *Grundwerte* basic values of life in the Spirit. Galatians 5:19-21; 2 Corinthians 6:14 - 7:1; cf. Romans 1:29-31; 13:13; 1 Corinthians 5:10f and 6:9f; 2 Corinthians 12:20f; Ephesians 4:31 and 5:3-5; Colossians 3:5-8; 1 Timothy 1:9f and 2 Timothy 3:2-7.

Spirit: love, joy, peace, patience, gentleness, goodness, kindness, faithfulness and self-control. These basic biblical values are those to which every Christian and every culture must conform. One can neither justify holding to one's own contrabiblical cultural values nor uncritically adapting unbiblical values of the new culture. The values of each culture must be held up carefully to the standard of God's values. The reminder of Paul in Romans 12:2 still holds: don't be conformed to the world (and it's non-biblical values) but be transformed by the renewing of your mind. As a word of caution one must add that not every cultural value recorded in Scripture is approved by the Lord. One must carefully distinguish between those to be emulated and those not to be. One commonly held cultural value, for example, derives the submission of wife to her husband from the Genesis 3. From this passage the curse, as a result of the Fall into sin, is equated quasi with a divine ordinance. One should not conclude that labor in food production should not be eased because the curse preprogrammed it. Nor would one not want to ease the labor pains of the mother because this too is part of the curse. But some all too quickly jump to the conclusion that "the woman's desire shall be for your husband and he shall rule over you" is a divine ordinance to be fulfilled rather than a part of the curse - unhealthy dependency upon the man - from which Jesus Christ freed the woman - and the man. The challenge is for missionaries to filter their own culture through the eternal values of Christ.

A helpful concept from Marvin Mayers, who was himself a missionary and my former professor in intercultural studies, which helps both the expatriate and national missionaries, is the six pairs of contrasting basic values: dichotomizing vs. holistic, declarative vs. interrogative, time-oriented versus event-oriented, goal-conscious versus interaction-conscious, prestige ascribed versus achieved, and vulnerability as a strength versus weakness. This list of values is not complete but if the missionaries, during analysis, can grasp these, they "can then derive the primary motivational values of a society."[35] For purposes of training missionaries to serve in or with other cultures, this tool was developed for the assessment of self and others. Not all of these pairs of values are as mutually exclusive as they may appear. For example, in observing the way Jesus allowed His ministry to be interrupted with the personal needs of people as contrasted to His sense of mission and feeling compelled to move on to another city to preach, Jesus probably could be rated as 8/8.

---

[35] Marvin K. Mayers, *Christianity Confronts Culture*, 147-70.

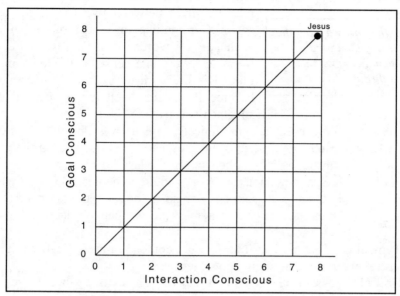

Figure 1: Goal/Interaction Consciousness (adapted from Mayers,
Christianity Confronts Culture, Zondervan: 1974)

Jesus would be seen as 100 percent on goal-consciousness as well as 100
percent on interaction-consciousness.[36]

When missionaries are in the process of deciding which values they
will hold to, those of their own culture or (in some cases) contrasting
biblical values, they are in essence asking themselves the question: "To
whom do I belong?" It is a question of whether their country, their own
sense of identity, have more hold on them than their identity with their
Lord?

Communication

Another outgrowth of culture, also integral to it, is communication.[37]
This need to communicate is in fact much deeper than the word itself
implies. The root meaning is drawn from the Latin word *communio,* de-

---

[36] Mayers, *Christianity Confronts Culture,* 147-70. See Appendix C for diagrams
of the six pairs of basic values.
[37] Cf. David W. Johnson, *Reaching Out: Interpersonal Effectiveness and Self-
Actualization* (Englewood Cliffs: Prentice-Hall, 1972).

noting the basis for all verbal and non-verbal communication i.e., relationship (communion). Communication is not strictly from a sender to a receiver; it is between two (or more) persons.[38] Communication is then more than an exchange of words; it is an exchange of lives. In a supreme sense, it is God's mingling His life with ours: "the Word (logos) became flesh and dwelt among us and we observed his glory . . . full of grace and truth."[39] Not the only way, but the best way God used to communicate with us was through His Son. The writer of Hebrews describes the progression: God spoke in the past in many ways through His prophets but in the last days He has spoken to us through His Son. No amount of words could come near to saying what God had to say to us so He sent His Son so we could begin to understand some of His message. This was a message we can observe and with which we can interact.

> *Not the only way, but the best way God used to communicate with us was through His Son.*

Typical of his American missiologist contemporaries, Kraft explains God's revelation in communicational terms:

> God (1) seeks to be understood, (2) recognizes that what the receptor will understand depends as much on the receptor's perception as on how he (God) presents the message, and (3) realizes that it is his task to stimulate the receptor to produce within the receptor's head the desired meanings. God, therefore, is (4) receptor-oriented in the way he goes about presenting his messages. He attempts to (5) present those messages with impact in (6) person-to-person interaction within (7) the receptor's frame of reference via (8) credible human communicators who (9) relate God's messages specifically to the lives of the receptors and (10) lead the latter to revelational discoveries.[40]

---

[38] The following are resources for Christian communicators in a cross-cultural setting: Charles Kraft, *Communicating the Gospel God's Way* (Pasadena: William Carey Library, 1985) and *Christianity and Culture*; Eugene Nida, *Message and Mission*; David Hesselgrave, *Communicating Christ Cross-Culturally* (Grand Rapids: Zondervan, 1978); Harvie Conn, *Eternal Word and Changing Worlds* (Grand Rapids: Zondervan, 1983); Edward Hall, *The Silent Language* (Greenwich: Fawcett, 1985); Louis Luzbetak, *The Church and Cultures;* and Marvin Mayers, *Christianity Confronts Culture.*

[39] John 1:14.

[40] Charles Kraft, *Christianity in Culture,* 170. For further discussion on this topic: see his chapters on receptor-oriented revelation and dynamic equivalence.

Others are far less receptor-oriented in their understanding of communication.[41] This reaction to psychological models of communication in America at first prevented the incorporation of any wisdom of the social sciences into the spiritual world of missions. One need only study Jesus' interaction with His contemporaries - His followers, interested people or even His opponents, to see that He mastered the art of communication. He was not prone to only one-way communication, although He did preach to people. His ministry is recorded far more as one of interacting with people in two-way communication, listening as well as speaking.

Communication is more than words. Indeed, to be effective, it profits from the use of many avenues to insure that the message conceived in the heart and mind of the sender comes to the heart and mind of the receiver in a form close to the original.

Communication can be most simply defined as, "getting your message across." The problem that arises in most communication and especially in cross-cultural communication is that the intended message of the sender is not the one that the receiver hears. There are many things that interfere. Much of the message is filtered out by the sender himself and by the receiver. That which is filtered out by the sender lies in the perception the receiver has of him. It is startling for missionaries to realize that "just as much emphasis is given to the carrier of the information as to the content."[42] It is the communicator, the missionaries, who either lend credibility to the message they communicate or distract from it. "Communicators isolated from their receptors by stereotype barriers tend to find the impact of their message low."[43]

While the content of the message is communicated by symbols, the value of the message is attached to the sender and the circumstances. That which the sender filters out is conditioned by three distinct proesses: 1) selectivity - receivers take in only that which is acceptable to them, that which fits into their worldview, is what they can comprehend;

---

[41] Hans-Werner Gensichen, *Glaube für die Welt: Theologische Aspekte der Mission* (Gütersloh: Gerd Mohn, 1971), 191-92, and the Roman Catholic *praeparatio evangelica* concept prefer to see the majority of the responsibility with God; it is His job to prepare the receivers. This is a position emphasizing the absolute sovereignty of God in evangelism, away from the responsibility of human beings, recipients or messengers. It is reminiscent of the parable of the sower in Mark 4, with the sower sowing the seed irrespective of whether the seed falls on fruitful or barren land. This is indeed one part of communicating the gospel but is it the whole picture?

[42] Eugene Nida, *Religion Across Cultures* (Pasadena: William Carey Library, 1968), 68.

[43] Kraft, *Christianity and Culture*, 395.

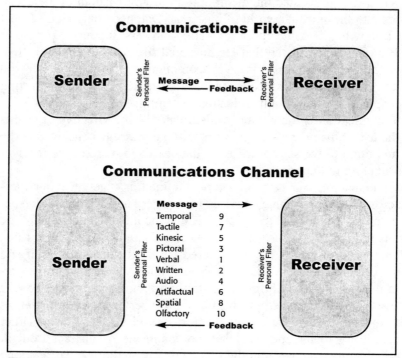

Figure 2: Communication Filters (adapted from Agape International Training, 1974)

2) skewing - receivers filter in but alter the concepts and reinterpret them; and 3) restructuring - receivers put contents together into new combinations.[44] Filters such as worldview, learning and experiences, beliefs and attitudes, and personality, if they are not identical to those of the sender, all can alter the message. The fact that these filters can actually distort the message intended, indicates that the recipient is indeed very active in the communication process.

---

[44] Nida, *Religion Across Cultures*, 74-77.

Only two avenues can be classified as verbal communication, the verbal and the written, which are the ways one tends to rely on most. [45] Yet these avenues, when not used in combination with other avenues, are those which leave the least impact. The other eight avenues (in the numbered order) create increasing impact and lasting retention of the message. And when one reflects on the avenues of communication, one sees how complicated it can be to be a credible messenger. "To overcome the barrier created by a stereotype, communicators need to act in a way that identifies them not with the stereotype but with the human being to whom they seek to communicate."[46] Other dimensions that enhance credibility include: perceived expertise on the topic of discussion, honorable motives, expression of warmth and friendliness, dynamism rather than passivity of the sender, and the fact that other people view the sender as credible.[47] The complex nature of communication underscores the necessity to solicit feedback often especially in a multicultural team. Without continual correction of perceptions, misunderstandings are pre-programmed. This is perhaps wearisome after the newness wears off, but it is as necessary to work on good communication to enhance team relationships as in any relationship.

Psychologically, communication can be summarized as: "It's not so much what you say but what I hear/feel/sense you saying." Existential philosophy describes communication as the listening, sympathizing, and actively responsible openness of one person for another. Dietrich Bonhoeffer reflects on the theological basis for this when he explains that only in the work of God the Holy Spirit does the other become *Du* (you) to me. This is because every human *Du* is the image of the divine *Du*, in contrast to Kierkegaard's extreme individualism in which *ich* (I) doesn't require a *Du* to exist. Bonhoeffer adds that God can make every person a *Du* for us.[48]

Communication has its theological mooring in God, *The Communicator*, who as *Logos* became a human being. There is no artificial separation of the messenger and the message. This thought is continued in Paul's writings describing his evangelistic and discipleship activities as being gentle as a mother tenderly caring for her own children: "So deeply do we care for you that we are determined to share with you not only the

---

[45] The diagrams are from *Dynamic Equivalence . . . To Communicate Effectively*, lectures in Agape International Training, Arrowhead Springs, 1974, by E. Thomas and Elizabeth S. Brewster.

[46] Kraft, *Christianity and Culture*, 395.

[47] David Johnson, *Reaching Out*, 66.

[48] Dietrich Bonhoeffer, *Sanctorum Communio* (Munich: Kaiser, 1954), 32.

gospel of God but also our own selves, because you have become very dear to us."[49]

With the information revolution in this age of cyberspace the future of true communication is at stake. More and more the "I - you" relationship is being replaced by "I - computer." Children, especially, are mesmerized by the computer and computer games. They have a feeling of mastery over their own world and can work at improving their skills. But they are not interacting with someone who knows them by name and can speak specifically to them as unique individuals. Yet the computer synthesizes this feeling, even uses the name typed into it to give a sense of personalness. It gives feedback but how often have I been frustrated with pre-programmed answers that didn't really answer my computer questions. The computer can never replace a person and it must remain under the control of each person who programs it or uses it. Even the prophet of computer software, Bill Gates, predicts that the information highway will have massive outworkings on the whole of our lives. He predicts the emergence of a world culture through the use of the information highway.[50] But this information highway is at best a means to an end; it is

> *Forces that tend to depersonalize our culture and us must be kept under control.*

impersonal. This will have massive implications for relationships and teamwork. Martin Buber chose people over books, even though people had been a source of disappointment to him far more than books. He would still enjoy being in his room and reading a good book but only because he could once again open the door and a person would look up at him.[51] Forces that tend to depersonalize our culture and us must be kept under control, not such an easy task in the face of problems and stress, which confront us.

Language

Although language is only a part of communication it is basic to it and integral to missions. For this reason the work of Bible translators, who do not mechanically translate the message into another language but

---

[49] 1 Thessalonians 2:8.

[50] Bill Gates, *Der Weg nach vorn (The Road Ahead)* (Hamburg: Hoffmann and Campe, 1995), 397.

[51] Martin Buber, *Begegnung, Autobiographische Fragmente* (Gerlingen: Schneider), 88f.

first are deeply involved with the people learning their language, is indispensable. "Faith comes from hearing the message, and the message is heard through the word of Christ," writes Paul in Romans 10:17. Language serves not just to communicate; it is especially an expression of thoughts and feelings.[52] It is a primary means of establishing and maintaining relationships. Such a sophisticated means of communicating is unique to human beings, and as such, a mark of personhood. God, who is a person, speaks. He speaks not just into void but to us; He wants to relate to us. The contents of His spoken word together with His acts in history tell us the degree to which He wants to relate to us. No relationship is so intimate, so all encompassing, so wonderful. His words express that beyond doubt; they express His thoughts and feelings towards us. His words comfort, encourage, chide, condemn, correct, and express desire, joy, love and care. His words, as all words, are not neutral vehicles; they are loaded with connotations and denotations. The mere choice of words can give rise to pleasure or anger. Because words alone are not the perfect expression of thoughts or feelings, they are guilty of producing misunderstanding, necessitating a context of relationship in which words can be rightly understood.

In most situations missionaries will be using a language other than their own mother tongue. It goes without saying that the context in which words are used must be carefully studied to produce mutual understanding. In some cases one will be choosing expressions in the new language that are close equivalents - not direct translations - of concepts, and begin to fill them with new content through teaching, preaching and counseling.[53] The Holy Spirit has promised to give wisdom, of which missionaries can avail themselves in translation of God's word. There was an era in which it was thought less than productive to translate the Bible into tribal languages, but thankfully, it has been acknowledged that the mother tongue is the heart language. Without spiritual nourishment in the heart language, spiritual life will dwindle.[54] Jesus probably spoke four languages: Hebrew, the religious language; Aramaic, the common language of His day; Latin, the official language of the occupiers; and Greek. He was prepared to use whichever language was appropriate in a given situation to make His message understood whether, in a synagogue, on the street, preaching to a crowd

> *Without spiritual nourishment in the heart language, spiritual life will dwindle.*

---

[52] E. Dammann, "Sprache," Müller and Sundemeier, *Lexikon missionstheologischer Grundbegriffe*, 447.

[53] Dammann, ibid., 448.

[54] Dammann, ibid.

or speaking to His accusers while on trial. At Pentecost, the birth of the church, all those present heard the message of Peter in their own language. This was truly a miraculous phenomenon produced by a loving God, eager to have His people understand this new chapter of His history and His personal work in their lives. It was, in a sense, the reversal of confusion of languages due to the building of the tower of Babel. Whereas the tower builders were usurping the status and power of God, the humble followers of Jesus at Pentecost were in place to hear from God and obey His word. Speaking the language which others understand is sometimes very humbling, but it is meeting the others on their territory and not expecting them to make their way to you. Expecting the other to learn your language is just another form of cultural imperialism. This should not even be open to discussion: the message of the gospel should come to the nationals in their language.[55]

Trust

Trust is the basis of all relationships. It is associated with a firm belief and confidence in the honesty, integrity, reliability and justice of another. Trustworthiness is the basis of credibility. Without trust a relationship cannot continue to grow. Without trust a person is unable to form relationships. A breach of trust will cause a sudden break in the relationship, which, if not resolved, will cause a deterioration of the relationship.

Trust is a primary pillar upon which our relationship to God is built. His call to us is to believe in or trust Him (*pistis*). God's call can be seen as releasing us from our fear of a terrifying God - His invitation to "Fear not!" as extended to Abraham, Isaac, Jacob, the prophets and the Israelites. Jesus repeated this invitation on such occasions as when He revealed the glory of God, coming to His disciples walking on water and at the

---

[55] There are few exceptions to this rule, I think. The exceptions are not for the long-term missionary but for short-termers who, because of the limited time available in the host culture, communicate in another common language. And, it is important to note in this context, that short-term missions are more effective if coupled with a long-term strategy. If God's word is to take root and change a people and a culture, it must come to the people in their heart language. This may be achieved by national Christians, who know the common language, and who are then theologically trained, serving their people as missionaries and pastors. Or the long-term missionaries learn the language to communicate God's word to the people. In both cases the strategy is long-term and involves learning the heart language.

Mount of Transfiguration. The trust-building Psalms picture God as a fortress and shield, a place of security and protection. This call reduces the distance to God.[56] Jesus calls God *Abba*. Faith in Him is justified because He has demonstrated His trustworthiness. He has established a covenant with us, strangely enough, because He has put in us the potential of trust and trustworthiness.[57] He makes Himself vulnerable and takes this risk of having His trust reciprocated or not reciprocated. The trust that God places in us builds our self-confidence; we are not only fallen people, we have the image of God in us and God has chosen to trust us. In contrast to self-abasement and self-mistrust, self-confidence grows with such knowledge. This is the basis for freedom to engage in relationships in a "culture of trust."[58] The trust relationship to God must be the primary one because He is the only perfectly trustworthy One, the One who can hold us when we weather the storms of breech of trust and disappointments in other primary relationships. Trust in oneself must grow into trust of others. And trust of others needs to be kept open-ended to include even more people. Jesus corrected His disciples when they excluded others outside their disciples' group who were also doing ministry. "Whoever is not against you is for you."[59]

Not that trusting others is without discretion. Bonhoeffer described his atmosphere in the Nazi prison in 1942 as the air being "contaminated with mistrust" but "we have learned not to trust the mean ones but to completely entrust ourselves to the trustworthy."[60] Akin to the building of trust to self and trust to others, trust in God results in trust for the future. Fatalism is banned. Whereas Strunk claims that optimism is uncritical and based on the past with trust being future-oriented based on a break with the past to follow Jesus, I see this same optimism as a foundation for a trust that is able to follow Jesus. It is a trust based on the past acts of a faithful, trustworthy God whose character never changes. His conclusion is nevertheless valid, that there are two opposite principles of life: one takes steps to make life secure and the other builds trust. This process of building trust he sees as a primary responsibility of the church.[61]

---

[56] Reiner Strunk, *Vertrauen: Grundzüge einer Theologie des Gemeindeaufbaus* (Stuttgart: Quell, 1985), 20f.

[57] Strunk, ibid., 23f.

[58] Strunk, ibid., 31f.

[59] Luke 9:49f; Strunk, *Vetrauen*, 35f.

[60] Dietrich Bonhoeffer, *Widerstand und Ergebung*, (Hamburg: Siebenstern Taschenbuch, 1970), 21.

[61] Strunk, *Vertrauen*, 38.

Trust is necessary for life and personal growth. Psychologists usually agree that basic trust is established during the first two years of life through the relationship to the primary person in our lives, traditionally our mother. The capacity for trust is etched out in us and continues to develop. Children are resilient and can usually compensate for delays in development. But as a result, they suffer as adults from deficits in this area. Delay at any stage of personal development results in, among other things, personal immaturity. This immaturity is usually evidenced in bitterness, anger, hatred, jealousy and resentment.[62]

Team relationships are built on and maintained by trust. Mission teams have the benefit of operating on an initial reservoir of trust, i.e., certain assumptions have been made which lend themselves to forming an immediate bond. The strongest is the common faith in the Lord Jesus Christ. There is the assumption that the team will operate on a basis of Christian love and acceptance rather than competition, for example. There are many more assumptions which serve as expectations for the team. Although it is important to discover individual deficits in trust in the application process and delay going to the field until some growth has taken place, we will nevertheless have missionaries with undetected deficiencies on our teams.[63] It's important to extend love and grace to them in the growing process.

A breach of trust occurs when words or actions do not concur with one of these many assumptions or expectations. If the time span is short, a breach, as such, may not occur. Bewilderment may hold it in suspension for a time and, if positively resolved, avoid creating a rift. In a multicultural team there are many, many opportunities for misunderstandings and resultant breaking of trust. If the "reservoir of love and acceptance" is deep and full, these misunderstandings and subtle "attacks" on trust can be withstood, but only if the misunderstandings are cleared up as they occur, with relatively little time lag. Dealing with misunderstandings as they come up and in a culturally appropriate way is a sign of good will. In this way the reservoir of trust that was there initially is preserved.

> *A breach of trust will cause a sudden break in the relationship, which, if not resolved, will cause a deterioration of the relationship.*

---

[62] Marjory Foyle, *Honourably Wounded* (Bromley, Kent: MARC Europe, 1987), 127. Dr. Foyle also mentions that the team problems that come to the surface are "yesterday's problems." These problems out of the past are the ones that should be dealt with; the problems between missionaries, in this case, are secondary. The primary problem should be dealt with first.

[63] See chapter 5 for detailed information on selection of missionary candidates.

Disagreements need not precipitate a breach of trust. Two mature missionaries such as Paul and Barnabas were not always in agreement over their plans. One serious disagreement over adding a new missionary to the team caused them to rethink their plans and eventually go separate ways, Barnabas taking John Mark with him and Paul with Silas, as a new team. They were not reluctant to express their own opinions and convictions, neither were they afraid to risk taking a totally different way than originally planned.[64] Abraham and his nephew Lot solved a dispute among their herdsmen by agreeing to part as well. There will be cases when convictions are so strong and disagreements so sharp that one must split up the team rather than break trust and destroy relationships. The end result of the development of John Mark indicated that this was a wise way to go; the trust between Paul and Barnabas was not broken; Barnabas "discipled" John Mark until he was such a trustworthy missionary that Paul even sent for him. Team relationships should not just follow a pattern of conflict-avoidance. Trust

> *Trust involves risk, feedback, solving problems, forgiveness, acceptance, unconditional love and risking again.*

must grow if the relationships are to deepen and "grow up in every way into him . . . joined and knit together by every ligament with which it is equipped, as each part is working properly, promotes the body's growth in building itself up in love."[65] Trust is transferred but must always be learned with new people in a new situation. It involves taking a risk, giving and receiving feedback, solving problems, mutual forgiveness, acceptance, and unconditional love and then risking again.

Conflict Resolution

The early church was not immune to conflicts. In fact there are many allusions to conflict between groups in the church itself, between leaders of the church, between individual church members. Where there is a fight there is also, even when it is hidden, human desire for power in play.[66] Some of these conflicts were based on cultural differences. The church in Jerusalem with its sub-groups of Palestinian Jewish Christians and Hellenistic Jewish Christians was concerned about the lack of care

---

[64] Acts 15:37-39.

[65] Ephesians 4:15, 16. Paul's detailed description seems to exclude individualistic efforts.

[66] Karl Rennstich, "Streit und Konflikte in der Bibel," unpublished, 1996, 4.

for the Hellenist widows (Acts 6:1-6). Some conflicts were more of a doctrinal nature, inevitably mixed with culture, however, for example the discussion over whether "heathen" converts could be baptized without being circumcised (Cornelius in Acts 10). The resolution of such conflicts took different forms: whereas in the Acts 6 account a "clear, theological and socio-psychological solution" was found (the groups operated as sub-groups within the same church with their own leadership), in the Acts 10 account a "communicative solution" was found, Peter using the best of his theological training to justify the situation.[67]

A word study of New Testament expressions translated "fight" shows that these were never used positively, as fighting against evil, for example. Although conflicts are inevitable when cultures and people clash, fighting or warring is rejected and to be avoided.[68] "Have nothing to do with stupid and senseless controversies; you know that they breed quarrels." (2 Timothy 2:23; cf. Titus 3:9)[69]

The level of our ability to relate to people determines how happy and effective we are as persons. And our inability to resolve conflicts leads to the undermining of trust and the destruction of relationships. Paul's insistence on "preserving the unity" in the body of Christ is not a luxury; it's a necessity. In most cases, problems that are successfully solved lead to a deeper intimacy and enhance the quality of our relationships.

What is the nature of unity that Paul strives for? It is not that we all have to share the same opinions. It is rather that we are there for one another and can share our opinions and receive feedback without ourselves as persons being put in question or criticized. If we do indeed belong together in the body of Christ, the conflicts cannot be ignored; they need to be named and dealt with. The greatest commandment and rule of communication of any kind, especially in solving conflicts, is love. Paul

> *The level of our ability to relate to people determines how happy and effective we are as persons.*

writes that we are to deal in truth, speak the truth in love (Ephesians 4:11-14). In the preceding verses mentioning unity, Paul emphasized genuine outworkings of this dealing in love: humility, gentleness and patience. Often these very qualities are the ones missing in an attempt to resolve

---

[67] K. Rennstich, ibid., 9f.

[68] K. Rennstich, ibid., 4.

[69] *Eris* (strife, contention), *eritheia* (faction), *antilogia* (strife, dispute), *maché* (strife, fighting), *philoneikia* (strife, contention) and *logomachia* (dispute, strife of words) are the Greek expressions used to indicate the presence of enmity listed in W.E. Vine, *An Expository Dictionary of New Testament Words* (Old Tappan: Revell, 1966).

conflicts; rather one is so concentrated on defending one's own interests that there is rarely a hint of "looking out after the interests of others" (Philippians 2). It is important then to check one's own motivation (Is it a reaction out of hurt or bitterness wanting to get revenge or to vindicate oneself?) before beginning to resolve the conflict at hand. A conscious decision must be made to deal in the power of the Holy Spirit and not in the energy of the "old self" (Ephesians 4). Emotions must not be "controlled," i.e. not concealed, but rather expressed under the leading of the Holy Spirit so there are mutually constructive benefits. It is best not to let the problem "stew" over a period of time, which gives the enemy of our souls the opportunity to distort the perspective and destroy unity (1 Peter 5:8, 9), but to begin to deal with the issue "before the sun goes down," today (Ephesians 4). The interaction should not be a mere flinging of emotions onto the table, but that which builds up and results in blessing (Ephesians 4:29). God is at work even in such negative situations; we should be attentive to what the Holy Spirit wants to do through this conflict, not "quenching" His influence (Ephesians 4:30). The discussion and the relationships are not to be characterized by destructive anger, bitterness, and insults, but rather by friendliness, helpfulness and forgiveness (forgiveness to the extent that Christ forgave us - Ephesians 4:31, 32).[70]

Power

One cannot speak of the encounter of cultures without dealing with the issue of power. It is said that power corrupts and absolute power corrupts absolutely.[71] This axiom unfortunately tends to be verified irrespective of the area of society it affects - government, business, family or church. Lord Acton believed that every form of power contained the germ of evil in it which infected the carrier of power.[72] The highest form

---

[70] Lianne Roembke, "Interpersonal Relationships and Problem Solving," unpublished lecture developed for Agape International Training. Cf. Duane Elmer, *Cross-Cultural Conflict* (Downers Grove: InterVarsity, 1993) and Donald Palmer, *Managing Conflict Creatively: A Guide for Missionaries and Christian Workers* (Pasadena: William Carey Library, 1990).

[71] This is first cited in a letter from Lord Acton to Mandell Creighton on 5. April 1887, who wrote of this in his five volumes on the history of the popes during the Protestant Reformation.

[72] Lord Acton, ibid.

of morals could not prevent corruption. Acton was convinced that the corruption of power was a theological problem.[73]

Cultural imperialism is a particularly subtle form of power plays. No nation is exempt from the exertion of cultural imperialism in the form of nationalism in its history: Germany with its exaltation of the Aryan race and plotted destruction of all else, Japan with its imperialist wars in China and Korea, the early (Spain and Portugal) and later (England, the Netherlands, Belgium, Germany, Russia) European colonizers of Africa, Asia and the Americas, as well as the tribal imperialism of the colonized nations.

The presence of power is a fact of life with which nations, societies, companies and families must deal. In contrast to Lord Acton, I believe that power, in and of itself, is not evil; but the abuse of power is. This abuse is sometimes subtle and at times unconscious, at other times overt and consciously self-exalting and destructive. The saying, "power corrupts" is almost inevitably true because of the fallen nature of human beings. This tendency leads them to use the power at their disposal to seek their own benefit and not look after the interests of others first, as Jesus did.[74] Jesus powerfully defined leadership as humble service when He washed His disciples' feet as an example to them. He chided His disciples when they asked about leadership positions and rebuked those who used their position as a platform for power plays. It is no coincidence that He, the Almighty God, was incarnated as a helpless child who had laid aside His rights to power.

The sin in the Garden of Eden was the sin of power. Adam and Eve's desire went beyond the truly good life they had to the deceptiveness of

> *Power is particularly insidious when linked with pride.*

wanting to know more, to have more and to be more than is right.[75] They were not content with their creaturely status; they wanted to be like God. This craving for power is destructive, causing a rupture in our relationship with God.[76] King Saul's rabid envy of David as a sign of his grasping for power in his powerlessness against David's popularity. "He would rather have murdered than have allowed power to slip through his fingers."[77] Power is particularly insidious when linked with pride. Pride, which normally

---

[73] Karl Rennstich, *Korruption: Eine Herausforderung für Gesellschaft und Kirche* (Stuttgart: Quell, 1990), 40f.

[74] Philippians 2:3f.

[75] Richard Foster, *Money, Sex and Power: The Challenge of a Disciplined Life* (San Francisco: Harper and Row, 1985), 175.

[76] Foster, ibid., 176.

[77] Foster, ibid., 176.

accompanies the destructive form of power, is also accompanied by a sort of blindness, a sense of strangeness to reality.[78]

Augustine was convinced that the desire for power was the ruling force in the affairs of the city, in political life. Thomas Aquinas, building upon this thought, said that power needed to be tamed, which he thought only possible under the authority of the Word of God and Church teaching.[79] John Calvin also proposed holding back the power of the powerful. Calvin's thoughts were used by Harrington (1656), Locke (1659), and Montesquieu to formulate their philosophies of government which were later reflected in the separation of powers in the new Constitution of the United States. "From a Christian perspective the concentration of power should be prevented, that is, held in check."[80] This is a challenge today, not only in government but in the church and in missions.

Power especially in relation to hierarchical structures is currently an explosive issue for many women, not just for feminists. L. Schottroff sees evil in the structuring of hierarchy in and of itself.[81] She dreams of a church that renounces such structures, serving one another, in which the real power is the power of God's Word. M. Josuttis questions whether attacking structures of power is getting to the real root of evil. He contends that one cannot just do away with such structures. Some structures are, for a time at least, necessary and good. Parents, for example, must exercise power over their children for a limited period of their lives.[82]

Others have problems when speaking of God as almighty. The experiences of Auschwitz caused D. Sölle to question the omnipotence of God.[83] Sölle criticizes J. Moltmann sharply in his portrayal of God suffering with Christ as He died on the cross.[84] As I understand it though, her criticism emanates from a false understanding of the trinity. Jesus in His suffering cannot be separated from God; they are one. M. Josuttis admits that God's omnipotence is problematic. One may not just apply

---

[78] Foster, ibid., 178. One begins to believe the press releases about oneself, says Foster.

[79] Church teaching became a power in and of itself, needing to be checked. For this Jan Hus gave his life.

[80] Karl Rennstich, "Geld and Macht in ökumenischen Beziehungen," unpublished, 1996, 5.

[81] L. Schottroff, "Über Herrschaftsverzicht und den Dienst der Versöhnung," in L. and W. Schottroff, *Die Kostbare Liebe zum Leben* (Munich: Biblische Inspirationen, 1991), 134.

[82] Manfred Josuttis, *Petrus, die Kirche und die verdammte Macht*, (Stuttgart: Kreuz, 1993), 31.

[83] D. Sölle, *Leiden* (Stuttgart: Kreuz, 1973), 35.

[84] Jürgen Moltmann, *Der gekreuzigte Gott* (Munich: Kaiser, 1972), 201.

philosophy or psychology naively.[85] He would agree with Foster that power is a fact of life and the resultant good or evil depends on how one handles power.

Another important area of power to be reckoned with is referred to by Paul as "principalities and powers" in Ephesians 6:12. "The Bible speaks of very real cosmic spiritual powers that manifest themselves in the very real structures of our very real world."[86] This is not prescientific thinking. Those who deny the existence of such powers are usually the Western materialists who have arbitrarily stricken them from their categories. Such powers are created realities (Colossians 1:16) which have rebelled against God, which seek to enslave and destroy (Galatians 4:8-10).[87] The collective force of such powers is greater than the sum of their parts, Foster maintains. He cites such hideous dimensions in the workings of the Ku Klux Klan and Nazi Germany.[88] My visits to Dachau and Auschwitz convinced me that there were more than depraved humans at work there. The ability to discern the spirits at work in such situations is one of the gifts of the Holy Spirit (1 Corinthians 12:8-10).[89] It is often the pioneer generation of missionaries who suffer the most for encroaching upon the kingdom of this world. Loss of life, health, family members as well as terrible battles with depression have been their lot then and now.

---

[85] Josuttis, *Petrus, die Kirche*, 34.
[86] Foster, *Money*, 180.
[87] Foster, ibid., 181.
[88] Foster, ibid., 180f.
[89] Foster deals with the issue of battling with the spiritual forces seriously. First, one must ask for the gift of discerning spirits, inviting God to teach us all it means. Secondly, we should gather around us a group of faithful believers to listen to what one another is learning and listen collectively to God. Thirdly, we begin by dealing with the "demons" within, with those areas of misuse of power that affect us, so we become free to not fight against those powers in kind. The Holy Spirit comes along side to comfort and encourage as He convicts. We let our hearts be conquered by the Lamb. Fourth, we renounce all of our misuses of power; we have nothing to lose. Fifth, we reject the use of the weapons of this world in defeating the powers, and make use of the power of the Holy Spirit. Sixth, we use the weapons of spiritual warfare in Ephesians 6 which tear down strongholds (2 Corinthians 10:4).

Leadership

One area in which power tends to be concentrated without proper checks and balances is leadership in the church and in Christian organizations. Karl Rennstich traces this back to an improper understanding of ministry and ordination.[90] In short, he points out that ordination is for serving the other members of the body of Christ in gathering them and building them up so that they in turn can make use of their spiritual gifts for the use of the church. The danger is that this power can be corrupted. The prophet Amos condemned the lack of righteousness and truth and corruptibility of the elders in Samaria and the prophet Isaiah the elders in Israel. They "raped the laws, falsified the truth, despised righteousness and got rich off the little man, the poor and the weak," preached the prophets. This in spite of the fact that their responsibility was to protect and to teach the Word of God entrusted to them.

This distortion of power can also infiltrate the ministries (= services) exercised in the church by the members of the body of Christ who have received the gifts of the Spirit of God for the purpose of serving. Paul states clearly that not one gift is better than another nor to be exalted over another; all are necessary for the smooth functioning and growth of the body. Only Jesus is the head of His body. It is clear that no authority can be exercised without respect to the whole of the body. "Not by power or by might but by my Spirit says the Lord of hosts," (Zechariah 4:6). God's power is wholly other; His power is in love, manifest in Christ.

There is also a "creative" aspect to power. Joseph, after he was sold into slavery, later imprisoned, freed and rose to a position next to Pharaoh in Egypt, had power to rescue his brothers and their families in time of dire need. William Wilberforce used the power of his office to help abolish slave trade.[91] Many peacemakers, non-politicians working behind the scenes in Israel, South Africa, former Yugoslavia, and elsewhere, are using their power and influence creatively and constructively to mend relationships.

There is also a creative aspect to power.

Jesus said the smallest is, in reality, the greatest (Luke 9:48). The Apostle Paul wrote in seemingly contradictory terms of strength being present in weakness (2 Corinthians 12:9). And Dietrich Bonhoeffer, who was at the mercy of the powers that be, wrote of his experience at the hands of Hitler's SS Black Guards, when he had to die to all his hopes

---

[90] Karl Rennstich, "Vom Ältestenamt Über Ordination und Priesteramt zur Theologie des Laientums" unpublished, 3f.

[91] Foster, *Money*, 196f.

and dreams. "When Christ calls a person, he bids him come and die."[92] The zenith of spiritual power is the crucifixion. At a time when all the powers of Satan were rallied to defeat the power of God, God used the death of Christ to defeat these powers. And we have been freed from those powers, never to have to be enslaved to them again. As Josuttis writes, the cross of Christ regenerated power. The crucifixion of Christ is the powerful solution to all tensions and contradictions in life.[93]

There are biblical injunctions for leaders that are binding to all cultures. Where, on the one hand, obedience is required to those in authority (Hebrews 13:17), leaders are cautioned not to "lord it over" them and to "shepherd the flock." The authority (*exousia*) of leadership is loaned to them by the Lord, and they are responsible directly to Him for the way they shepherd. The power (*dynamis*) is not exerted on others; it is rather that power or strength that is given from the Holy Spirit to leaders and all Christians who avail themselves, to carry out His ministry. In addition to the God-given authority team leaders carry, they may also have other resources of authority that make their teammates willing to follow more readily their leadership: the authority of competence, the authority of position, the authority of personality and the authority of character.[94] These resources can be further developed. Great leaders, as Jesus Himself has shown, are servants first and foremost (Mark 10:43, 44). They seek the good of those they lead, not being consumed with organizational or (God forbid) personal goals of success. When the team members sense the leader has their best interests at heart (*agape*), cheerful participation and obedience will follow respect.

> God's power is wholly other; His power is love, manifest in Christ.

While all relationships in life involve power one can learn how to use it for the good of others. The desire for excellence, while noble, should not be a cover for the seductive powers of greed and prestige. Creative use of power produces unity. Foster gives seven marks of creative power which apply to team members and leaders alike. 1) *Love* for the other expels the egotism in power. This is *agape*, self-sacrificing love. 2) *Humility* is power under discipline, which realizes that power is a gift not a given and expresses gratitude. 3) *Self-limitation* - "The power that creates refrains from doing some things - even good things - out of respect

[92] Dietrich Bonhoeffer, *The Cost of Discipleship*, transl. R.H. Fuller (New York: Macmillian, 1963), 7.

[93] Josuttis, *Petrus, die Kirche*, 205.

[94] William Oncken, Jr., "The Authority to Manage," Circular No. 36, (Dallas: Oncken, October, 1970), as quoted in Ted W. Engstrom, *The Making of a Christian Leader* (Grand Rapids: Zondervan, 1976), 112-13.

for the individual."[95] Jesus often refused to use power at His disposal. 4) *Joy*, not an insincere frivolity, results from the exertion of creative power. 5) *Vulnerability* lacks the symbols of human authority; it is self-chosen meekness, which looks powerless. It is the power of the "wounded healer," to borrow from Henri Nouwen's phrase. This power leads from weakness because it knows that in weakness Christ's strength is made perfect (2 Corinthians 12:9-10). It is power that does not dominate but patiently waits. 6) *Submission* to the ways of God. Creative power is to "submit to one another out of reverence for Christ" (Ephesians 5:21), the overriding command. Since there is no such thing as being more or less submissive there is no power struggle.

> *"Submission is power because it places us in a position in which we can receive from others."*

Apollos submitted to Priscilla and Aquila when they took him aside to correct his teaching (Acts 18: 24-26). "Submission is power because it places us in a position in which we can receive from others."[96] We have access to their vast resources of wisdom, counsel and encouragement. 7) *Freedom* comes from creative power that does not bind or crush people or their hopes (Matthew 12:20). It frees people to be all that God created them to be; it frees them even from the pressure to please others. Again, this power is best kept from abuse in a system of checks and balances both from "above" the team leader and within the team itself. Team leaders can use this power to facilitate the competence of others, not promote feelings of inadequacy. And the team members use their power as the mighty tool of encouragement. An important criterion for the multicultural team: Is the team characterized by the love of power or the power of love?

The cultural backgrounds of the team members will determine how they perceive the leadership. Everyone will tend to look at the exercise of servant leadership through their own cultural glasses. They should be quick to observe and slow to judge. And they should be wise enough to call their own cultural values into question. For example, through the effects of antinomianism in most Western cultures the term "obedience" has very negative connotations. Especially in Germany the terms *Führer* (leader) and *Gehorsam* (obedience) can hardly be used

> *The cultural backgrounds of the team members will determine how they perceive the leadership.*

today without eliciting a negative, sometimes emotional reaction; these terms have been discredited by Hitler. For Germans then, it is imperative

---

[95] Richard Foster, *Money,* 203.
[96] Foster, ibid., 206.

that the power not reside solely in one person, insuring keeping absolute power in check.

In summary, power and its use is a fact of life. The decision of how people, groups and organizations use power is crucial: creatively, for the good of others, or destructively, for their own selfish purposes and the detriment of others. Because of human falleness, building in checks and balances of power is healthy and wise.

Money

There is hardly another area of life which is more prone to the misuse of power than the area of finances. And there is hardly a more taboo subject of discussion than money. But Jesus spoke more about money than about any other area of life, except the kingdom of God.[97] "Sell your possessions and give to the poor . . ." (Luke 12:34). "For where your treasure is, there your heart will be also" (Matthew 19:21). "But the worries of this life, the deceitfulness of wealth and the desires for other things come in and choke the word, making it unfruitful" (Mark 4:19). "Woe to you, teachers of the law and Pharisees, you hypocrites! You clean the outside of the cup and dish, but inside they are full of greed and self-indulgence" (Matthew 23:25). Foster categorizes the effects of money on us twofold. The "dark side" of money is the grip it has on us based on our past; there may be a lack of security and a fear that grips us. This can be overcome with a spirit of trust. The "light side" of money is the way we can use it to enhance our relationship with God and benefit others.[98]

Jesus "personified" *mammon* (Aramaic for "wealth") as a god, which people worship. Foster deduces from this that money is not neutral but rather a power that seeks to dominate us. "Perhaps the most insidious form of syncretism in the world today is the attempt to mix a privatized gospel of personal forgiveness with a worldly (even demonic) attitude to wealth and power."[99] This power seeks devotion as a rival god.[100] In cases in which people had been consumed by this devotion (Zacchaeus

---

[97] Foster, ibid., 19.
[98] Foster, ibid., 22f.
[99] "The Willowbank Report" of the Lausanne Committee, 1978, Ralph Winter and Steven Hawthorne, *Perspectives on the World Christian Movement* (Pasadena: William Carey Library, 1981), 531.
[100] Foster, *Money*, 26f.

and the rich young ruler) Jesus called for a complete renunciation of this
god. Money, Foster observes, has many of the characteristics of deity: it
can give security, power, freedom, and can induce guilt.[101] But these are
false securities. Jesus called the wealthy farmer
who tore down his barns to build bigger ones to
keep his honestly earned grain, a fool. His security was falsely rooted. We attach an incredible
amount of personal worth and prestige to money.
In this age of rising unemployment, people are
searching for and governments are hoping to

> Money has many of
> the characteristics
> of deity: It can give
> security, power,
> freedom, and can
> induce guilt.

create jobs. But such "meaningful" work, to have value in our society,
dare not be non-paid volunteer work even if it is meaningful and, in
many countries of the Western world, covered by relatively good unemployment pay. The sacrifice of prestige is too great.

Money is tied to missions. In the New Testament one sees several
methods of securing finances for mission work. Our Lord was supported
by patrons, including notable women.[102] He was not wealthy by any
standard; He owned no home or property. The Bible says that although
He was rich, He became poor for our sakes.[103] The accruement of wealth
was the furthest from His mind. His advice to those who were obsessed
with their wealth was to sell everything they have and give to the poor.[104]
But Jesus was comfortable being invited to dine with the rich and yet
bold enough to speak a message that confronted them with repentance,
financial implications included. After hearing Jesus' message, Zacchaeus, a tax collector of ignoble repute, repented and repaid four-fold
those he had overtaxed.[105] Jesus moved with ease among all circles of
society, and did so with a clear conscience. He sent His disciples out on
short evangelistic projects without resources or even a change of clothes.
They were to be guests of those who were receptive, but never to impose
themselves on others.[106]

The Apostle Paul wrote often about finances. In addition to financing
his ministry sometimes by his own business (tentmaking), he willingly
accepted contributions. He built his case on the Old Testament principle
that the ox that threshes should not be muzzled (Deuteronomy 25:4), that
they who preach the Gospel should live from the Gospel (1 Corinthians
9:14). This he describes as a right; the worker is worthy of his salary.

---

[101] Foster, ibid., 28.
[102] Luke 8:3.
[103] 2 Corinthians 8:9.
[104] Luke 18:18-25.
[105] Luke 19:1-10.
[106] Luke 9:1-6; 10:1-22.

Whether this salary is taken or not is a matter for the individual to decide, it nevertheless remains a right.[107] In some cases Paul refused his rightful salary. This was qualified, however; he did not take money from the people to whom he presently ministered. This had to do with his sensitivity to the misuse of a certain practice in his culture - teachers who taught for profit. He refuted any accusation of this kind: "For we are not peddlers of God's word like so many; but in Christ we speak as persons of sincerity, as persons sent from God and standing in his presence."[108] Roland Allen reflects, "It is strange how often he refers to it [finances], what anxiety he shows that his position should not be misunderstood."[109] On the other hand, Paul thanks the believers in Philippi for the financial care they showed for him.[110] He showed a definite inner independence from the power of money; he knew how to deal with hunger and need, as well as abundance.[111] But greed was not his motive for preaching the Gospel. "He refused to do anything from which it might appear that he came to receive, that his object was to make money."[112] He encouraged churches to be self-supporting,[113] but did not discourage them from supporting other churches in need.[114] Voluntary, cheerful giving was to characterize the church.[115] His counsel regarding giving was: "I do not mean that there should be relief for others and pressure on you, but it is a question of a fair balance between your present abundance and their need, so that their abundance may be for your need, in order that there may be a fair balance."[116]

Historically, missions have established a mixed picture of credibility in finances. Lack of credibility has resulted - sometimes inadvertently, sometimes intentionally, in an unholy alliance with mammon. Karl Rennstich relates the story of the missionary, Dr. Karl Gützlaff, called a "Friend of China," who, because he wanted to make inroads to preach the Gospel, accepted an offer as a translator on a ship trading in opium. As incredulous as this may seem today, his "internal conflict" over this decision of translating for British opium traders Matheson and Jardine

---

[107] Karl Rennstich, "Paulus als Geschäftsmann," unpublished, n.d., 2f.
[108] 2 Corinthians 2:17.
[109] Roland Allen, *Missionary Methods St. Paul's or Ours? (Grand Rapids: Eerdmans, 1995, first published 1912)*, 49.
[110] Philippians 4:16.
[111] Philippians 4:12.
[112] Roland Allen, *Missionary Methods*, 51.
[113] Galatians 6:6.
[114] 1 Corinthians 16:3.
[115] 2 Corinthians 9:7; 8:3-4.
[116] 2 Corinthians 8:13-14.

was rather easily quieted by their offer to make it worth his while. If the trade flourished they would publish the newspaper, posters and leaflets he needed for evangelism! And his first trip as translator was not his last.[117]

But history is also full of notable exceptions. Thank God for the Mother Theresas of today and the St. Francis's of yesterday. The Dominican monk Bartholomé de las Casas (1474-1566), stood alone in his battle against the corruption of the Spanish of his day in Central America. He demanded that the European "Christian" colonialists pay retribution for the damage they had done in the trading of weapons and slaves. This challenge was echoed centuries later by Christian Gottlieb Blumhardt, Albert Schweizer and others.[118] In 1675, Philip J. Spener, a father of the Pietist Movement, challenged Pietists with a "conversion to the future" in his *Pia Desideria*. He saw the necessity to redistribute goods. His view was that everything belonged to God and he was just a steward. His neighbor was not to request of him, but he could freely give to his neighbor when he can't be helped in any other way.[119] As Rennstich notes, "Long before the German intellectuals discussed the issue of human rights, the Pietists of Southwest Germany, such as Ostertag and Blumhardt [directors of the *Basler Mission*], were involved with this issue and its connection to commerce."[120]

Money and lifestyle, though not synonymous, are almost inseparable. The amount of money one has often determines the lifestyle one leads, i.e., how much money is put into purchases of house, clothes, food, and what is deemed necessary for living.[121] Greed, as one of the deadly sins, is defined as desiring more than what

> *Greed is desiring more than what one has or having more than enough in a context when some have less than enough.*

---

[117] Karl Rennstich, *Die Zwei Symbole des Kreuzes: Handel und Mission in China und Südostasien* (Stuttgart: Quell, 1988), 26-28.

[118] Rennstich, "Mission und Geld. Einführungsvortrag zum Missionstheologischen Symposium Mission und Geld," unpublished, 1996, 25-26.

[119] Karl Rennstich, *Mission und wirtschaftliche Entwicklung* (Munich: Kaiser, 1978), 184.

[120] Rennstich, "Mission und Geld," 23.

[121] Many recent books written about a simpler lifestyle are frankly written to ease the pressure of the Westerner, making life more livable. Others, such as Richard Foster's *Freedom of Simplicity* (San Francisco: Harper and Row, 1981) and Ronald Sider's *Rich Christians in an Age of Hunger: A Biblical Study* (Downers Grove: InterVarsity, 1978) are geared specifically to sharing God's resources, the biblical principles of being led by the Spirit and not by the god of mammon.

one has or having more than what is enough in a context when some have less than enough.[122] This sin is as deadly for the Western missionaries as it is for those among whom they work.[123] A preoccupation with material things is also very detrimental to the credibility of the gospel. What constitutes "preoccupation" is also culturally evaluated. A preoccupation with things can be the time involved in purchasing, setting up, using, repairing those things the missionary, for example, judges as "necessary," but which are looked upon by others as "luxury." Jonathan Bonk emphasizes however that Christian stewardship is not something we *do* primarily but rather something we *become* - a way of living. He believes this is a process of self-examination (with feedback from others) in the light of the Holy Spirit.[124] The social responsibility missionaries assume in their context (actually of Christians in any context) is a telling indication of where their hearts are. Are they willing to give of their treasure, their resources, their time? Or are they so wrapped up in their "mission" that they refuse to see the wounded one lying on the street on their way to an appointment? Not one of us is exempt from this temptation.

John Stott sees parallels and contrasts in the parables of the Good Samaritan and the Prodigal Son in Luke's Gospel which picture both responsibilities of Christians: evangelism and social action. The victim in the parable of the lost son is the son himself, who is a victim of his own sin (personal sin). In the parable of the good Samaritan, the victim is the man who is mugged by those who sinned against him (social sin). Both conditions should arouse the compassion of Christians. In both parables there is a rescue and a display of love which triumphs over prejudice. In both there is a sub-plot, an emphasis on what kind of behavior is to be condemned: the elder brother of the lost son deserves condemnation for refusing to become involved in evangelism and leaving his brother in his sins; in the parable of the good Samaritan, it is the priest and the Levite who resist the call to social action.[125]

> "We affirm that Good News and good works are inseparable."
> The Manila Manifesto

It has been heartening to see the move of Evangelicals towards a holistic form of ministry, with social action an integral part, similar to their predecessors such as Wesley and Wilberforce. The moving forces behind this "conversion" were the mission churches in Asia, Africa and Latin America, who knew no dichotomy between "horizontal and vertical the-

---

[122] Jonathan Bonk, *Missions and Money* (Maryknoll: Orbis, 1982), 80f.

[123] Bonk, ibid., 79.

[124] Bonk, ibid., 131-32.

[125] John Stott, *The Contemporary Christian* (Leicester: InterVarsity, 1992), 346f.

ology."[126] A turning point in this whole discussion for Evangelicals was the Lausanne II Conference in Manila. Working through tensions that could be felt, the wording of the "Manila Manifesto" captured the consensus of the delegates. While holding to the primacy of evangelism, it was acknowledged that "we are called today to a similar integration of words and deeds [as that of Jesus proclaiming the kingdom of God and demonstrating its arrival by works of mercy and power] . . . we also affirm that Good News and good works are inseparable."[127] Anna-Maria Sauer in her research on the social responsibility in the Lausanne Movement, concurring with K. Bockmühl, concludes that the kingdom of God, living under the rule of God, means to live as Jesus, for God and for one's neighbors.[128] J. Stott pleads with Christians to enter into the heart world of other people, their *Angst* and alienation, "for it is impossible to share the gospel with people in a social vacuum, isolating them from their actual context and ignoring their suffering."[129] Jesus consistently identified Himself with the poor and the weak. But He went further than that; in bringing the good news to the oppressed He simultaneously spoke a word of judgment to the oppressor.[130] This vindication of the oppressed in the name of righteousness is not replacing power with another form of destructive power; it is allowing God's righteous power to right the wrong without allowing evil to gain a hand.[131]

> *Jesus consistently identified Himself with the poor and the weak.*

Women

It is encouraging to see the serious biblical scholarship that has gone into researching the subject of "women" in recent decades, liberating women from false interpretations of the Bible and from role expectations

---

[126] Karl Rennstich, "Die soziale Verantwortung der Christen heute," unpublished, 6.

[127] "Manila Manifesto" in *Proclaiming Christ Until He Comes* (Minneapolis: Worldwide, 1990), 30. These words were followed by appropriate words of repentance for previous narrowness of concerns and vision.

[128] A.-M. Sauer, "Die 'soziale Gerechtigkeit' in der Lausanner Bewegung 1974-1989" unpublished, 1992, 83.

[129] J. Stott, *The Contemporary Christian*, 360.

[130] "The Willowbank Report," 530.

[131] The issue of power is handled more extensively under the section "Leadership styles, authority and decision-making" in chapter 4.

that are purely cultural.[132] The then one hundred year old pamphlet by Catherine Booth, "Female Ministry: The Right of Women to Preach the Gospel"[133] (admittedly along with the conflict between the expectations in my environment and my sense of having to suppress the exercise of spiritual gifts), was my first impetus to research personally the subject of women in the Bible. To my amazement amidst

> *Neither man nor woman alone, but together they bear and reflect the image of God.*

what was otherwise careful biblical scholarship, I discovered a bias of interpreting the few obscure statements about women through cultural glasses, making these ambiguous passages the norm of doctrine. One would never have dared to do that with other Scripture passages, leaving the door open for the accusation of heresy. Leaving the questionable passages (1 Corinthians 11 and 14; 1 Timothy 2) to the end of my study I began by looking at where women were included, particularly in descriptions of believers in the body of Christ. The results of letting key passages of Scripture speak for themselves in context were amazing and convincing. First, in the Genesis 1 account of creation it states specifically that God created man and woman in His image. Neither man nor woman alone, but together they bear and reflect the image of God. Genesis 2 further states that the woman was created as a "help" (Hebrew *ezer*, often translated "helpmate," weakening the meaning). Further study of the word reveals that in 13 cases it refers to God as our help, a subordinate connotation

> *The woman was not made to serve her husband but to serve **God** with her husband.*

being totally absent.[134] The woman was made not to serve her husband but to serve **God** *with* her husband. Both are needed to reflect more completely the image of God.

Second, women held the offices of prophet (Miriam, Hulda, Deborah) and judge (Deborah) in the Old Testament, with no indication that this was against the will of God.

---

[132] Fortunately, the list of references on this subject has grown significantly in the last two decades. A popular book based on cross-cultural missionary experience is Kari Torjesen Malcolm, *Women at the Crossroads: A Path beyond Feminism and Traditionalism* (Downers Grove: InterVarsity, 1982), Aidá Besançon Spencer, *Beyond the Curse: Women Called to Ministry* (Nashville: Thomas Nelson, 1985), is a thorough handling of the biblical passages related to this issue, as is Gilbert Bilezikian, *Beyond Sex Roles* (Grand Rapids: Baker, 1985).

[133] Catherine Booth, "Female Ministry: Woman's Right to Preach the Gospel" (first published in London: 1859; reprinted New York: Salvation Army, 1975).

[134] Spencer, *Beyond the Curse*, 26-29.

Third, that Jesus had a circle of women disciples traveling with Him was against the cultural values of His time and showed that He valued women. He spoke with women about theological subjects (John 4), He trained them with the seriousness that the Rabbis trained their followers ("sitting at the feet of . . ." Luke 10:38-42 cf. Acts 22:3 - Paul sat at the feet of Gamaliel) and He chose women as the first witnesses of His resurrection, although women were not recognized as witnesses by the courts of His day.

Fourth, the commands of Jesus were directed equally to the women, as well as the men, who followed Him. The women were to become His witnesses and ambassadors, too.

Fifth, the Holy Spirit was poured out on the daughters as well as the sons (Acts 2, cf. Joel 2). Both women and men were to prophesy and teach as a result.

Sixth, the Holy Spirit gave and gives spiritual gifts to all believers, men and women alike, so that they can serve the Lord and other believers. These gifts are not distributed according to status, education, race or gender , but rather according to the sovereign will of God (1 Corinthians 12:1-11).

Seventh, in the body of Christ all barriers of status, gender and culture are removed: Galatians 3:26-28 proclaims the magna carta for all believers, "there is neither Jew or Greek, slave or free, male or female, for you are all one in Christ Jesus."

Eighth, the office of priest, once reserved for men and Levites, was given to all believers (1 Peter 2:9).

Ninth, even discipleship in the church is described with "female" as well as "male" characteristics (1 Thessalonians. 2:7-12). These characteristics were practiced by the Apostle Paul and are guidelines for all believers in relating to the new believers whom they disciple.

Tenth, the believers, men and women, are all co-heirs with Christ (Galatians 3:29; Ephesians 1:11) and will rule with Him.[135]

Eleventh, women in the early church held responsible positions for which we ordain people today: apostle - Junia (Romans 16); prophets - Anna and Philip's four daughters; teachers - Priscilla. There were no pastors, male or female, mentioned, but leaders of churches among whom were: "the elect lady" in 2 John 1, "the elect sister," Phoebe, Euodia, Syntyche, Priscilla, Tryphaena, Tryphosa, Chloe, Lydia, the mother of Mark, Nympha, Apphia and possibly Stephana.[136]

---

[135] Lianne Roembke, "Die Frau aus biblischer Perspektive" unpublished, 1987.

[136] Spencer, *Beyond the Curse*, 96f.

This is but a short summary of my findings relating to the position of women according to biblical revelation. These statements are normative statements for every woman and form the basis of her expectations of how God wants to use her. There are other statements correcting specific situations in particular congregations, which are described in the New Testament. These are descriptive of the problems then rather than prescriptive for women's ministry today.[137]

In the modern missionary era it has not always been self-evident that women were missionary-material. Mission agencies were reluctant to send single women, and married women were not counted.[138] J. Hudson Taylor and his wife Maria set a precedent in the founding of the China Inland Mission in 1865 by stating in their articles that wives are missionaries in their own right and have the same privileges as their husbands. Single women have the same privileges as men and can be sent independently to pioneer areas.[139] H. Taylor was convinced that if Chinese women were going to hear the gospel, women missionaries must be allowed to go into the interior and face the hazards as well. Robert Morrison, Gützlaff and Lobscheid had all previously advocated the use of women missionaries but it was Hudson Taylor who set the precedent on a wide basis.[140] They were not without opposition, however. Julius Richter criticized him publicly in the "Missionary Review of

> By 1894 there were thirty-three women's foreign missionary boards which had sent one thousand single women as missionaries.

---

[137] A. B. Spencer, ibid.; K.T. Malcolm, *Women at the Crossroads* (Downers Grove: InterVarsity, 1982), in German: *Christinnen jenseits von Feminismus and Traditionalismus* (Giessen: Brunnen, 1987), and Catherine Booth have sections in their books dealing with the so-called problem passages about women from the Apostle Paul. Additional resources are: Alvera Mickelson, ed. *Women, Authority and the Bible* (Downers Grove: InterVarsity, 1986); Gilbert Bilezikian, *Beyond Sex Roles* (Grand Rapids: Baker, 1985); Patricia Gundry, *Woman Be Free!* (Grand Rapids: Zondervan, 1977) and *Neither Slave nor Free* (San Francisco: Harper and Row, 1987); Myrtle Langley, *Equal Woman* (Hants: Marshall Morgan and Scott, 1983); Mary Stewart Van Leeuwen, *Gender and Grace* (Downers Grove: InterVarsity, 1990); Janet L. Kobobel, *But Can She Type?* (Downers Grove: InterVarsity, 1986) and Paul Tournier, *The Gift of Feeling* (London: SCM, 1982), in German: *Rückkehr zum Weiblichen* (Freiburg: Werder, 1982).

[138] Klaus Fiedler, *Ganz auf Vertrauen: Geschichte und Kirchenverständnis der Glaubensmission* (Giessen, Basel: Brunnen, 1992), 39.

[139] Klaus Fiedler, *Ganz auf Vertrauen*, 67.

[140] Daniel Bacon, "From Faith to Faith: The Influence of Hudson Taylor on the Faith Missions Movement," (Deerfield: D. Miss., Singapore, 1984), 64.

the World" in 1898 saying how "unbecoming and repellent to our German ideas was this free employment of single sisters in the midst of entirely heathen districts," to which Hudson Taylor replied "suggesting that Richter view the situation from a Chinese standpoint instead of through 'German or European eyes.' "[141] What was viewed as irresponsible at first proved itself effective through their significant contributions in the face of great danger and was imitated by other societies.[142] Missionary wives and in some cases clergy, such as Rev. David Abeel in China, led the way in calling for single women, free from domestic duties that burdened the wives, to form women's missionary societies and come and reach the women for Christ. America led the way, followed by England, but the concept met resistance on the European continent. By 1894 there were thirty-three women's foreign missionary boards which had sent one thousand single women as missionaries. There was a flocking of women to the mission field in the 1880s and 1890s.[143] It was not long before this posed a threat to some men. In the early 1900s the women's missionary societies were absorbed into denominational missions, sometimes much against the desires of the women who feared losing the limited power they had struggled so long to attain. Missionary statesman A. T. Pierson advocated an equal role for women, not barring them from leadership: "If Priscilla be the equal of Aquila, let her take rank by him, and if by superiority Priscilla outranks Aquila, let us not fear to put her name first."[144] But, alas, Pierson's egalitarianism was not contagious.

> "If Priscilla be the equal of Aquila, let her take rank by him, and if by superiority Priscilla outranks Aquila, let us not fear to put her name first." A. T. Pierson

Historically, women have been freer to exercise their spiritual gifts in pioneering situations, primarily because of the absence of men. But not all women have stepped into such a vacuum with the assurance that they were "God's person for the job." Gladys Aylward, the single "little woman" in China, once confessed her insecurities:

> I wasn't God's first choice for what I've done in China. There was somebody else . . . I don't know who it was - God's first choice. It must have been a man - a wonderful man. A well-educated man. I don't know what happened. Perhaps he died. Perhaps he wasn't

---

[141] Walter Liefeld and Ruth Tucker *Daughters of the Church* (Grand Rapids: Zondervan, 1987), 318.

[142] Bacon, *From Faith to Faith,* 65f.

[143] Liefeld and Tucker, *Daughters of the Church,* 301.

[144] Liefeld and Tucker, ibid., 312, as quoted from A. T. Pierson's publication: *Missionary Review of the World 14,* "The Outlook for the Twentieth Century," March, 1901, 167-68.

willing . . . And God looked down . . . and saw Gladys Aylward. . .
. And God said - "Well, she's *willing*!"[145]

Once it was acknowledged that women could make significant contributions in missions, women in pioneer areas knew no boundaries. It was only after they had worked hard to build the church (and hospitals, orphanages, etc.) that men were sent in to take over leadership. This was hard to swallow for most. After Dr. Helen Roseveare had built her own hospital (literally building the kiln and firing the bricks with her own hands, supervising the workmen and training the medical workers) the mission turned over the leadership of the hospital to her new male colleague.

> She knew she hated Dr. Harris' takeover . . . In her terms he'd "just taken over" Nebobongo, *her* place, which she'd built up out of nothing, out of her dreams, out of her heart, out of the money she'd raised . . . Then she found she couldn't take it. Perhaps she had been her own boss too long. But she had lost everything. She had always taken morning prayers; he took them now. She had always taken the Bible class: Dr. Harris took it now . . . Everything that had been hers was now his.[146]

And this situation is not unusual. Some women have been obliged to suppress their spiritual gifts which would otherwise have put them or kept them in leadership or positions of influence. The assumption that women's gifts are only for support ministries or for ministries exclusively with women and children, as important as these ministries are, is not valid. Sometimes a confinement of the areas of ministry for women has been observed in deference to the host culture. Sending agencies are often at a loss to know what to recommend to Western women missionaries, in particular, who are used to freedom of movement and dress, who are used to a voice in decision-making and ministering within a broader spectrum of possibilities. Wives are not content to be just "trailing spouses" when God has called them, along with their husbands, to minister according to their gifts. Those of the host culture need the opportunity to study the Scripture in the context of the Bible times, without the cultural bent of the expatriate missionaries. Often, however, the limitations made for women missionaries in the name of the host culture are in

> *The building of God's kingdom and the body of Christ both suffer when all Christians are not exercising their God-given gifts to the fullest.*

---

[145] Phyllis Thompson, *A Transparent Woman: The Compelling Story of Gladys Aylward* (Grand Rapids: Zondervan, 1971), 182-83.

[146] Alan Burgess, *Daylight Must Come, the Story of Dr. Helen Roseveare* (London: Pan Books, 1975), 129.

reality an accommodation to the home culture of the missionaries and hardly in keeping with the Scripture.

God's Spirit sovereignly gives gifts to God's children without respect to gender, race, status or education, i.e., to men and women alike, at His discretion. The building of God's kingdom and the body of Christ suffer when all Christians are not exercising their God-given gifts to the fullest. Men and women in their relationship to one another also suffer when women's gifts are repressed. This is an area in which God's norms in Scripture (as opposed to cultural norms then) take precedence over those of culture. Unfortunately, since the absorption of women's missionary societies into other mission agencies, the place of women in positions of leadership and influence has been downplayed and limited. But God's call is still valid today to let the daughters of the church be co-heirs with the sons in the Lord Jesus and share the priesthood of all believers.[147]

---

[147] Additional sources in the area of women in missions in German are: Veronika Elbers, "Die Dritte Welt Missionare - Ein Interview mit Lotje Pelealu, Indonesische Missionsgesellschaft," *Evangelikale Missiologie,* 2/1992; Christa Conrad, "Die ledige Missionarin und ihr Dienst," *Evangelikale Missiologie*, 1/96; "Partnerschaftliche Zusammenarbeit von Männern und Frauen in deutschen Glaubensmissionen: Neuentdeckung - oder Rückkehr zu den Anfängen?" *Evangelikale Missiologie*, 3/94; Marjory Foyle, "Stress als Single," *Evangelikale Missiologie*, 4/95; Christa Conrad, *Die ledige Frau in der Glaubensmission* (Bonn: Verlag für Kultur und Wissenschaft, 1997). Lynn Smith und Ingrid Kern, *Ohne Unterschied? Frauen und Männer im Dienst für Gott.* (Giessen: Brunnen Verlag, 2000); Cornelia Mack und Friedhilde Stricker, *Begabt und Beauftragt. Frausein nach Biblishen Vorbildern.* (Holzgerlingen: Hänssler, 2000)

2

CREDIBILITY FACTORS IN

COMMUNICATING THE GOSPEL

Biblical Principles and Examples that Relate to Credibility in Communicating the Gospel

The Bible gives several examples of attitudes of "sent ones" (*apostolos*, the word used for missionary) and the adaptations they were willing to make and made to insure correct understanding of the message they were communicating and the God they represented. The zenith of all examples is our Lord Jesus Christ Himself, in particular, His incarnation and His sacrificial death. The Apostle Paul writes of Jesus' incarnation, that He, although He was God, with all the rights and privileges that entailed, emptied Himself (*ekenosen*).[148] He gave up all these rights and privileges as the Lord of Creation and identified Himself fully with His creatures. He came as a helpless baby in humble surroundings. He identified with people, ate, worked, lived among them, and finally died the most horrible death of any social outcast.

This is indeed the epitome of all humility. Kraft describes Jesus as breaking out of the stereotype[149] of what had come to be perceived as a predictable, impersonal God. This is what gave God credibility because it caused humankind to take God seriously. Even if the stereotype is a positive one, it removes the personalness of the one involved because

---

[148] Philippians 2:5-8.
[149] Stereotyping is the predisposition almost everyone has of categorizing people based on prior experience/hearsay. It is recognized in such statements as, "*All* Americans do that!" or "*All* Germans behave that way," saving oneself the effort of getting to know the individual personally. It therefore depersonalizes. See Kraft's discussion on the negative effects of stereotyping in *Christianity and Culture*, 156f.

one behaves too predictably, almost instinctively towards this person. This, of course, is a risk. Jesus risked not being respected at all by giving up His rights. Most of the Pharisees and members of the Sanhedrin did not respect Him because He didn't meet their

Stereotyping depersonalizes.

expectations, their stereotype of the Messiah, despite His fulfillment of Old Testament prophecies. Instead He earned the right to be heard by living among, listening to, eating with, understanding and helping the people He loved. This kind of empathy and participation in life with the people is part of the identification process. He was and is Emanuel, "God with us" in our misery and our joy, in every sense of the word. And because of His close proximity to humankind and all the problems we face, through Him we can understand the message of God as never before in history. The writer of Hebrews expressed it so well: "For we do not have a high priest who is unable to sympathize with our weaknesses, but we have one who in every respect has been tested as we are, yet without sin." And "although he was a Son, he learned obedience through what he suffered."[150] This is the example for missionary service. For Jesus said, "As the Father has sent me, so send I you."[151] If "the servant is not greater than his Lord,"[152] then Jesus' example is a pattern for all "sent ones."

What exactly does incarnational sending/going involve? Incarnation means literally "becoming flesh," taking on human form. It is best defined by Jesus' example. He came as a learner. The Almighty laid aside His rights and began as a baby to learn language, culture, a trade, even God's laws from His parents and later through interaction in the synagogue. He learned for thirty years before He began formal ministry.

His identification was not a blind appropriation of all cultural values, but those carefully filtered through the Word and character of God.

Through His identification with the people He came to serve, He earned respect; He did not have it because of the status of His family or His country. He grew in favor with God and people.[153] He was careful not to take on the negative aspects of His culture (the legalism of the Pharisees, denial of taxes to the imperialists, racism, sexism, etc.), and He took care to live out the love of God in all of His dealings with people. To do this He did not deny principles of righteousness, however. His identification was not a blind appropriation of all cultural values, but those carefully

---

[150] Hebrews 4:15; 5:8. cf. 2:10, 17, 18.
[151] John 20:21.
[152] John 13:16.
[153] Luke 2:52.

filtered through the Word and character of God. He did not only teach and preach in theory; He lived an observable life full of integrity. His secrets were not personal but theological, which were able to be understood by those with spiritual discernment. His lifestyle was transparent, open to imitate and to criticize, as many did. But no one could have said He was aloof, distanced from the people He served.

John Stott calls it the "cost of the incarnation, of entering into our condition in order to reach us." [154] The emptying and humbling of Himself involved sacrifice, for example, sacrificing His right to be worshipped and served as Ruler of the Universe with the Father. The temptation in the wilderness was an offer of the enemy to short circuit this process of identification and sacrifice, which Jesus rejected. The climax of His incarnation and ministry was the giving of Himself in death as a ransom. This is the ultimate test of the second most important commandment - loving the other. The Apostle Paul says we are to "do nothing out of selfish ambition or vain conceit, but in humility consider others better than ourselves."[155] Jesus calls us to similar costly identification with those to whom He has sent us. Giving up what one knows and has practiced in order to be a learner of the elementary order again is costly. Stott calls it the "self-humility of his incarnation."[156] The Gospel of John characterizes Jesus in His incarnation as "full of grace and truth." One often thinks of these contrasting qualities as paradoxical, which, in the same person would tend to neutralize one another, i.e., one cannot at the same time be 100 percent full of grace and 100 percent full of truth. Dealing in grace and truth seem to be mutually exclusive. On the contrary, they are the ultimate combination for the Christian and especially for the cross-cultural missionary. There is a reluctance to apply this paradoxical principle to mission; but the Bible clearly teaches that suffering is the path to glory, death the only way to life and only in weakness is the power of God made evident. "In the shadowy image of Isaiah's suffering servant, suffering was to be the condition of his success in bringing light and justice to the nations."[157] As unpopular as the thought is over against the personal success of the "prosperity Gospel,"[158] Jesus Himself could not avoid suffering. Mission, doing the Father's will, is inevitably connected to suffering. Jürgen Moltmann links qualities of love and suffer-

---

[154] John R. W. Stott, *The Cross of Christ* (Leicester: InterVarsity, 1986), 179.
[155] Philippians 2:4.
[156] Stott, *The Cross of Christ*, 205.
[157] Stott, ibid., 291.
[158] The prosperity gospel is the notion that only God's blessings - not ill-health, financial setbacks, etc. - will follow the truly obedient Christians, including health and wealth. Thus suffering, for the Christian, has been done away with.

ing together in the character of God. "Were God incapable of suffering ... then he would also be incapable of love." And "the one who is capable of love is also capable of suffering, for he opens himself to the suffering which is involved in love."[159] This is a powerful concept for missionaries and those in multicultural teams in particular.

Another aspect of this concept is what Kraft calls "reverse identification." Jesus' "credibility, though made possible by his identifying with us, was cemented by the fact that *we can identify with him.*"[160] In this process, differences fade into the background. The bond that is created supersedes the suspicion and dividing effects of any differences. What draws us to Jesus? His humanity, feeling, sympathizing, weeping with those close to Him and those whom He encountered; His temptations, in His care for His mother, in being treated unjustly, in loneliness and perhaps especially in His being abandoned; these all draw us strongly and powerfully to Him. We can identify with Him at these points and "cement the communication bond in such a way that we will never recover from the impact."[161]

Jesus identified Himself with the poor and needy (Matthew 25:34-40) and He identifies Himself with a suffering church (Acts 9:4). He did not come as a god, aloof, immune to pain, stoic in the face of needy people. He suffered and suffers with them and calls those of us who follow Him to suffer too. There is no exemption for missionaries, those "sent ones" as the Father sent the Son. One should not expect the road to be easy.

Why and how did the Father send the Son? We can deduce from such summary passages as Luke 19:10, that Jesus' primary interest was to seek and to save the lost. And He did this in the posture of a servant (Mark 10:45; cf. Luke 22:27). To minister, to serve is not the same as "having a ministry." Larry Poland honestly pointed out the vast difference: "I seldom catch myself wanting to *serve* others (with them in control) or to *serve* them on their terms. This kind of motivation is alien to my basic desires - another way of saying that my basic motivation is sinful."[162] The true motivation is love, love that reaches both bodies and souls and compassion that expresses itself whenever needed.

Stott gives four marks of dialogue essential in evangelism, which relate to an incarnational lifestyle and incarnational communication:

---

[159] Jürgen Moltmann, *The Crucified God* (Minneapolis: Fortress, 1973), 220-230. See also Kitamori's work *Theology of the Pain of God*, 1946.

[160] Kraft, *Christianity and Culture,* 177.

[161] Kraft, ibid., 177-78.

[162] Larry Poland, "Serve or minister?" *Expressions*.(A former publication of Campus Crusade for Christ for their missionaries serving internationally) Vol. 4, No. 8. Aug/Sept. 1987.

authenticity, humility, integrity, sensitivity.[163] And Jesus, as illustrated, exemplified them all. Why is it necessary to listen, to enter into dialogue? Proverbs 18:13 gives a word of wisdom: "To answer before listening - that is folly and shame." True listening is entering into the situation of another, sympathizing, allowing our prejudices and preconceptions to be reformed by the new realities.

Did the incarnation mean Jesus changed His personality? Did He behave differently with the Samaritans than with the Jews? His approach was obviously different, but His personality was consistent. He was harder on some than on others because they claimed to have the truth, but compassion was not lacking. He was also misunderstood; some didn't like the way he celebrated with "outsiders" (sinners). Others didn't approve of the way He and His disciples overlooked some of the laws. He was faithful to the commands and character of God and was consistent in communicating God's love. This is incarnation; this is the essence of missionary service. It is this attitude, the posture of a servant that sent ones should share with their Lord.

> *Did the incarnation mean Jesus changed His personality?*

It is also this process that causes missionaries much grief and hardship because the process is one of denial. This is not self-negation. It is not a destruction of the person God created us to be. But it is a careful filtering of what our culture and sinful nature have added to the image of God in us. "We may even say that in the Incarnation God 'encoded' His infinite qualities in the limitations of human language and human form, and showed us what He is like by His acts within history."[164]

A different personality was not required, but a new, understandable form. This, of course, required limitations, a step one is hesitant to take in Western cultures that shout out the virtues, yea, the necessity of developing oneself to the fullest. In some cases this process of identification is almost seen as self-abrogation. But the Spirit of God calls for self-control in all areas of life. And it is certainly unrealistic to expect to develop all areas of one's life and gifts simultaneously even under optimum circumstances. The God who created us knows what can be developed and when. Emotionally, however, there are feelings of loss. This is normal; one may need to go through the grieving process in giving these gifts back to the Giver to await His timing in using them again. The grieving is only one side of the coin; God's blessing for obedience is the other. There are advantages and disadvantages, benefits and losses to *every* situation in life. One need not fear the losses in God's will, providing it

---

[163] Stott, *The Cross of Christ*, 71-73.
[164] Eugene Nida, *Message and Mission,* 23.

is not a lack of personal responsibility. The Apostle Paul describes his own process to the Corinthian church:

> *For though I am free with respect to all, I have made myself a slave to all, so that I might win more of them. To the Jews I became as a Jew, in order to win Jews. To those under the law I became as one under the law (though I myself am not under the law) so that I might win those under the law. To those outside the law I became as one outside the law (though I am not free from God's law but am under Christ's law) so that I might win those outside the law. To the weak I became weak, so that I might win the weak. I have become all things to all people, that I might by all means save some. I do it all for the sake of the gospel, so that I may share in its blessings.*[165]

These statements are all-inclusive. No category of people in Paul's acquaintance seems to have been omitted with whom he was not willing to identify in order to win some to Christ. He was willing to go to virtually every extreme in order to communicate the gospel in terms that could be understood by his hearers. Their understanding was his criterion, not his preaching. He did not obligate them to take a cultural (or sub-cultural) leap to decipher the message. He came to them, used their language and symbolism in their context. Romans 14 indicates that his practice was removing stumbling blocks. Nothing, or very little, perhaps just the content of the message itself, was so sacred that it couldn't be changed or adapted to fit the context. This is not syncretism. It does not compromise the truth. It is grace and truth. But discerning what really is the truth, what is the message, and what are the cultural appendages is crucial. Nothing could be better than the crucible of a multicultural team to help filter (or burn) out the impurities of cultural baggage. Hardly any area of life, personal and ministry, is left without the challenge of holding it up to the standards of God's Word and calling one's own cultural values into question.

Paul's main focus was not self-preservation; his identity was secure in Christ. He was not threatened by encountering a new culture and was therefore free to listen and to adapt. His main purpose was to communicate the message of God in a way that could be understood by his hearers. And Paul's was also not a mere theoretical teaching or preaching; he was a father, a mother, a mentor to the new disciples. His teaching was in the context of relationships.[166]

---

[165] 1 Corinthians 9:19-23.
[166] 1 Thessalonians 1:7-12.

Historical and Cultural Factors that Relate to Credibility

Missionary sending has been perceived as being primarily from West to East, from North to South. But there has been a definite shift in missionary activity in and out of countries in which the majority of Christians live today. Most would agree with the mission executive who said the most significant thing that has happened in world missions in this generation is: "The rise of mission agencies and missionaries in Africa, Asia, and Latin America. The growth rate of this movement overshadows the growth rate in North America and Europe over the same period of years."[167]

Multicultural mission teams have been on the scene a long time, beginning with Apostle Paul himself. God's vision for the church explained in the book of Revelation is that those of all languages and people groups be represented in His church. No one culture is allowed to take the Gospel captive. It is Christ who makes us, not we who make Christ. It is He who makes His multicultured church into one coordinated, functioning body. He is the vine; we are just the branches. We are united in belonging to Him and in celebrating Him. This is highly symbolized when we are in communion together at His table. This one faith has many forms.

> *We are not even aware of most of our ethnocentric biases until we face another culture.*

But even if the sending countries represented in the teams were mostly Western, many cultural adjustments within the teams themselves were necessary. More than one hundred years ago the *Basler Mission*, for example, had teams composed of Germans, Swiss, English, Africans, Indians and Chinese. The trend now, however, is towards an even more complex cultural mixture, representing many continents, language, status, and economic groupings. The fastest growing group of missionaries continues to be those from the *Two-Thirds World* (i.e., the non-Western world which now includes the Central and Eastern Europeans and can rightfully be called the *Three-Fourths World*).[168] And some pre-

---

[167] Jim Reapsome, "Interview with Wade Coggins" *Evangelical Missions Quarterly*, Vol. 20, No. 2, April, 1984.

[168] Larry Keyes and Larry Pate, "Two-Thirds World Missions: The Next 100 Years," *Missiology,* 189-206. The spiritual hunger and resulting increase in the church in Central and Eastern Europe since the Fall of Communism is producing a number of missionaries from this region. "Should they be classified as Western or non-Western? Or should they simply be classified as Central and Eastern European missions? They are like the Two-Thirds World missions in a number

dict the major concentration of missionary activity in the new Millennium will most likely be re-evangelizing the pagan West. If interpersonal relationships among team members are the Achilles heel in a monocultural team, this problem then becomes increasingly complex in a multicultural team. There is a growing need for mutual understanding among team members to facilitate more effective ministry. Some even question the desirability of such teams if the energy of the missionary is consumed internally, solving team and personnel problems rather than "making disciples of all nations," as our Lord commanded us. This is indeed a valid concern.

Ethnocentrism is an extreme form of individualism, where the individual in his natural unchecked egocentrism assumes the world revolves only around him and his interests. This person is oblivious, even hostile, to others. Ethnocentrism "is defined as the practice of viewing alien customs by applying the concepts and values of one's own culture."[169] The accompanying dangers of ethnocentrism are obvious: pride and superiority, which need to be dealt with in the heart of us all. We are not even aware of most of our ethnocentric biases until we face another culture. Actually, every person and culture is guilty of ethnocentrism; in some it is more blatant than others. Every culture assumes it is inherently the best and its culture is the standard of measurement in judging other cultures. "Full cultural objectivity is impossible, but an awareness of the vagaries of our selective ethnocentrism is very helpful."[170] Jesus warned against such ethnocentric prejudice in commanding us to take the log out of our own eye before we concern ourselves with the speck in our brother's. The value of seeing the world anthropologically, deducing from traditions and institutions the worldview behind them, is that it raises our self-awareness of our own ethnocentrism and increases our willingness to correct it.[171] In this light the imperative of mission is seen by an African church leader as follows:

---

of ways: (1) They are emerging late in the history of global missionary activity. (2) They will be sent from developing countries. (3) They will likely develop indigenous sending models which will be peculiar to their own region and circumstances, rather than modeled after Western missions. (4) They will be sent from parts of the world not traditionally considered to be Western."

[169] Robert B. Taylor, *Introduction to Cultural Anthropology* (Boston: Allyn and Bacon, 1973), 64.

[170] William A. Smalley, "Respect and Ethnocentrism," William A. Smalley, ed. *Readings in Missionary Anthropology II*, (Pasadena: William Carey Library, 1978), 712.

[171] Smalley, ibid., 713.

Christian mission like Christian faith represents the amalgam of a *residuum evangelium*, Graeco-Roman culture, and European cultural additives. Those who engage in mission then need to be sensitive to the distinction between the non-negotiable *residuum evangelium* and the negotiable cultural trappings, to attempt to divest the mission of the cultural trappings of the particular part of the world and to enable the investiture of the authentic cultural trappings of the new context. Thus mission becomes at once a *kenosis* and *skenosis*.[172]

In reflecting on the effects of the contributions of missionaries in years past, Joachim Wietzke expresses gratitude, but on the other hand explains that the missionaries were "children of their time bound to their

> *We must confess our sin of linking the Gospel too closely with worldly powers and religious-cultural imperialism.*

contemporary political and economic conditions and carrying their ideological and religious convictions and prejudices." Their sin was indeed great. And we must confess our sin of linking the Gospel too closely with worldly powers, religious-cultural imperialism. "We have to confess our guilt for having presented the gospel in a triumphalistic and paternalistic way obscuring the biblical reality of the cross and the cost of discipleship."[173] Harvie Conn poses the question each missionary and each multicultural mission team must wrestle with:

How can one avoid restructuring the meaning of the gospel as presented in the original source when communication takes place between sources and receptors who have different cultural backgrounds? What factors are important for the communicator in seeking to insure "the closest natural equivalent" of the gospel, first in meaning and, less importantly, in style?[174]

In addition to avoiding negative repercussions in communicating the gospel by overlooking or disregarding cultural factors, anthropological understanding provides a key that could facilitate better communication and receptivity of the gospel. Kraft suggests that one can even predict

---

[172] John S. Pobee, "Christian Mission Towards the Third Millennium: The Gospel of Hope." *Missions Studies*, International Association of Mission Studies, Vol. V-1, 1988, 9.
[173] Joachim Wietzke. "Introduction," *Missions Studies*, International Association of Missions Studies, Vol. V-1; 1988, 2-3.
[174] Harvie Conn, *Eternal Word and Changing Worlds,* 148.

receptivity to the Gospel as well as fine-tune appropriate innovations and create better behavioral impact of Christian teaching.[175]

The view missionaries have of themselves and their task can facilitate this process. One would hope that the Western missionaries draw their self-understanding as leader from a biblical one, as servant of the church, rather than from the Western cultural practice of leadership. An understanding of the *emic-etic* distinction can promote a healthier perception of one's role as an outsider in the host culture as facilitator, empathizer, mirror, catalyst, source of cultural alternatives. The terms *emic* and *etic* were first coined in 1954 by linguist, Kenneth Pike, drawn from the terms *phonemic* vs. *phonetic*. The etic viewpoint is from outside the culture using one's own culture and presuppositions (or randomly selected presuppositions) as the backdrop. In contrast, the emicist attempts to view the culture from within, without any preconceptions or absolutes, in the way linguists would approach a language without given structures. The emic point of view is the insider's view and is discovered inductively.[176]

In applying this concept to translation of the Bible, Kraft pleads for the use of "dynamic equivalence."[177] This is a "dynamic equivalence transculturation" of the message as we participate in God's communication, a "dynamic equivalence theologizing" as we reflect on and communicate God's truth through our culture-bound perceptions and a "dynamic equivalence churchness" as each new generation, in its own cultural experience, produces an appropriate church vehicle, utilizing its own cultural forms for the transmission of God's meanings.[178] Unfortunately, many Western missionaries insist that their converts convert both to Christ *and* to a "particular western *emic*, ethnic understanding and verbalizing of theology."[179] Jesus formulated theological truth in the terms of His hearers. Paul used the same *emic* approach when becoming a Jew to Jews and a Greek to Greeks.

Could a trained multicultural team help reduce this problem of transference and keep the message "purer?" Theoretically, the chances would

---

[175] Charles H. Kraft, "Can Anthropological Insight Assist Evangelical Theology?" Christian Scholar's Review 7, nos. 2-3 (1977), 191 as quoted by Harvie Conn. Ibid., 150.

[176] Harvie Conn, *Eternal Word*, 151. Louis Luzbetak, *The Church and Cultures,* 150.

[177] "Dynamic equivalence," a model developed by Eugene Nida from linguistic and communication theories, captures the meaning and spirit of the original without being bound to its linguistic structure (formal correspondence).

[178] Charles Kraft, *Christianity and Culture*, 41.

[179] Charles Kraft, ibid., 300.

be much better of reducing the problem of transference of the culture with the gospel. And in practice this is also the case. If, as Proverbs says, "As iron sharpens iron, so one person sharpens another,"[180] then brothers and sisters in Christ from different cultures, serving together invariably encounter opportunities to reveal one another's blind spots and to correct their communication of the message. This, however, does not occur automatically. There are too many variances in cultural values that work against this process just happening. There are, for example, values which people in certain cultures hold dear, which do not allow vulnerability or direct communication. An attempt to force the issue can only make matters worse. Adopting a passive "live and let live" attitude shuts off communication as well. Attempted correction without solicitation of correction has been known to create misunderstandings followed by less communication and has, on occasion, led to the dissolving of a team. The multicultural team at its best is *the* best, but at its worst, it can be disillusioning and destructive. It can be destructive to both ministry and missionary. Kraft, basing his opinion on the ten propositions of theologizing from Robert McAfee Brown, in fact, recommends this kind of interaction as basic to theologizing: "An etic approach to Christian theologizing, on the other hand, attempts to compare and discover universally applicable theological categories of Christianity on the basis of analyses of many emic varieties."[181]

> *The multicultural team at its best is THE best, but at its worst, it can be disillusioning and destructive.*

Expanding on this thought in his frame of reference, John Pobee says, "a de-imperialized mission should also be a 'skenosis,' a tabernacling of the Word of God in the specific [in his case] African context." While he does not believe it is possible to have an a-cultural Word of God, he protests strongly against exalting the expression of one particular in translation "as *the* true expression, all others deemed false, if not devilish."[182] Pope Pious XII claimed: "When the Gospel is accepted by diverse races, it does not crush or repress anything good and honorable and beautiful which they have achieved by their native genius and natural endowments."[183] Ernst Troeltsch believed, however, "that Christianity and Western culture are so inextricably intertwined that a Christian can say little about his faith to members of other civilizations, and the latter in turn cannot encounter Christ save as a member of the Western

---

[180] Proverbs 27:17.
[181] Kraft, *Christianity and Culture,* 293-94.
[182] John Pobee, "Christian Mission Towards the Third Millennium," 9.
[183] Pope Pius XII. "Evangelii Praecones," 1951. Raymond Hickey, ed., *Modern Missionary Documents and Africa.* (Dublin: Dominican, 1982), 97.

world."[184] Klaus Fiedler, however, points to the change in culture as a natural process of international contact, not just a premeditated or unconscious result of missions. It's not that Christianity becomes more African, he says, rather it's the role it plays. Africans want to give up parts of their culture (as do we all) that have lost their function and incorporate parts of other cultures that they judge as valuable. What is deemed African is not that which has its roots in the past, rather that which meets the present needs of Africans.[185]

A key to understanding the foreignness of the gospel, quite apart from the cultural trappings alluded to by Niebuhr, is that all cultures, Jews, Greeks, Romans, medievalists and moderns, Westerners and Orientals have rejected Christ because they saw in Him a threat to their culture.[186] The Gospel in the person of Christ is a stumbling block, says the Apostle Paul; there is no getting around the offense caused by the message itself and the revolutionary change of heart *(metanoia)* it requires of each who embraces it. But one must be ever so careful not to taint, cover, mutilate or distort the message by adding cultural requirements as additional stumbling blocks. Paul's message to the Galatian church applies here: to do so is *anathema*.

In an ever-shrinking world, in which contact with other cultures and subcultures can hardly be avoided, we have no choice but to learn to deal with the new dynamics and problems which such cultural complexity creates. And this duty is a privilege indeed. North American Indians have a word of caution for relating to others; "Do not judge another man until you have walked one mile in his moccasins."[187]

How does learning the local language relate to credibility? In my survey results and everything I have read or heard, with very rare exceptions, speaking the heart language of the people is second in order of importance only to loving them. In fact, the tedious, sometimes grueling, yet exciting process of language

> *Speaking the heart language of the people is second in order of importance only to loving them.*

learning speaks volumes of love to the nationals. "Not speaking the language of the country can suggest an insult: in effect, you are saying,

---

[184] Ernst Troeltsch, *Christian Thought,* 1923, 21-35.

[185] Klaus Fiedler, *Christentum und afrikanische Kultur; Konservative deutsche Missionare in Tanzania, 1900 bis 1940* (Bonn: Verlag für Kultur und Wissenschaft, 1993), 17.

[186] Fiedler, ibid., 4.

[187] A sign over the counter in a cafe in the village of Supai in Northern Arizona, quoted by Robert T. Moran in *International Management,* March 1988, 66.

'Your language is not important enough to merit my time and effort.' "[188] It is not the degree of perfection to which the language is spoken, but rather the fact that one is going to the trouble of learning it, soliciting correction and continuing to learn it. (It is indeed a never-ending process.) This posture of being a learner connotes humility, willingness to hear, understand, share and contribute, all of which, in most cultures, give the learner credibility and, by association, their message as well. It means active involvement with the people, not isolation and, because of the many mistakes made, a high degree of vulnerability. Almost anyone likes to help someone who expresses a need for help. The missionary becomes a real person removing the aura of mystery and suspicion.

Advantages of a Multicultural Team

What are the advantages of multicultural mission teams? First, one of the more obvious advantages of such a "colorful" team is that it reflects the body of Christ more fully and completely. This means there is a variety of different Christian persons with whom non-Christians or new Christians can identify. No one type of spirituality (or denomination) is superior to another. All are on equal footing. Pride and ethnocentrism have no place. All individuals are appreciated for who they are and for their unique contributions to the team. Such teams can be a foretaste of that day, when, before the Lord, Christians from "every nation, from all tribes and peoples and languages"[189] will proclaim His glory together. There is a richness and obvious interdependency in the inner workings of such a team.

Second, the network of resources and breadth of experience brought from the home countries of such a team can be of major benefit. This set of resources is broader and deeper than what mere quantity can offer. A more exact estimate of what might or might not work in the new host culture can be predicted by analyzing what has or has not worked well in the various cultures represented on the team. There is a greater willingness to try something unfamiliar in such a pluralistic situation.

Third, these multicultural teams can perhaps best pioneer new areas, new ministries, even new countries. The presuppositions are at a minimum; the openness to other ways is great. Such a team helps keep the message of the gospel purer, freer from "cultural baggage." Every culture

---

[188] Ted Ward, *Living Overseas* (New York: The Free Press, 1984), 151.
[189] Revelation 7:9.

or subculture has tended (consciously or subconsciously) to attach cultural values to the biblical message and biblical values and proclaim both with an equal emphasis. This has produced many negative effects throughout the history of missions, the worst of which is "throwing out the baby with the bath water," i.e., a rejection of the message of the gospel along with the cultural trappings in which it was encased. Because members of a multicultural team challenge one another in their presuppositions, much of the dross of these cultural trappings, the barriers or non-essentials to the gospel, are filtered out. A purer gospel is communicated. Generally speaking, missionaries who have worked in multicultural teams are in a healthy position to recognize and question the anti-Christian elements in their own culture and to live and communicate the gospel accordingly.

3

ADJUSTMENT OF THE MISSIONARIES TO THE

HOST CULTURE

The Adjustment Process

The adjustment process is multi-faceted and complex because so many new, unpredictable things avalanche upon the missionary at once. Handling changes in so many areas of life simultaneously produces a great amount of stress and requires a lot of flexibility. The entrance of the gospel alone and the spiritual potential this creates will most likely be countered by great opposition from the enemy of our souls. This is not to be underestimated in the process of moving to a country and getting settled. If one takes into consideration all the stress elements involved in getting prepared for this major move (e.g., support development, deputation, travel, leave-taking from family, friends, church, colleagues, support group, moving, mission orientation/training phase, changes for spouse and children, etc.), it is no wonder that today, when traveling to the field is a matter of only 8 to 48 hours in most cases instead of 8 weeks, the missionary arrives needing a vacation. A list of stress factors[190] modified to include items listed above might indicate that most

---

[190] See Figure 3: "Stress Factors as a Result of Life Changes."

"Medical studies show that if too many stress points accumulate during any one year, there is a great likelihood of developing significant physical or emotional problems. The Holmes-Rahe Stress Test was designed to identify the number and severity of stress factors experienced by an individual during the preceding year. Note to Figure 3: A total of two hundred or more stress points can indicate the presence of or likelihood of burnout." Flournoy, Hawkins, Meier, Minirth, *How to Beat Burnout* (Chicago: Moody, 1986), 116-17.

* Starred factors in the table are those listed by Holmes and Rahe. Other similar factors are estimates based on the experiences of missionaries. These factors

missionaries could be candidates for burnout in this initial phase. These new stresses and their effects are not to be underestimated and should be the basis for extending much grace to newcomers.

But stress can have a positive effect as well. The positive effects can far outweigh the negative effects of stress *if* one has the mindset to receive them in this way. The initial phase in most cases also brings with it a buoying effect, sometimes called "the honeymoon phase" because of the euphoria of finally getting to the people and place one has prayed for and dreamed of. The initial encounters (apart from perhaps customs office formalities and the like) are usually exhilarating. The positive effects of stress cause the adrenaline to flow, thus spurring one to action. This initial phase can increase one's conscious dependence upon God. One can go a long way on this jet stream of exhilaration, if one chooses. But the choice to do so must be made beforehand. For most mission agencies today, missionary applicants are screened for qualities including a relatively healthy self-concept and trust in God and His sustenance, because compounded stress factors tend to cause old problems and patterns to surface with new intensity.[191]

The tension at this juncture between wanting to relate to the people of the new culture and wanting to feel comfortable and reduce stress is very real. This can lead in one of two directions: towards the new culture or away from it. Nostalgia may arise in great proportions and with it the desire to escape to that which is familiar, through books, videos, letter writing, e-mailing or activities with other expatriates. But the missionaries who resist this great temptation at the outset and move towards the new culture single-mindedly, will not regret the benefits and basis for long-term ministry they are creating.

---

were confirmed by Dr. Paul Meier, co-founder of the largest group of psychological clinics, Minirth-Meier New Life Clinics.
[191] See chapter 5 for further discussion of selection factors.

Figure 3: Stress Factors as a Result of Life Changes

Events	Scale of Impact
Death of a Spouse*	100
Divorce*	73
Learning a new language - total immersion	70
Marital separation*	65
Jail term*	63
Death of close family member*	63
Personal injury or illness*	53
Marriage*	50
Fired at work*	47
Finances cut off	47
Marital reconciliation*	45
Spiritual opposition	45
Retirement*	45
Change in health of family member*	44
Pregnancy*	40
International move (incl. re-entry)	40
Sex difficulties*	39
Gain of new family member*	39
Business readjustment*	39
Furlough/constant travel	39
Change in financial state*	38
Financial support loss/dire need for support development	38
Death of a close friend*	37
Change to a different line of work*	36
Change in number of arguments with spouse*	35
Opposition of family to move	35
Debts totaling over one year's salary	31
Foreclosure of mortgage or loan*	30
Change in responsibilities at work*	29
Son or daughter leaving home*	29
Trouble with in-laws*	29
Outstanding personal achievement*	28
Spouse begins or stops work*	26
Begin or end school*	26
Change in living conditions*	25
Revision of personal habits*	24
Trouble with boss*	23
Change in work hours or conditions*	20
Change in residence*	20
Change in schools*	19
Change in recreation*	19
Change in church activities*	19
Change in social activities*	18
Debts less than one year's salary	17
Support maintenance	17
Change in sleeping habits*	16
Jet lag	16
Change in number of family get-togethers*	15
Change in eating habits*	15
Vacation*	13
Christmas*	12
Minor violations of the law*	11
Spouse's or children's stress	10

(adapted from Flournoy, Hawkins, Meier, Minirth, *How to Beat a Burnout*, Moody: 1986, pp 116-117)

The missionary, if he or she has normal relational potential, *will establish* bonds with someone when he arrives; it remains to be seen with whom. A small booklet on the subject of bonding has been the object of controversy. Drs. Betty Sue and Tom Brewster, working as consultants to many mission agencies, developed a process of bonding, allowing the newly arrived missionary to bond first with the residents of the host country (including, of course, the missionaries of that host country in the team). Their principles were precipitated by their own birthing experience. They contend that, for example, as with ducks, bonding with humans does take place and it is important for both parents to enter into the process consciously. To prepare to establish a bond with the nationals, one has to plan to limit the initial contacts primarily to nationals from the time of arrival in the country. This usually means living with a national family, who speak little of the missionary's mother tongue in order to encourage learning the language from the outset in a natural context. The prerequisite is that one has learned the LAMP method of language learning[192] prior to arrival. The benefits of the missionary being at once perceived as a learner has many positive benefits in creating cords of affection and acceptance with the nationals.[193] Having personally coached many new missionaries, I have not seen any who have regretted their decision to restrict their *initial* contacts with other expatriate missionaries in order to concentrate on getting to know and allow themselves to be formed by the new culture and people. Conversely, I know of many who, in retrospect, have wished they had gone this way. The decision literally needs to be made months before one gets on the plane. The personal conviction on the part of the missionaries is important. They should not be forced against their will to follow this intensive bonding procedure or they may very well be setting themselves up for rejecting the people and being personally rejected initially. It is only fair to the other missionaries in the team to know this is the desire of the new missionary so they can adjust their expectations and preparations accordingly. It is helpful if a resident missionary who knows about the bonding process can set up an appropriate living situation for the first six to twelve weeks with native-speakers of the language and serve the incoming missionary as a resource. It is possible, even in a highly organized society such as Germany, to find such a situation upon arrival, if necessary. And families can do it successfully, too. The parents' contagious attitude of trusting God in this adventure sets the atmosphere and expectations for the

---

[192] E. and T. Brewster, *Language Acquisition Made Possible.* See further details in the section "Language" in chapter 4 of this book, also in Winter: *Perspectives.*
[193] Brewster and Brewster, *Bonding and the Missionary Task* (Dallas: Lingua House, 1982).

children. They should not be abandoned, but rather be a central part of all the goings-on in this phase. Children's observations and reactions will give good insights as well. In addition to using the "honeymoon phase" for establishing a strong mutual bond with the people, taking advantage of this initial bonding process carries with it the benefit of using the "grace period" to the maximum.

The "grace period" is an observable phenomenon during which time greater allowance is given by the nationals towards the missionaries for their cultural faux pas. These cultural mistakes, which every foreigner makes, are excused because they are new and they are given the benefit of the doubt in their ignorance. One can actually gain a lot of acceptance by laughing at oneself and one's own mistakes during this time. If missionaries continue to be learners, correcting their behavior from their mistakes as well, they will enjoy even more grace beyond this initial period. I have seen this principle nullified only in a situation where the number of new expatriate missionaries at a given time so exceeded the capacity of the one national missionary, that she eventually was exhausted by the demand. This was not true for the bonding effects for those who pursued relationships/cultural guides in the community, however. It was merely a case of overload for the one national. There is almost everything to be said for - and nothing to be said against - having the new missionaries establish their bond in a new country initially with the people of that land and not with the expatriate missionaries. If there are foreseeable circumstances that would hinder living with a national family for a short period of time, such as the birth of a child or a troublesome teen, it would almost always be better to postpone the arrival of the missionary family until a bonding situation is possible.

> *There is almost everything to be said for having the new missionaries establish their bond initially with the people of that land and not with the expatriate missionaries.*

Children are in the process of learning their mother tongue as well as the new host language. Care should be taken to use languages consistently in certain contexts. Most advise keeping the mother tongue as the home language for the sake of the children, their fluency and their being comfortable in relating in the country of origin. This, of course, slows down the language learning process of the parents, making it, however, by no means impossible. Some parents have decided, with success, to immerse themselves in language/culture at alternate periods of time; the children are then well cared for by one parent and each of the parents has the unhindered opportunity to bond and learn. The national language may be used between the parents and children in public. Older children may even be embarrassed if the national language is not used with them in public. But the parents should avoid interspersing both languages in conversing with the children; this has been known to cause mixing of the categories of languages for children. It is important for children to be able to sort out which language belongs to which context.[194] Parents of young children are stretched in different directions through multiplied responsibilities. The mission must exercise wisdom in giving time for language learning to both parents. One cannot do everything in the name of expediency (i.e. the attitude, "We need this man for the job now!" and, therefore, only he is given time to learn the language well) and expect positive long-term results. Some couples have postponed having children at this juncture of their lives with all the changes and stress. But there are many factors to be considered, personal and cultural. One can certainly plan as wisely as possible and trust

> *The mission must exercise wisdom in giving time for language learning to both parents.*

God in these matters as well. Children are not a disadvantage in language learning; they are an entrée into most cultures, most of the time.

When missionaries come as a couple or family, these primary relationships are not to be sacrificed at all costs to learn the language. One needs much wisdom to find the right balance for each person involved. Some couples have chosen to separate for a time of initial language learning. Some have said as a rule they would speak the new language (primarily with others) until a given time, e.g. 9 p.m. each evening, and then feel free to converse with the spouse in their mother tongue. This is hard and can produce additional stress for the couple. It is not without good reasons that Hudson Taylor required his missionaries, the men as well as the women, in the China Inland Mission to have a certain level of Chinese fluency before they married. In our mission we have advised married couples to stay within one language level[195] of each other in the

---

[194] Much has been written for the benefit of missionary children, especially in the last two decades. For example, Edward Danielson, *Missionary Kid*, (Pasadena: William Carey Library, 1984). Suffice it to say here that children are excellent language learners if not forced to learn or made to feel inferior. However, care should be taken for any person in a primary relationship with the child to use the same language (preferably that adult's mother tongue because children learn from them) consistently with the child, even if the child replies in another language. Because different languages form different categories in which one then classifies reality, the resultant confusion of categories, if the languages are mixed, may cause the child to develop in his reasoning capacities more slowly.

[195] See Brewsters' *Language Acquisition Made Practical* for a description of these language levels.

learning process. This avoids adding some stress or a sense of competition in the relationship with one feeling left behind and eventually alienated from the culture and people. For single and married alike, avoiding the temptation to compare one's progress (or lack thereof) with another's is of utmost importance.

If missionaries sense their own insecurities and want to have their self-confidence reinforced, they are likely to be tempted to reverse their commitment to language learning and bonding to the host culture. It somehow feels more comfortable to find one's place in the existing team of missionaries first. This secondary bonding with the expatriates on the team must come, too, but it is not to confuse nor replace the primary bonding with the people, to which one needs to learn to communicate on a heart level. And when the team is multicultural as well, the pull may be even greater for some, or non-existent for others. One tends to escape to that which feels comfortable. This primary initial bonding process is of utmost importance in a multicultural team, otherwise the direction of adaptation is unclear. *The normative culture to which all team members adapt is the host culture, not the cultures of one another.* There will be adaptations to other team member's cultures represented but they will not be as extensive and, as such, are not normative. The majority culture represented in a given team, or the culture of the team leader, may consciously or unconsciously exert an amount of pressure to move towards or adapt to that culture, but if it is not the host culture, it should not be made the normative culture for the team. This often precipitates a great deal of frustration for those missionaries from minority cultures.[196]

> *The normative culture to which all team members adapt is the host culture, not the cultures of one another.*

The adjustment process during the initial period of entry into the new culture focuses primarily on language. Assuming the posture of a learner is key to anyone coming into a new situation or culture. One of the most obvious things the missionaries must learn is the new language. It is no great virtue for new missionaries to come to the new location with a semi-mastery of the language, especially if they have learned it in another context. The identification - reverse identification[197] process plays a role here. If the local people see them struggle with learning their language (and what language comes easily?) they become emotionally tied to them, sympathetic with their willingness to struggle to communicate with them. And the missionaries become emotionally bonded to them

---

[196] This issue is discussed further in chapter 4.
[197] Kraft, *Christianity in Culture*, 177.

when they help them understand not only the language but also the context of all that they are learning, easing the stress they feel in the newness of it all. Language, although one of the basic sources of culture shock is also the area in which there are the largest number of cues to interpersonal relationships. Newcomers to a culture lose the status and security of their education and intelligence. Smalley's description is one with which many veteran missionaries can identify:

> The very exercise of language study itself gives some people acute culture shock. Many people have a mental block against practicing something they do not understand. But they can never understand a language until they have practiced it enough so that they are familiar with it. They find themselves in a vicious circle - unable to learn, unable to get along without learning . . . Many an overseas American who started out to learn a language has ended by rejecting it . . . less and less study, more English contacts, perhaps illness, animosity against teachers, bitterness against the people who make you stick to your books, blame their own failure on the antiquated system of study . . . Some people turn to errand-running and do administration, do busy work to make them feel that their time is too full to be spent in language study. Some people are constantly making trips, off on one pretext or another, and never learn.[198]

Such escape mechanisms only offer temporary relief. A properly prepared bonding process plunges one into language learning, with daily motivation to learn to communicate the most basic of needs and desires. Care should be taken not to resort to one's mother tongue or another common language too often. An ideal host family during initial bonding should not speak much of any other language in common with the missionary except the one the missionary needs to learn. And care should be taken not to confuse the language learning process with the use of other common languages, e.g., Spanish or English and the local language. This may confuse language categories for the new missionary.

Implications for the multicultural team are legion. Resorting to the use of English in the team presents a real hurdle, for example, to those whose mother tongue is not English, who also need to learn the local language. As cumbersome and lonely as it may feel at the outset, it is precisely this need for non-superficial communication and meaningful relation-

> *Resorting to the use of English in the team presents a real hurdle to those whose mother tongue is not English.*

---

[198] William A. Smalley, *Readings in Missionary Anthropology, Vol. II*, 698.

ships that drives and continually motivates new missionaries to learn to express themselves in the new language. This process will be short-circuited if English or another common language is resorted to too often.

All other factors being equal, the more time one spends totally immersed in the culture and language - actively involved, not passively absorbing, without escaping, the quicker one will learn. This includes "escaping" through reading or writing in the mother tongue, too. After I had learned a certain amount of German, I decided to begin to take my spiritual nourishment exclusively in that language. I read the German Bible, the first gift given to me, and made exciting new discoveries. It took longer, but the study was more careful and, consequently, was fresher to me than the English translations I'd come to know so well. A songbook was the next addition. I began keeping my journal in German. This is not to say that I never heard a sermon, song or tape in English, but I didn't allow it to be my primary source of spiritual intake in those initial years.

A reasonable minimum of time in one's mother tongue will be needed, in primary relationships, in communication to the family, friends and mission in the home country, but the language learning time must be protected by missionary, supervisor and mission alike, almost at all costs! Most likely one will not have such an opportunity for concentrated language learning later and then the patterns of relating to people, and especially the pronunciation, will have been set and will be very difficult to correct. One learns from one's mistakes, therefore our mission has the policy that for long-termers the proximity to other missionaries should be minimal during the months of intensive language learning. Also the missionary should have no other official job responsibilities at this time. This time is sacred but it requires lots of discipline to hold to it in the throes of culture shock. A successful bonding, however, minimizes culture shock. "The one who feels at home does not experience culture shock."[199] Learning in this way, one feels more and more at home.

Today there are many methods of language learning available for most languages. Prior to arrival in the country, the missionaries should weigh the advantages and disadvantages of each method accessible in their situation. As mentioned before, family factors are significant considerations. Optimally, the language should be learned in-country and only from native speakers. This is critical for establishing patterns of correct pronunciation from the outset. Incorrect pronunciation and grammar may be cute the first weeks, funny the second month but it embarrasses both the missionary and the nationals and especially the accompanying

---

[199] Brewster and Brewster. "Bonding and the Missionary Task" in Winter and Hawthorne, ed., *Perspectives on the World Christian Movement*, 455.

national missionary (diminishing the credibility of the church/mission) in the long run. Enough cannot be said for starting off with discipline in this area and inviting the correction of the nationals again and again. The nationals will probably be reluctant to give feedback initially and need to be convinced over and over that the missionary really wants it. The missionaries, in turn, need to accept critique graciously, and correct themselves accordingly. On the other hand, the nationals should appreciate how difficult it is for the missionaries to be continually vulnerable, thus correcting them gently, yet without hesitation or exaggeration of the mistake. It is not at all helpful for the national to make jokes about the missionary's pronunciation or imitate it. It defeats the purpose.[200]

Because pronunciation is so important I highly recommend a combination of methods of language learning including the LAMP method.[201] To use the LAMP method exclusively requires a high degree of discipline or the cooperation of a group of missionaries. Where there are no language schools, however, it is the best method. Even with a highly systematized language such as German, I found it most helpful to use LAMP for my initial six weeks before going to language school to learn the grammar and thereafter for pronunciation and vocabulary in particular. In addition to criteria such as the family situation, the availability of certain methods and the structure of the language, the personality of the missionaries themselves plays an important role. As mentioned, the LAMP method requires discipline but a gregarious personality is quite an asset. A group situation, however, can compensate for shy personalities. It takes some insight to structure the drills necessary to correct one's mistakes, too. I can not pretend to be a sanguine personality, but I profited greatly from learning the LAMP method prior to going to the field, using it upon arrival, during the four months of language school and using the LAMP principles thereafter. I found the structure of the school, despite the temptation to spend time with other foreigners in school rather than Germans, gave me the needed sense of progress and the grammatical structure to organize my learning. I lived with Germans, however, and was therefore forced to use the language daily. My language helpers were the most critical factor in forming pronunciation, as well as those who continued to correct me (to this day). My greatest difficulty, in addition to job pressures, was my hesitancy to risk using the language. It helped that I used my initial six weeks to listen, learning to

---

[200] Soliciting and giving feedback is discussed in more detail in chapter 6.

[201] See Brewster and Brewster's book named: LAMP (or the newest edition called LEARN) for a detailed description of the method and discussion of language helpers.

discern new sounds and beginning to recognize words and phrases in conversation. But, as Luzbetak reminds us,

> perfectionism and fear of a strange culture are, in fact, as detrimental to apostolic work as the disregard for cultural differences. Fear that leads to inactivity is like the fear of making a mistake in speaking a foreign language. If fear keeps one from speaking, the foreign language will never be learned.[202]

In a handbook[203] written for Campus Crusade for Christ missionaries (called "International Representatives") in Europe, the process of adjustment during the first two years of missionary service has been outlined after they had completed a period of service in the home country and a preparatory course (Agape International Training). Of course, there are many variations of this pattern due to the criteria mentioned above, but the handbook gives a picture of what it is like to balance all these priorities at once and nevertheless relax in the fact that "to everything there is a season."

Another important activity which goes hand-in-hand with acquiring a new language is learning about the culture. Using the acrostic KEEPRRAHT,[204] the new missionary can begin to observe the various areas found in every culture: **K**inship, **E**ducation, **E**conomics, **P**olitics,

Kinship
Education
Economics
Politics
Religion
Recreation
Association
Health
Transportation

Religion, **R**ecreation, **A**ssociation (status, class system), **H**ealth and **T**ransportation. In this process is important not to rely on just one authority, thus one must validate one's observations properly. Regional and tribal differences are to be noted and not to be confused. For the missionary with a bent towards research, this exercise is great fun. Care must be taken to view the people of the culture not as informants or mere culture-carriers, but as real people with real needs. The investigative process can also form close bonds and will most likely be understood that way by the people one questions often. The missionaries will not just be accumulating facts about the culture new to them but will also be in a better position to weigh the cultural values they begin to discern. Many values will not be obvious but will be perceived by reading between the lines or feeling the differences that may not initially be able to be explained. Of-

---

[202] Louis J. Luzbetak, *The Church and Cultures,* 221.

[203] Lianne Roembke based on Campus Crusade for Christ's Agape International Training: *International Representatives In-Field Training Handbook,* unpublished, 1980. Revised 1981.

[204] KEEPRRAHT is cited in Brewsters' LAMP, 132. They further attribute it to John D. Donoghue.

ten they may have to consciously tell themselves, "It's not wrong; it's just different," as they attempt to understand their new situation. They will be taken again and again to the Scriptures to seek discernment on areas in question, being careful not to rely on their prior culturally-tainted opinions but to discover God's Word anew. They will understand themselves and their culture in contrast to that which they are learning.

Very few missionaries go through the process of entering a new country unscathed. Culture shock or culture stress may be defined as exchanging one set of known behavioral cues for the unknown cues. The result is a continuous series of jolts in which the world doesn't make sense. It feels like a game in which someone suddenly changed all the rules and didn't inform you. The shock effect comes from the feeling of being out of control and not in the know. Some symptoms of culture shock are: a negative and suspicious view of the 'strange' people and their ways and values, homesickness, loneliness, boredom, lethargy, a tendency to withdraw, rising stress, an overall feeling of dissatisfaction, disgust, irritability, depression, physical illness, especially chronic headaches and hypertension, exhaustion, an overconcern about one's health, excessive drinking or some other questionable compensation, inappropriate outbursts of anger, hurt feelings, feeling undervalued.[205] Some physical illness during this time can undoubtedly be attributed to the spiritual battle that is waging and the enemy's attempt to discourage and disable the missionaries. Other mild factors are the result of the disorientation the new missionaries feel. One missionary, returning to his home country for his first furlough, yelled at a passer-by who had thrown some litter onto the sidewalk. He was tired of seeing this be done in his host country and overly reacted to it being done in his home country. Suffering from an extreme case of loneliness during culture shock, however, another new missionary became involved in an illicit sexual relationship and had to leave the mission. It is very important for missionaries to know for themselves which values are biblical, unchangeable and which values are open to discussion. They will be otherwise most vulnerable to temptation.

If one can look back after a few months (and every interval thereafter) and see that the world is beginning to make more sense and some things have even become second nature, then culture shock is happily losing its effects. If the shock effect persists, i.e., one either doesn't learn the rules and/or does not want to play by them, one should get professional help to discover the point(s) of resistance and perhaps reconsider a long-term stay.

---

[205] Luzbetak, *The Church and Cultures,* 204.

Lest one think that the effects of culture shock are less when a Westerner moves to a Western country or an Asian to another Asian country, M-2 cultural moves produce as much culture shock as M-3 moves.[206] The forms used may be similar, but the meanings are different. When one thinks of adjustments on the mission field, food, climate and health concerns in general, are the most obvious. But actually the most difficult adjustments are not physical but rather psychological and social.[207] These changes are in no way to be underestimated. This, of course, is multiplied in a multicultural team situation in which one is adapting to one's colleagues as well.

What are some appropriate ways of coping with culture shock? In addition to continuing to discover new things in language and culture, recognizing the stress points, eating a balanced diet, getting regular, enjoyable, culturally appropriate exercise, taking an occasional break and doing what one enjoys - reading a book, listening to music, painting, baking, cooking, writing poetry, taking pictures; setting realistic goals

> *The most difficult adjustments are not physical but rather psychological and social.*

for language progress, reducing expectations in other areas of life, discovering new interests in the country, laughing (watching a video occasionally, reading a joke book, sharing funny mistakes with other missionaries), being patient and forgiving with oneself and others, doing one thing in which one can see progress quickly so one feels good about oneself, and, above all, making national friends as soon as possible. Nothing will make one feel at home more quickly than learning to enjoy the nationals and to enjoy that which they enjoy.

The importance of new friends and "substitute family" cannot be overstated. In fact, Jesus promised that those who leave this constellation of relationships will receive them back and that multiplied.[208] That is not to say there won't be lonely times, especially initially when neither the language nor the new ways of the people are understood. Making good friends is one of the most natural ways to begin to understand people.

---

[206] Ralph D. Winter has given us these categories for evangelism and mission: M-1 indicates evangelism within the same culture; M-2 is to a sister language/culture, not as easy and requires different techniques; M-3 is to a totally strange language/culture and is considerably more difficult. ("The New Macedonia," Winter and Hawthorne, *Perspectives on the World Christian Movement* (Pasadena: William Carey Library,1981), 293-97.

[207] My surveys and interviews have borne this out. Luzbetak supports this: *Church and Cultures,* 205.

[208] Mark 10:29-30.

Although expectations of friendship are culturally defined, Luzbetak points out that

> friendship anywhere in the world presupposes the following: (1) mutual understanding, (2) common taste, (3) common interests, (4) mutual support, (5) mutual admiration, and (6) mutual accessibility. Such traits will lead to mutual trust, affection, and identification.[209]

Learning the culturally appropriate verbal and nonverbal expressions of friendship will go a long way in the identification process and make the missionary feel very much at home. "Friendship is the foundation for mutual support on the field. Healthy intimacy with a few good friends can make the difference between making it on the field and going home emotionally broken."[210] And the leadership plays an important role in this. "Leaders who both value and model providing support for others will tend to have followers who do the same."[211] One often gets the impression from missionary biographies that missionaries were all self-starters, self-motivators,

> *Going native is a neurotic form of identification.*

self-sufficient or so super-spiritual, that they didn't need anyone but God. One needs to read between the lines or read primary sources such as diaries, to see their points of vulnerability.

One extreme manifestation of the attempt to adapt, of culture shock is "going native."

> Going native is a neurotic form of identification, a compulsion for belonging to the society whose culture is responsible for the cultural stress being experienced. One is driven uncritically to giving up even one's most cherished values, in order to be accepted by the community and thereby once and for all to be free of the discomfort of cultural stress.[212]

The host culture is romanticized rather than viewed objectively or critically; nor is one's own culture viewed objectively. It is rejected along with all others belonging to it (perhaps team members). This neurotic reaction comes not from altruistic motives but is compensatory behavior for ultimately selfish reasons.

Conversely, going anti-native is an uncritical acceptance of the home culture and its values as superior and rejection of those of the new cul-

---

[209] Luzbetak, *The Church and Cultures,* 325f.

[210] Kenneth Williams, "A Model for Mutual Care in Missions," Kelly O'Donnell, ed., *Missionary Care: Counting the Cost for World Evangelism,* (Pasadena: William Carey Library, 1992), 48.

[211] Williams, ibid., 49.

[212] Luzbetak, *The Church and Cultures,* 218.

ture as woefully inferior. It can be detected in generalized statements of judgment about the new culture and all-inclusive praise of the home culture. Suspicion, aggression and irritation peak out. Labeling, categorizing and stereotyping things and people in the new culture are perverted forms of humor attempted to relieve the discomfort of culture shock. Missionaries in both categories should be sent away (or home) to a place where there is a sense of normality for them to establish equilibrium or, if it persists, their assignment should be reassessed. In extreme cases the person "gone native" will resist these suggestions perhaps leave the mission and may even remain in the country. These are, however, symptoms of deeper problems, which surface in stressful situations. An attempt to meet these deeper needs in a less stressful situation is in order.

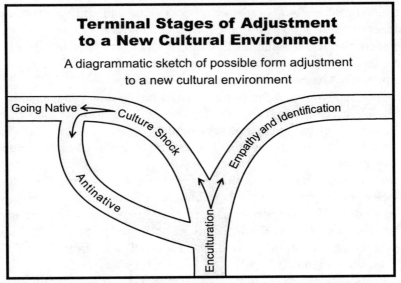

Figure 4: Terminal Stages of Adjustment to a New Cultural Environment
(adapted from Luzbetak, *The Church and Culture,* Orbis: 1988, 218)

Two phases of cultural adjustment have been described: 1) the honeymoon or tourist phase and 2) the stage of disenchantment, culture shock. The final two stages complete the cycle: 3) a period - long or short - of resolution and 4) the adjustment stage, in which one feels more comfortable, even at home, in the host culture. How one relates to the people during the stage of resolution is very important "for patterns of adjustment we form here tend to stay with us."[213] If the people of the new host culture sense attitudes of appreciation and acceptance from the missionary then the foundations for learning their culture and becoming one with them have been laid. Conversely, if the missionaries remain distanced at this time, "chances are that [they] will remain foreign and never identify [themselves] with nationals."[214] And this reflects on the gospel as well; it will also appear as distant and foreign to the people of the host culture. This stage marks the end of the bonding process and, with it, a decision to belong to these people (or not).

The adjustment stage (stage 4) continues in reality until another cultural change is made, either re-entry into the home country or another international move. During the phase of positive adjustment, serious incarnational identification takes place. The nationals know at this point if the missionary is a person to be invested in or just another short-termer who comes and goes.[215] Trust, the ultimate requirement for acceptance, is deepened between the missionary and the people. The missionary is moving toward being considered, if not an insider, then a valuable addition to their society.

One might question if it is even desirable to be considered an insider in a new culture. Are not the expectations too great for the newcomer to ultimately fulfill? Jacob Loewen expresses serious doubts about the credibility of the insider's role long-term.[216] He feels that outsider roles are probably more honest, better understood and safer. "Full acceptance of the alien is not dependent on being inside, but on transparent honesty and reciprocity."[217] Because foreigners can never really lay aside their cultural identity completely to fully become an insider, it is probably a matter of semantics when dealing in "outsider/insider" terminology. One should perhaps more appropriately speak in terms of identification, acceptance, mutual respect and

> *Biculturality may be a more realistic by-product of the goal of identification than becoming an insider.*

---

[213] Paul G. Hiebert, *Anthropological Insights for Missionaries* (Grand Rapids: Baker, 1985), 74-77.

[214] Hiebert, ibid., 76.

[215] No negative connotation of short-termers is implied here. But the categories must be clear to the nationals, in all honesty, for them to be able to create appropriate expectations. If missionaries give the impression they are staying long-term and then leave, there may well be feelings of abandonment on the part of the nationals. One relates differently to those who are there for short-terms.

[216] Jacob A. Loewen, "Roles: Relating to an Alien Social Structure," *Missiology*, Vol IV, No.2, (April, 1976), 217-42.

[217] Loewen, ibid., 240.

trust. Biculturality may be a more realistic by-product of the goal of identification than becoming an insider, as such. The intention is for the missionary to be a person of integrity who humbly attempts to understand others, who also loves and accepts them. There are, however, concrete trust factors in each culture which are viewed as credible.

One of the greatest mistakes missionaries can make is to think they know the culture and language well enough to stop learning. As in the case with spiritual development, one is either moving forward or moving backward, particularly in a culture that is rapidly changing. There is also a special temptation, particularly for Americans, whose culture, like it or not, is to some degree imprinting all but the remotest parts of the rest of the world. This is a result of the mass media explosion in the last half of the twentieth century. A great percentage of the world has tried a McDonald's hamburger, seen American television and movies and think, therefore, they have had a glimpse into the American home and family life. The image of Americans being rich has been perpetuated by media and tourism and missionaries will have to work hard to change this image that most people cannot identify with. These images affect the way most Western missionaries are perceived and are, therefore, not a problem just for American missionaries. Certain elements of this "media culture" are being assimilated into many other cultures; these cultures are in flux, too. On the one hand, it's attractive, perhaps status-enhancing, for them to know first-hand a person from this culture if they are positive towards the assimilation. On the other hand, it has grave backlashes in, for example, Muslim countries that are anti-Western at present, causing rejection by association for the missionary. For those nationals positively disposed, one can gain much mileage from the curiosity the media have created by allowing people of the new country to look into one's life and get to know one's God. It's a tightrope to walk, however, opening the windows and doors of one's life and home, yet not overwhelming them with gadgets or creating a chasm between lifestyles that is too big to cross. Although they are assimilating new values into their cultures, they still love their old culture without the Western artifacts. The points of identity and mutual trust must be worked on consciously.

Strange ways continue to feel suspicious. This can be observed presently in the East in Germany, where I now live. Many elements in the West German culture, which were new to them, were almost immediately absorbed as soon as the Berlin Wall fell. But other values have been subsequently imposed upon the East Germans and they resent it. There is also a nostalgic desire to keep some of the old values, which are quickly being destroyed by such radical changes. This warrants a study in and of itself. To my knowledge, no other nation, as a whole, has gone through such a culture shock without cultural guides to help them. Many of the rules have been changed for them almost overnight. When a culture changes so radically in such a short period of time, there is a sense of loss of personal identity. As a missionary, one is sometimes at a loss to know which values to identify with at present, knowing, however, that empathizing with the people in their confusion, anger and loss over the changes is most important.

One must remember that adjustment for the missionary is not a smooth, steady uphill incline that eventually plateaus. It often resembles the path of a roller coaster, with the seeming progress and emotions often plunging below the "desire to stay" line. Although it eventually smoothes out somewhat, there will still be stormy times, e.g., after furlough, with family and job changes, and with the development of the ministry. (See Appendix B)

Looking at the phases of adjustment is one way to mark the chronology; evaluating and assimilating certain values in the new culture is another process. While Hiebert postulates the process of evaluating other cultures from the world view level as follows: understanding -> appreciation -> informed judgment,[218] I tend to see the process of evaluating cultural values in the new culture with a view towards identification as follows: *observe -> understand -> assimilate -> appreciate*. Sometimes assimilation occurs unconsciously, without understanding, but not often on the part of adults. However, it is a

> Moving into the new culture involves:
> *observing → understanding → assimilating → appreciating*

known fact that the head is often in front of the heart, that the emotions follow a decision of the will. When a new cultural value is understood and a cognitive decision is made that, under the given circumstances, it would be better to assimilate that value, this is the course of action to follow. It may even be that, in the honeymoon phase especially, one is "infatuated" with new values and assimilates them quickly. But real appreciation is a step in which the missionary says, "I not only see that it's better, I like it that way!" There is no longer an inward "fight" to go against that which feels natural (own culture) in order to do what one knows to be appropriate in a given situation in the adopted culture.

To illustrate, inwardly I fought the German pattern of dialectic thinking (coming from a culture that has linear logic) when the discussions seemed endless and rather heated to me. Cutting off the discussion process for my German colleagues, however, was a serious insult, and was perceived as a lack of respect for each individual opinion, communicat-

---

[218] Paul A. Hiebert, *Anthropological Insights for Missionaries,* 99.

ing superficiality and an unwillingness to go through the process to get to a conclusion. Through feedback at many points over time, I finally understood this, but it still "felt" foreign to me and I "felt" that the raised tone of voice was very close to what "felt" like sin. Because of understanding the process and a conscious decision not to offend, I was able to participate in and endure this process long before I could appreciate it. Now I like it! This appreciation phase comes much later with some values than with others and for some types of people than others.

Not all adapting will look the same. In some cultures, during certain periods of history, under given circumstances, some missionaries will sense that the impact of their message will be enhanced by their changing. Others will sense the opposite (apart from total obliviousness to cultural sensitivity, that is). "Some Americans in Europe have been like large friendly dogs in a small room. Every time they wag their tail they knock over a chair."[219] [Note: One is allowed greater freedom with critique on one's own culture, but woe unto the outsider who takes the same liberties!] J. Hudson Taylor came to the conviction, despite harsh criticism from his co-workers, that national dress and hairstyle would lessen the cultural gap between the people and himself and pave the way for the understanding of the message.

Lars Peter Larsen, a Danish missionary, wrestled with his own adjustment process, "He could be highly critical of missions and their ways, but that did not make him ever want to masquerade as an Indian."[220] If he felt he were "masquerading" would have felt artificial, unnatural for Larsen, and he could not see it helping him accomplish his purpose in India. The intentions of Larsen and his wife were serious and decisions were made after reflection and prayer. "The Larsens 'agonized' over their affluent lifestyle and began to ask questions about the relations between Indians and Europeans."[221] They also spent much time learning Tamil and were careful to distinguish between communicating the gospel and transferring Danish Lutheranism.

> It's hardly debatable, that the mastery of the national language is a non-negotiable element of adaptation.

The Larsen's decision not to wear clothing native to India was apparently as much bathed in prayer and sound anthropological reasoning as J. H. Taylor's decision to do the opposite in China. Caution must be taken

---

[219] Alan Butler, in a speech to the Public Relations Society of America as quoted in *International Management*, June 1985.
[220] Eric J. Sharpe, "The Legacy of Lars Peter Larsen," *International Bulletin of Missionary Research,* Vol. 18, No. 3 (July, 1994), 119.
[221] Sharpe, ibid.

at the socio-economic level not to imitate (as in play-acting), but neither should there be "a conspicuous disparity between the missionaries' life-style and that of the people around them.[222] The question being asked was not whether or not to change on the surface, but rather: What impression is being created in the mind of the national? Is it advantageous for the sake of the gospel to change?

The extent to which missionaries should identify themselves with the people to whom they go is a matter of controversy. It's hardly debatable - though, unfortunately not always adhered to - that mastery of the national language is a non-negotiable element of adaptation.[223] Identification means being immersed in their culture, learning to think as they think, feel as they feel, do as they do.

What is the essence of cultural adjustment? A definition which I believe reflects the essence of incarnational thinking is: *removing the cultural obstacles which hinder clear, credible communication of the Gospel.* In the context of becoming "all things to all people," the Apostle Paul writes of enduring "anything rather than put an obstacle in the way of the gospel of Christ."[224] This, then, does not mandate the missionaries changing their ways 100 percent, nor changing in every area of life.

> *The essence of cultural adjustment is removing the cultural obstacles, which hinder clear, credible communication of the Gospel.*

It does require careful, prayerful consideration, evaluation of the new culture's values and the effect of the missionaries' values on the situation, feedback from nationals and resultant change, if required. The responsibility lies with the missionaries to do their homework.

Identification and the Missionary

The issue of identifying with the people of the new host culture evokes a sense of fear and loss in the minds of some. To them it means exchanging not only the familiar, but also that which one had grown to value for that which is unknown, to them unproven. How Jesus identified

---

[222] "The Willowbank Report," 521.

[223] The mastery of the language is commensurate with that which their job requires. While all missionaries should be able to communicate their faith in the national language, some missionaries will be called to preach and teach whereas others will be doing primarily bookkeeping or administrative tasks. Not all missionaries need to reach the same level of mastery to begin their ministry, but all missionaries should continue to grow in their language capabilities.

[224] I Corinthians 9:12b.

with others was discussed in the previous chapter. In this section, identification will be defined and illustrated by missionaries who have struggled with this issue.

Associated with identification are such concepts as: solidarity, involvement, taking up the cause of those with whom one identifies. There is nothing that would imply that one must exchange values, as such. Nida suggests that identification is a complex concept but one which "involves the totality of interhuman relationships." It is not imitation or the sentimental attempt to "go native" which indicates a loss of objectivity and realism. Imitation "creates contempt, the most important barrier to mutual understanding." He concludes with what might be used as a working definition: *"Identity means, not being someone else, but being more than oneself."*[225]

The stories and sacrifices of many missionaries could be cited to illustrate identification with the people one has grown to love. But there are many chapters of personal missionary history which would be perhaps more realistic and attractive if they had been written. Some are just now being written in retrospect. Perhaps the generations before have not been as vulnerable, but, to underscore the need, the present generation virtually demands vulnerability and self-revelation as a measure of credibility and a point of identification.

> *Identity means, not being someone else, but being **more** than oneself.*

Dr. Helen Roseveare, in my opinion, is just such a person. A missionary doctor in the days before, during and after the revolution in the Congo, she had her share of adjustments. She was determined to take care of all the sick she could, and her dream was to train Africans as medical workers. During her decades of service she made bricks, built clinics, did the bookkeeping and even coached soccer teams! As goal-oriented as she was, she listened to the counsel of her coworkers, her African pastor and colleagues. Her ultimate goal in life was to live for Christ and Him alone. At one juncture, after having rebuilt so much of what had been destroyed in the revolution and personally suffering indescribable humiliation and beatings, she was preparing to leave for a well-earned furlough, wanting to record her work and the graduation on film and cassette for her supporters at home. Then, due to a misunderstanding in the handling of funds, her students went on strike. There was no graduation of the medical aides. There was no grand farewell for the missionary. But the Lord was asking her, "You asked Me when you were first converted for the privilege of being a missionary. This is it: don't

---

[225] Nida, *Message and Mission*, 162.

you want it?"[226] He was reminding her of previous days when she had been willing to undergo even inhuman treatment for Him. "These are not your sufferings: they are Mine. All I ask of you is the loan of your body." At first the sense of privilege of being asked for something He needed overwhelmed her.

"You went home and told everyone that I was sufficient at *that* moment, in *those* circumstances. Isn't this true now, in today's circumstances?"

I tried to say: "But of course, Lord. You know it's true."

"No," He quietly rebuked me. "No. You no longer want Jesus only, but Jesus plus . . . plus respect, popularity, public opinion, success and pride . . . Jesus, *plus* . . . No, you can't have it. Either it must be 'Jesus only' or you'll find you have no Jesus. You'll substitute Helen Roseveare."

A great long silence followed - several days of total inner silence.

At last I managed to tell Him that with all my heart I wanted "Jesus only."[227]

There was a farewell after all, and the students who had gone on strike sang a self-composed song asking to be remembered as her sons and that God would blot out the memory of the wound they had tried to inflict in their stupidity. But the process of "Christ living in me" and identifying with the people sometimes asks a high price of the missionary.

Identification, as Jesus illustrated it, is in two directions: the missionary identifies with Jesus in His incarnation and suffering on the cross, and with the people whom he/she serves. This identification is costly. It may mean, as it has for many missionaries, giving up family, career, serving humbly under perhaps less-trained and less-experienced national leadership. "Each of these can be a kind of death, but it is death which brings life to others."[228] The Apostle Paul was no stranger to this. He described his own *kenosis*: after listing his credentials, an impressive list indeed, he moved his credits over to debits considering "regarding them as loss because of the surpassing value of knowing Christ Jesus my Lord."[229]

> *This identification is costly.*

In Philippians 2, just before the description of Jesus' identification with us as an example to us, Paul's charge to the church is: "Do nothing from selfish ambition or conceit, but in humility regard others as better

---

[226] Helen Roseveare, *He Gave Us a Valley* (Leicester: InterVarsity, 1976), 180.

[227] Roseveare, ibid., 181.

[228] Stott, *The Cross of Christ*, 291.

[229] Philippians 3:4-9.

than yourselves. Let each of you look not to your own interests, but to the interests of others. Let the same mind be in you that was in Christ Jesus."[230] Paul gave criteria for living together: "Don't look down on one another in order to reinforce your own ego or identity, but rather look up to Christ, the One who was not worried about His image by association."[231] The temptation to think that one's "God-given" goals, plans and programs are more important than the agenda others create is very subtle. One needs Christ's wisdom to consciously evaluate and discover God's priorities in the context of new values. It is easy to rely unconsciously on one's own cultural values instead of asking God the question again and again, "What is on Your agenda for me, just now?" The new, appropriate cultural values may never "feel right" and thus the resulting struggle, even suffering. "We do not [tend to] accept one another in love, but rather we try to remake those around us in our own image. This tendency is the negation of the principle of incarnation, which requires that we learn to think in the style of our neighbor."[232] It is a not-so-subtle egoism. It is the assumption that my ways, plans, etc. are the right ways and plans. Against this judgment of personal or cultural superiority we are severely warned!

Identification - how far? Eugene Nida presents four degrees of identification in terms of levels of communication which are important for our consideration:

1. At the lowest level: the message has no significant effect on the receptor's behavior and the message is essentially self-validating. (The train station is down the street.)

2. This level has no permanent effect on the total value system of the receptor, though it does affect significantly his immediate behavior. "Unless the source identifies himself with the message, the effect upon the receptor is largely nullified" (e.g., announcing a flood and preparing to evacuate).

3. This level affects a large segment of a person's behavior and changes his whole value system (e.g., repentance from adultery and faithfulness to wife). "In addition to identifying with his message, he [the sender] must also demonstrate an identification with the receptor, for the receptor must be convinced that the source understands his views, even though he may not agree with them." Something common in their backgrounds will give weight to the message.

---

[230] Philippians 2:3-5.

[231] Free paraphrase of Philippians 2:3-5.

[232] Sherwood G. Lingenfelter and Marvin K. Mayers, *Ministering Cross-Culturally* (Grand Rapids: Baker, 1986), 67.

4. Complete identification: "The message has been so effec-
    tively communicated that the receptor feels the same type of
    communicative urge as that experienced by the source. The
    receptor then becomes a source of further communication of
    the message."[233] cf. 2 Timothy 2:2.

One must carefully distinguish between outer and inner identity. Living in poor surroundings, if improperly motivated, is likely to separate.
So can living in a large home with all the trappings *if* "these things keep
one from people and serve as symbols of one's inner isolation or lack of
identity. In themselves, however, things are only things - it is only when
people attach values to them that they acquire meaning and serve to
thwart effective communication."[234]

This is getting to the heart of the matter. Not pretense, only integrity
is ultimately respected. "Inner identity does not mean it is necessary to
adopt the value system of those one seeks to communicate with; rather,
that it must be taken seriously."[235] This is both politeness and good psychology whether one is dealing adult to children and, most certainly,
adult to adult, as with equal partners. This is qualified, lest one might
mistakenly be led to think that love and
inner identity require no outer identity.
"Outsiders cannot live on the edge of a
community without coming to the attention
of insiders in a negative way."[236] The goal
of the missionary is to become as much an

> *The goal of the missionary is to become as much an insider as is necessary to be credible.*

insider as is necessary to be credible, to become a valuable person in the
host culture. Living on the periphery of the culture as an outsider drasti-
cally reduces effectiveness. The identification process is not abstract and
impersonal. "As a prerequisite to any type of identification, one must
recognize first that he is identifying with specific persons [rural farmers,
students, etc.], not with a generalization or type."[237] Granted, identification can only be partial, "if our communication is to be effective, our
identification should be as extensive as possible."[238] When the barriers of
opposition loom before us, that which we have in common in Christ is
cherished. Unfortunately, this is usually realized only in dire circumstances such as extreme persecution.

---

[233] Nida, *Message and Mission*, 164-66.

[234] Nida, *Message and Mission*, 163.

[235] Nida, *Message and Mission*, 164.

[236] Donald N. Larson, "The Viable Missionary: Learner, Trader, Storyteller,"
Missiology, Vol. 6, No. 2, 158.

[237] Nida, *Message and Mission*, 168.

[238] Nida, *Message and Mission*, ibid.

In some circles syncretism is feared as a by-product of cultural adaptation. Nida differentiates between change in form and change in content:

Indigenization consists essentially in the full employment of local indigenous forms of communication, methods of transmission, and communicators, as these means can be prepared and trained. Syncretism, on the other hand, involves an accommodation of content, a synthesis of beliefs, and an amalgamation of world views, in such a way, as to provide some common basis for constructing a "new system" or a "new approach."

He purports that rather than syncretism being a by-product of cultural adaptation, actually just the opposite occurs. "In fact, where there is no indigenization of the message, syncretism is usually greatest, for without indigenization there is no meaningful confrontation of religious systems and no intelligent 'yes' or 'no' to the claims of Jesus Christ."[239] This "backlash effect" may well occur without indigenization because the form of the message connotes "foreignness," thus resulting in its rejection and moving towards syncretism. John Pobee cites negative effects of the lack of cultural adaptation:

Mission produced split-personalities in Africa with the result that there is often a double insurance policy on the side of Africans . . . while in public they profess Christianity, they do not appear to have full satisfaction from it and against what the official church says, they go on to do their own thing along the lines of traditional Africa. [240]

The danger of exclusivism, missionaries withdrawing or associating only with others from their homeland, is ever present during periods of intense culture stress. Exclusivism behaves almost like a self-protecting reflex. But in this case the causes and effects of culture stress need to be re-evaluated. They may feel destructive, but are they really? Are they not indeed part of a healthy process, moving one towards a more fulfilling friendship and identification with the people?

Another form of withdrawal in the process of cultural adaptation is for missionaries to pull back into the safe nest of their homes, becoming so preoccupied with themselves that they cease to reach out, learn, adapt, and enjoy the new host culture. Such a withdrawal is indicative of a "survival mode" and a preoccupation with self/family that eliminates most active ministry. "It is the mutual responsibility of both husband and wife to see that each does not hinder the other from fulfilling his or her ministry . . . Care should be taken that family claims do not monopolize

---

[239] Nida, *Message and Mission,* ibid., 185.
[240] Pobee, "Christian Mission Towards the Third Millennium," 10.

the time and energies of either parent . . . A home that is absorbed in itself is not a truly Christian home."[241]

One national missionary, distressed over the fact that the long-term missionary and team leader was so absorbed with his family needs that he didn't have time to minister to the team, could see little justification for their being on the field at that time. The grace period for these missionaries was over long ago and the crisis situations left little room for ministry. It was clearly a time for change in leadership, at least temporarily, until the family regained their footing.

> *It is incumbent on the parents to continually direct their own and their children's attention outwardly and communicate a positive, trusting attitude.*

With all due respect to the needs of children, it remains incumbent on the parents to continually direct their own and their children's attention outwardly and communicate a positive, trusting attitude. Homes that only revolve around their own needs are neither exemplary nor helpful for the people or other missionaries. Even in crisis situations, the griefs can be shared and needs made known for the growth of all involved. But they dare not be so all-encompassing that the other real needs of team members, or ministry, are neglected.

Another danger is related to the contributions of missionaries. They need to be holistic in nature, not compartmentalized. This caution is twofold: the areas of ministry should not just be to the mind, but to the body and soul as well. And the missionary himself should not just allow his sphere of influence to be confined to the mental, or the physical, but also the social and deeply spiritual. Too often Western male missionaries are guilty of such compartmentalization. Often the most sincere compliment a missionary can receive sounds almost childish but reflects the integrated view of life most non-Western cultures share: "You are the first one who ever played with us." Play, as Nida conveys, is more symbolic than work and is closer to the area of human interpersonal communication.[242] This was also born out in my survey as a response from national missionaries.

> *Play is more symbolic than work and is closer to the area of human interpersonal communication.*

The emotions ran the gamut between being offended, to being disappointed that expatriate missionaries didn't choose to associate with them during their free time. Most often it was an oversight rather than premeditated. But it was hurtful nevertheless, be-

---

[241] Williamson, *Have We No Rights?* 67, 79, as quoted from The Overseas Manual of the China Inland Mission. Overseas Missionary Fellowship, 1955, 22.
[242] Nida, *Message and Mission*, 163.

cause it communicated that they didn't "like" them, also rejection, to a certain degree. It also gave the impression that the expatriate missionaries were not interested in the nationals; they were there to get a job done reflecting a non-integrated lifestyle not understood or valued by non-Westerners.[243]

Is this not our goal: identification to the degree that the receptors be-

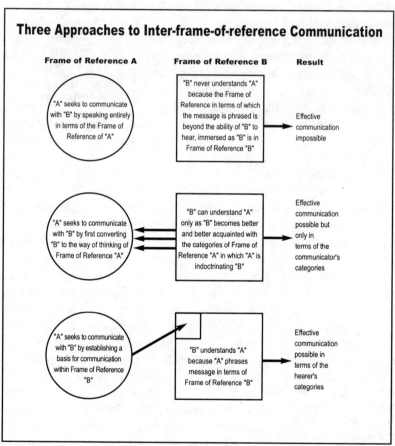

Figure 5: Three Approaches to Inter-frame-of-reference Communication (adapted from Kraft, *Christianity in Culture,* Orbis: 1979, 218)

---

[243] This area is discussed further in chapter 4, "Meeting Personal Needs."

come valid disciples of Jesus in their own right? Is not, then, complete identification on their terms a prerequisite?

As much as there is a need on the part of the messenger to identify with the people, there is also the need for the message to be communicated carefully in terms that the recipients understand in their cultural context. The contextualization of the message has been the subject of much more research, however, and is a topic in and of itself beyond the scope of this work. There are important points, which are mentioned as they relate to the subject of multicultural teams in chapter 4.

Charles Kraft outlines an identificational approach, which he says is more in line with Jesus' approach to people and with the practice of the early church. This approach starts with the felt needs of the receptors.[244] Felt needs, in contrast to real needs, are those of which the person him-

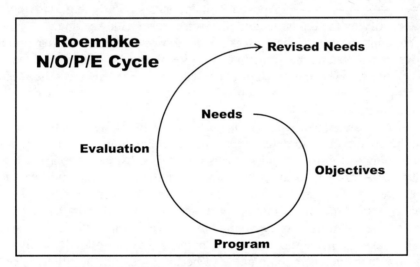

Figure 6: The Training Cycle (Roembke, unpublished)

self is aware. It is important, then, to start at the point of awareness; other real, deeper needs will surface in the process.

Dr. Lois LeBar made use of this principle in what she called the educational cycle of the church.[245] I revised it to use when enculturating and individualizing training for Campus Crusade for Christ staff in many countries of Europe as well as in the USA, Africa and Asia to the Train-

---

[244] Charles Kraft, *Christianity in Culture,* 154.
[245] Lois E. LeBar, *Focus on People in Church Education* (Westwood: Revell, 1968), 26f.

ing or N/O/P/E cycle.[246] The premise of approaching training or communication from the point of "need" is that one must bridge the gap, move
from the known to the unknown, touch persons at the point of their receptivity, then move on from there. Some needs are essentially brought
to the surface in the light of new information or responsibilities, e.g.,
when a new job description reveals a need for training or, in the case of
evangelism and discipleship, when the Bible sheds light on life.

Jesus used this approach with almost everyone He met - the Samaritan
woman, Zacchaeus, Nicodemus, the rich young
ruler, the blind man. He basically asked them
directly or indirectly, whichever was
appropriate, to articulate what they wanted.
Their interest was aroused, a bond was created,
a willingness to receive was expressed. The
Apostle Paul operated similarly, e.g., in Athens,
by identifying the unknown god they were fearing and seeking.

> In approaching training at the point of need, one must bridge the gap, move from the known to the unknown.

In communication theory it is a well-known principle that perception
governs understanding, sometimes in spite of what is said. Sometimes it
is the nonverbal communication that distorts the messages for the receptor; more often than not in a cross-cultural situation it is a matter of difference in perception.

A young Liberian who had been schooled in Western institutions in
his homeland once told Kraft that his understanding of John 3:16 was
something as follows, "God so loves Europeans that he accepts as Christian any African who turns his back on his own customs and becomes
converted to Western culture."[247] This is certainly a tragic distortion of
the truth God meant for him to understand, but indeed how he had perceived the conditions for receiving God's love. Perhaps the missionaries
didn't take his perception seriously; perhaps they were totally oblivious
to how their message communicated because they never solicited feedback.

---

[246] Lianne Roembke. "Using the N/O/P/E Cycle in Developing Staff Training"
unpublished. Based on the felt needs and moving to the real needs of people, one
develops concise, measurable, personal objectives, then suggested programs,
methods and materials to help meet these objectives. One then evaluates periodically, not primarily how good the programs are, but how well the objectives
have been met, before revising and continuing the process. This process is very
person oriented and is geared towards life change under the guidance of the Holy
Spirit using the Word of God.
[247] Kraft, *Christianity in Culture,* 289.

Adapting Without Hurting One's Identity

Perhaps a prior question must be considered first: What factors work against cultural adjustment? First, ignorance caused by cultural blind spots or lack of opportunity for training or research in this area can cause resistance to change. Second, personal insecurity, inability to change at a given time for psychological reasons, deficits in childhood or presently, may render the missionary temporarily incapable of changing. And third, there could be a basic unwillingness to change. In addition, there are other factors, such as some personality types or national cultural heritage, which are more rigid and tend to resist change.

That change is possible and desirable, is the basic assumption of every missionary who intends to effect positive change towards the gospel message. The question for missionaries is a practical one and re-volves around the degree of change necessary and their ability to change. "A searching test of identification is how far we [the missionaries] feel that we belong to the people, and - still more - how far they feel that we belong to them?"[248] As subjective as these criteria may seem, they nev-ertheless represent a very complex process. Balasundaram reflects posi-tively on the discernment of Lars Peter Larsen decision not to exhibit "that very form of subtle condescension" in wearing Indian garb. "He lived, as he should, a European; and yet made everyone, were he a Hindu or a Mohammedan or a Christian, feel perfectly at home in his good home - which was the centre of culture. He was incapable of racial feel-ing."[249]

The point is clear: no mere outward conformity is to be equated with identification and resultant credibility. This kind of integrity of person and respect for the other can only come from a non-judgmental heart of love. There is also a clear correlation between what is expected from the nationals and how ready the missionary is to change.

If we are to effect even a reasonable degree of identification, it is necessary that we first fully recognize our own motivations. Our interests in identification must not be some subtle projection of our unsatisfied desire to dominate, nor must they represent any con-scious attempt to escape from our own cultural milieu . . . not an attempt to dodge reality . . . to find a strange, exotic niche or think that we can compensate for our hidden failures by engineering the

---

[248] "The Willowbank Report," 521.
[249] "Dr. L.P. Larsen - An Appreciation," *Young Men of India,* April 4, 1941, as quoted in *International Bulletin of Missionary Research,* July 1994.

lives of others . . . We shall soon get stopped dead in our tracks by people who can see through our sham.[250]

In the case previously described, perhaps Balasundaram's history with Europeans, in general, and the contrast in attitude of the Larsens were the factors that gave them credibility. In countries without prior contact with other cultures or where the cultures are similar, the expectations for change are different. This the missionary needs to find out. Where there are expectations, however, and the missionary resists change, even in the smallest of things, credibility is questioned. For example, the most gracious of Germans will overlook the table manners of American missionaries who, in Germany, insist on cutting with their knife, laying it down, and switching the fork over to the right hand to eat - for a while, that is. But if the Americans begin to try to convince the Germans that their way is better they will only be stared at in disbelief. If the Americans proceed to load up their open-faced sandwich with layers of meat and cheese (even if they are increasing the protein without adding more carbohydrates or calories!), they are then thought of as wasteful, selfish or gluttonous. (This still is considered true although the shortages of the last war were 40-50 years ago. One puts only one piece of either meat *or* cheese on the bread. No Dagwood sandwiches! When there was a shortage of cake it was made to go further by putting it with bread, forming a "sandwich.") How can "such little things" affect the credibility of the Gospel one might ask? Such little things add up to a composite feeling of strangeness, oversight, and especially if one has been told about it over and over, these seemingly trifles can lead to a lack of respect and lack of credibility.

Finnish missionaries in Germany were sometimes misunderstood because each family built a sauna in their home. For the rest of the team, Germans, Swiss, Dutch and Americans alike, it was viewed as a luxury, or relatively high priced recreation at the time. Upon getting to know the Finnish culture, however, it became clear that a sauna is viewed by them as basic hygiene, like the bathtub or shower. They didn't really feel clean without steaming out the dirt. It also

> Evaluate with nationals which areas are necessary for credibility, which add to credibility, which are relatively neutral and which would discredit the message.

played a role in social/business intercourse, an informal atmosphere for continuing discussions with colleagues. (Not mixed, however. So much for the equality of the sexes!) So, is it permissible for Finnish missionaries in Germany to each have a family sauna? In addition to the criterion

---

[250] Nida, *Message and Mission*, 168-69.

of cost, the use of it is critical. Is it used to include others from the community or team (the living room principle of hospitality)? Or is it just perceived as exclusive and luxurious?

Some change is necessary for credibility and we have begun to answer the question: how far *must* one adapt? But the corollary question remains: how far *can* one missionary adapt without hurting one's identity? Which elements belong to the composite of a person's identity? Can one change each element as easily as another?

One can view one's personality as a set of concentric circles, with the innermost circle of values being those held to more dearly and, therefore, the values harder to give up or change. A good exercise would be to begin to evaluate one's personal values according to the resistance to change one senses: Circle A represents values one can change without feeling any loss or struggle. Circle B represents values one sees the need to change and intends to as one can. There may be felt resistance but it is mostly related to the comfort of habit, not real conviction about the inherent worth of the value. Circle C represents values one struggles with greatly to change; the need to change may or may not be clear, or the values themselves are closely linked to the perception of oneself. Circle D represents values one holds so dearly it would be very difficult, if not impossible, to change. The estimation of these values will be different from person to person.

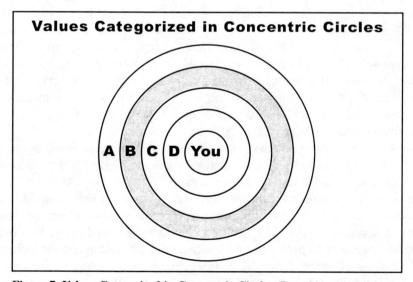

Figure 7: Values Categorized in Concentric Circles (Roembke, unpublished)

The list of values to be considered is endless. One can start with the more obvious: food, eating habits, dress, courtesy and manners, concept of time, concept of personal space, modes of transportation, form of housing, language, pronunciation, methods of hospitality, planning and scheduling of time, lifestyle, use of finances, view of property, concept of privacy, sanitary facilities, cleanliness, orderliness, punctuality, egalitarianism, health care, children's education, views of dating and marriage, "roles" of women and men, concept of freedom, methods of discussion, decision-making (logic), leadership style, measures of success, etc. (One can add to the list as one becomes more aware of one's own values or those of the new culture.)

And then the less academic but most important part of the exercise: Evaluate with *national* friends and colleagues, which areas are necessary for credibility, which add to credibility, which are relatively neutral, and which would detract from credibility (with the changes implied, of course). These should all be validated as well. Underlying this process one will sense either resistance and tension and/or the moving of the Spirit to be willing to be made willing to change in crucial areas. This is identification with Jesus. This is part of the call.

A relatively recent experience for me has confirmed the importance of this dynamic process. Although I had lived in West Germany for over 16 years and worked for several years with a team that traveled into East Germany before one ever thought about "the Wall" falling, it was quite another thing to actually uproot from my second home in West Germany and move to the East. It turned out that there was a sort of "entrance fee" to be paid. In 1991 housing was hard to get in West Germany but it was at a premium in East Germany. And, whereas some of my colleagues were able to get housing in other Eastern European countries, I didn't have the leverage of offering a "hard currency" against theirs, since the West German Mark was already the currency of the East. The use of bribery was not an option, though the offers kept coming (pay DM 10,000 for our "improvements" and you can have the apartment). It took two years, with many disappointments and blind alleys, before my East German colleague, Doris Döring, was able to eventually offer her smaller apartment in a three-way-trade for us to get a larger apartment together. Not every apartment was available to us because the government limited the number of rooms and square meters per person. In the two intervening years Doris allowed me to live in her already crowded apartment as we looked daily for adequate space to live and work. I learned the "East German" ways of entertaining guests, dealing with bureaucracy, politics, repairmen; learned to tread carefully

> *How far can one missionary adapt without hurting one's identity?*

with people's political backgrounds; even learned a new dialect of German. I was absorbed into Doris' circles of friends and family. The delay was indeed a blessing in disguise. Many times I felt pushed to my personal limits to change, and I supposed the expectations from me were even higher than from a new arrival because: (1) I had lived in West Germany so long and had visited East Germany so often and (2) culturally speaking, East Germany was being shoved rapidly in the direction of West Germany in the unification process and I, of all people, was looked to as a cultural guide - when I was in need of one myself!

In evaluating one's values in concentric circles, it becomes apparent which values are so closely attached to one's personal identity that the attempt to change - even the thought of it - literally hurts. Is this feeling of hurt an indication that one has gone too far in changing? It is indeed an indication that one has touched an area, a value, that is so closely tied to personal identity that the missionaries don't feel as if they could still be themselves if they changed. The feeling may border on self-denial. However, this identification process, described before as becoming more than what one already is, is comparable to another conversion: "When we first believed . . . we experienced a reintegration of our whole person and life. We did not lose our original identity nor wipe out our past life, but we entered into new relationships with both God and our fellow human beings."[251]

The missionaries are experiencing inner conflict encountering a new culture and are subconsciously or consciously questioning themselves and the values of the new cultures as well. To balance out the cumulative effects of the stresses caused by many changes at once, "a missionary needs to feel an adequate degree of security so that survival does not become a major daily question. Having to fight for survival takes away energy and concentration . . ."[252] Missionaries need to learn to pace themselves well in stressful situations and sometimes pull back or take a break. It is not uncommon to feel the stress of role ambiguity. The mission should be careful to outline clear and reasonable expectations for *all* missionaries, married and single women included.[253] Frustration may take the form of rejection, not only of the new culture but of oneself. "The person suffering from culture shock may feel that he is a failure, that he had no business coming overseas in the first place, that he cannot possibly make good." The blame may be turned inward for every mis-

---

[251] Sherwood G. Lingenfelter and Marvin K. Mayers, *Ministering Cross-Culturally,* 123.

[252] LeRoy Johnston, "Core Issues in Missionary Life," Kelly O'Donnell, ed., *Missionary Care,* 42.

[253] Cf. section on Women in chapters 1and 4 for further discussion.

take, every lack of success. "The rejection may even be focused on God. It was God who called him into missionary work and sent him to this place. God is to blame for making such a terrible mistake."[254]

How can this inner conflict be resolved and the "inner conversion" accomplished? First, the basis for personal security in the midst of all change is recognizing that our identity, indeed our value, is in Jesus Christ. We are loved unconditionally by Him. We have been accepted, redeemed and called by Him. He does not and will not expect the impossible from us. And He knows us so very well. It is based on this love and our trust in His integrity that we can face change of this magnitude positively, without fearing the loss of our identity or a portion of it. It is indeed exhilarating to be buoyed up by God's love in the throes of change.

One's faith in a reliable, personal God is strengthened. Facing radical change, then, is a process of resting in God's love and protection and being willing to let Him change one. It is a conscious releasing of one's "rights" to retain what one feels belongs to one's being. It is the "emptying" of oneself, as Jesus emptied Himself. But this emptying, ironically, brings fullness.

> But this emptying, ironically, brings fullness.

As Smalley comments: "We tend to respect what we like or learn to like."[255] "In order for the missionary to become an effective communicator in a cross-cultural setting he/she must be trained to think and act biculturally . . . Nothing in our culture prepares us to function in another culture."[256] This does indeed call for a another conversion.

And second, in order to resolve this inner conflict, the necessity for change must be based, not on the missionary's resistance or willingness to change, but on the determining of the credibility of certain values which the national and the missionary evaluate together. Here a definite distinction needs to be made between cultural adaptation and syncretism. The warning is clear; indigenization is not to be equated with an uncritical acceptance of a culture. Both individuals and societies are subject to change under the higher authority of the gospel. "Indigenization is communicating the gospel in ways that challenge them in their personal and corporate lives with God's call to discipleship."[257]

The issue is to learn not to withdraw because of the pain of culture shock or to fiercely hold on to one's cultural values, but, as quickly as possible, to let that tension motivate one to develop a degree of bilin-

---

[254] William A. Smalley, *Readings in Missionary Anthropology, Vol. II.,* 697.
[255] Smalley, ibid., 712.
[256] Lyman E. Reed, *Preparing Missionaries for Intercultural Communication* (Pasadena: William Carey Library, 1985), 5.
[257] Paul G. Hiebert, "Critical Contexualization," *Missiology* Vol. XII., 289.

gualism and biculturalism. "Sometimes the person suffering from culture shock discovers his own emotional insecurity. He finds himself behaving childishly . . . projecting his problems upon others . . . For many it is a time of renewed commitment to Christ."[258]

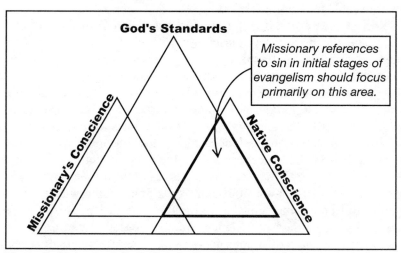

Figure 8: Juncture of God's Standards and Human Conscience (adapted from Priest, "Missionary Elenctics: Conscience and Culture," *Missiology Volume XXII No. 3,* American Society of Missiology: July, 1994, 300)

Another aspect concerning change and perceived need for changing on the part of the missionary involves the area *of elenctics.*[259] The essence of the concept is that one's view of sin is culturally conditioned, although most missionaries would claim they base their definition of sin on the Word of God alone. It is however more culturally tainted than one would admit. Anthropologist, missiologist and son of missionary parents Robert Priest explains, "American missionaries [for example] internalize deeply held moral ideas about punctuality, egalitarianism, individual rights, privacy, cleanliness, etc., which derive much more clearly from

---

[258] Smalley, *Readings in Missionary Anthropology II,* 699-700.
[259] Dutch missiologist J.H. Bavinck and his followers, David Hesselgrave and Klaus Müller, are calling for a missionary science under the name of "elenctics," which is based on the Greek word *elenchein* meaning "to bring to shame, convict, convince, reprove, rebuke." Cf Klaus Müller, "Elenktik: Gewissen im Kontext," Kasdorf and Müller, eds., *Bilanz und Plan: Festschrift zum 80. Geburtstag von George W. Peters* (Lahr: Johannis ed. VLM, 1988).

their culture than from the Scriptures." [260] One cannot assume that some-one, even a trained missionary, can adequately distinguish the biblical from the cultural aspects of his values. "The missionaries' consciences will tend to function both on moral sentiments learned from Scripture and on moral sentiments derived from culture - each set of moral senti-ments affecting the way the other is viewed, the two not being intuitively distinguishable to conscience." [261]

R. Priest contrasts the congruity (or lack thereof) of the native con-science and the missionary conscience with God's moral norms as re-vealed in Scripture. His point is: the missionaries tend to begin with and concentrate on the points of sin which go against the missionaries' cul-turally-conditioned conscience. But this does not touch the national con-science.[262] The beginning point and content of their preaching and teaching should be at the *juncture of God's revelation and the native conscience*, the missionaries' conscience notwithstanding. One reason for this is that one does not respond to that about which one has not de-veloped a conscience. This sensitivity comes only in time with exposure and response to God's Word through God's Spirit. Otherwise the nation-als will be deemed unresponsive to the message just because the Word was not applied to their conscience. Another reason is that one tends to judge others by one's own conscience. This becomes apparent when the nationals are critical of the missionary on an issue of their (nationals') conscience which the missionaries do not perceive in their own con-science. This has devastating implications for the credibility of the mes-sengers in the new culture. They can quickly be labeled as hypocrites. The disparity in consciences would cause those from a Muslim culture, for example, to question the sexual modesty of all but the most carefully dressed missionary. The issue is: What in the person of the missionary communicates virtue, integrity and love to them? This perspective is most helpful in focusing the attention of the missionary in the adjustment process, namely on God, His revelation and the people and their reac-tions.

> Becoming conscious of, and analytical about, our own cultural glasses is a *painful* business. We do best by learning about other people's glasses. Although we can never take our glasses off to find out what the world is 'really like' or try looking through any-

---

[260] Robert J. Priest, "Missionary Elenctics: Conscience and Culture," *Missiology*. Vol. XXII. No. 3. (July 1994), 300.

[261] Priest, ibid.

[262] Priest, ibid., 302.

one else's without ours on as well, we can at least learn a good deal about our own prescription.[263]

Personal pain is not enjoyable but it is often not unhealthy. Change that challenges one's identity, then, is not necessarily bad. Unlike the value of most Western cultures, pain is not to be avoided at all costs. Pain and suffering, biblically speaking, are part of the sanctification process, part of God's plan of conforming us to the likeness of His Son. And certainly pain endured in a cross-cultural situation for the sake of the Son is, in the end, healthy and even desirable (if it is not sadistic). This means that if missionaries *feel* like they are losing an important part of their identity, this may not necessarily be the case, in reality. It could, in fact, be that they have built their personal or cultural values on a faulty foundation which needs to be evaluated primarily in light of God's Word but also with respect to the effect of those values on the host culture. The shock of self-discovery, perhaps feelings of defeat instead of the success enjoyed in the home culture, sometimes can be the beginning of healing.

In all honesty most missionaries have to admit, they bring some of the pain upon themselves by their unwillingness to change. If they were willing, as the Apostle Paul, to count all things in our history of prior successes as loss, in order to gain Christ, they would surely experience much more of the heart of Christ. It is often a matter of focus. Is the focus on the losses or on the gains? The question of whether all the pain of adjustment is worth it has to be answered by each individual missionary. The question should actually be put into better perspective: Is knowing Christ worth the pain?

Is knowing Christ worth the pain of adjustment?

Veteran missionary Mabel Williamson's reminder, that missionaries are guests, with the responsibility of adaptation on their side, not expecting the people to adapt to them, is warranted.[264] I remember that while visiting Nairobi, Kenya to interview national and expatriate missionaries for this research, I made a trip to the post office. I realized back at the house that the man at the counter had charged me twice as much for the large quantity of stamps I had purchased. The expatriate missionary basically told me to forget the loss; I wouldn't get anywhere protesting. But I wanted to not only reclaim my loss but also to see if I could find a key to dealing with the post office agreeably. The next day at the post office, wearing the same dress in order to be recognized I luckily found the same man behind the counter. Weighing my words carefully, I

---

[263] Roger M. Keesing and Felix M. Keesing, *New Perspectives in Cultural Anthropology,* (New York: Holt, Rinehart and Wilson, 1971), 21, [emphasis mine].
[264] Mabel Williamson, *Have We No Rights?* (Chicago: Moody, 1957), 36.

began "Hello! Do you remember me? I think I made a mistake yesterday. I think I paid too much for the stamps." To my surprise, without another word of explanation or any questions asked, he pulled out the equivalent amount of stamps and pushed them over the counter towards me. I thanked him politely. Now, I would have to live there longer and have similar experiences to validate this observation, but I reasoned that accusing him would embarrass and/or anger him. I was the guest there and it was I who needed to learn to recognize and count the currency. So suggesting that it was my mistake was the only reasonable approach to take.

Mabel Williamson, in asking the question of how far to adapt, says it is the responsibility of the missionary to be a gracious, not a demanding guest, so for the people there is "profit in pursuing my acquaintance" and profit "in listening to the strange stories of Someone called Jesus that I am so fond of telling."[265] Hospitality is a high value, a norm for most peoples. It is also a biblical value (Hebrews 13:2). Missionaries who offer hospitality, whether guests announce their arrival or just come by, will want their guests to feel at home. This is not always easy, because, for the Western missionary in particular, our privacy, our sense of convenience and comfort, need to undergo drastic alteration. Even our sense of belonging to ourselves will have to become secondary in order to develop a sense of belonging to others, which the rest of the world so values.[266]

Many are the times when missionaries will want to echo the words of an old pilgrim's prayer, "Lord, grant me the serenity to accept the things I cannot change, the courage to change the things I can, and the wisdom to know the difference." In most areas it's a matter of trusting the God who called us to this "impossible situation." Even in what would seem to be a black and white situation, such as cleanliness, M. Williamson can say, "Surely in cases where adhering strictly to the rules of hygiene would hinder the fulfilling of our commission, we can trust the One who sent us forth to look after us."[267]

So how far can one adapt without losing one's identity? In summary, the process of adapting to another culture is not without pain. It includes "challenges" to the identity, where the missionaries will have to decide how important a given practice or value is to their personal identity. It involves *kenosis*, emptying oneself to be filled with new values, biblical

---

[265] Williamson, ibid., 16.
[266] Smalley, "The World is Too Much With Us," *Readings in Missionary Anthropology Vol. II*, 702.
[267] Williamson, *Have We No Rights?*, 31.

values and values that, though perhaps biblically neutral, communicate the message of the gospel to the people much more clearly.

Is there a real danger of adapting too far so that one's identity is hurt? The examples of the way Jesus, Paul and the early church appealed to people to change, without condemning them if they didn't, is the best guideline to follow if a missionary is resisting change on this basis. No one changes convictions, behavior or values permanently if it is done only under pressure. If one is consciously, under the guidance of the Holy Spirit, referring to God's Word, and evaluating with the people before changing, there is no danger of hurting one's identity, as such. One is becoming bicultural and bilingual, more able to move with ease in one's adopted country as well as in one's homeland. The only real danger is insensitivity to the people or change, or rejecting one's own culture for neurotic reasons. Sometimes the national's feedback and "demand" for change is well meant, yet excessive, exerting too much pressure on the missionaries. They, then, need to be honest about their desire for feedback and about their capacity for it, as well. This will enhance trust, if communicated in the right way.

But certainly one evidence of God's love is that it cares to solicit feedback. Where feedback is not sought and perceptions not checked out, there may well be a backlash that totally surprises the missionaries. Such an incident was recently reported in Romania with the comment:

> According to Novak, the fact that the Romanian people reacted with hostility towards the foreign mission agencies is primarily their own fault. They provoked the attacks themselves, particularly the young evangelists, because they seriously upset the more conservative sensitivities of the Romanian people by wearing too casual of clothing. [268]

This does not represent a rejection of the Gospel based on theology or ethics, but rather based on a cultural offense. The cultural trappings discredited the message, in all probability because no one sought feedback as to why the young workers were getting negative reactions.

Adaptations perceived as masquerading or condescending are eventually counter-productive. No national is fooled by superficial or artificial change, a change which is not motivated by a heart of love. And conversely, genuine *agape* love allows many cultural errors to fade, even those one is not aware of. An American missionary in Ghana

There seems to be no limit to change as long as it is willing change, not forced on the person.

once asked his African director's advice concerning cultural appropriate-

---

[268] *Idea Spektrum,* 21. September 1994, (My translation).

ness in a particular situation. His reply was, "John, you're likely to make many cultural blunders as an outsider. My people expect you to. But, they're also willing to overlook those blunders, if they sense you love them. Love indeed covers a multitude of blunders." [269]

How far can one adapt? Apart from the undesirable extreme of "going native" with its denial of the home culture, there seems to be no limit to change as long as it is willing change, not forced on the person. On the contrary, the negative effects on credibility seem related more to unwillingness to change.[270] This underscores the role the will plays in change and the necessity for the Holy Spirit to liberate the missionaries from that which personally binds them, to be free to change and identify with the people.

---

[269] John Austin quoting Dela Adadevoh (Campus Crusade for Christ's Life Ministries Director for East Africa) in *InsideR*.

[270] Robertson McQuilkin, "Six Inflamatory Questions - Part 2," *Evangelical Missions Quarterly,* Vol 30, No. 3.

4

ADJUSTMENT OF THE MISSIONARIES TO ONE

ANOTHER

It is obvious that the more cultures represented in a team, the more complex the team dynamics become. And it follows that it is more difficult to operate in the team. One missionary interviewed said that more than two cultures "add stress to an already stressful situation."[271] Another said, however, for him, "the more cultures, the merrier!"[272] Personality types differ, of course, as does the ability to cope with differences. One missionary warned, "mixed teams in a culture where no one is at home [no nationals on the team] may be very risky."[273] An African missionary commented that multicultural teams "should be given priority for it is the proof of what Christ does in people, being of one mind, breaking down the walls of culture and color."[274]

Getting to know one's teammates is, at first, most exciting. It's a smorgasbord of inviting nuances promising to enrich one's own life. But reality soon sets in when the most normal ways of interacting become gnawing irritations or puzzling encounters. Kalevi Lehtinen, Finnish evangelist and former Director of Campus Crusade for Christ in Western Europe, has had much experience in multicultural teams. In training missionaries for such teams he contrasts, for example, the methods of conversation for Americans and Finns. The American begins, "How are you this morning? What have you been doing lately?" It's always a question. The other person is not expected to give a profound long answer, only to

---

[271] Lianne Roembke, survey results (see Appendix A) and interviews with national and expatriate missionaries in Asia, Africa, and Europe. Because of the sensitive nature of some questions and answers, anonymity of the responders was assured. Therefore the details of those quoted are withheld.

[272] Roembke, survey, ibid.

[273] Roembke, survey, ibid.

[274] Roembke, survey, ibid.

say, "Fine, thanks. What about you?" And so it goes, question - answer after question - answer. Once one topic has been exhausted they change to another. Unbeknown to the American, the Finn is beginning to feel interrogated, being challenged to give information he had no intention of revealing. And, to top it off, it's a one way street. Only the American is doing the questioning; only the Finn is answering. Why this is so uncomfortable to the Finn is explained by the Finnish method of conversing. "One Finn says something, shares something from his own heart, but does not end that with a question; he just stops. And then the other Finn shares something about how he feels about the issue. And then the other responds." To each in his/her own culture the expectations are clear. But what happens when a Finn and an American meet? It might well proceed as follows:

The American says, "How are you this morning?" And the Finn feels, "Oh, he's interested in how I feel." And then the Finn gives a ten-minute long, profound answer, analyzing his feelings, particularly at that moment. And then he stops. He expects the American to respond and share from his life. But the American cannot respond because the Finn has not asked the question. There is a five-second long, uncomfortable, quiet moment and neither of them knows what to do. And then the American, because he has been trained to take the initiative, asks another question. Then the Finn responds. He gives another ten-minute long, good answer and stops. And then there is an uncomfortable silence, and then the American asks another question, and the Finn tries to answer. And at the end of the discussion, both of them feel that it has been an unfair situation. The Finn feels that he has been in a "third-degree" investigation. He has been pushed into the corner and he has had to share his heart and the American has taken advantage of it and has not opened up his heart at all and shared at the same level. And the American feels that it has been unfair because the Finn has taken the opportunity to talk about himself and has not given the American the same opportunity to do it. So that's a very, very hard and frustrating situation.[275]

This example of two different methods of communication[276] causing misunderstandings is cited in full to give opportunity for the reader to identify with both parties involved. It is precisely this process of understanding and empathizing with one another that must take place in the multicultural team. It is not enough to make an enlightening observation

---

[275] Kalevi Lehtinen, "Through the Prism," unpublished, 4.
[276] See also the section on "Communication" in chapter 1.

and then continue in old cultural patterns, assuming others must understand me and adapt to my ways. Nor is it wise to pull back, assuming I cannot communicate in such a way as to be understood. In the above example, after these observations have been made, in order to move closer to one another, the American could attempt to volunteer more information about himself instead of waiting to be asked. The Finn could learn to take the initiative to ask. Apart from this dynamic within the team itself, all will be learning appropriate ways to discuss in the host culture and this will, hopefully, soon become the team norm. As in any other of life's relationships, one dare not stop talking to one another. One must give feedback again and again, clearing up misunderstandings when something strikes one as strange or incomprehensible.

The following fictitious case study was written at the height of frustration by one American missionary empathizing with a national teammate, who, though from the host culture, was in a minority on the team. The expatriate American agonized over how to communicate this, so the other Americans and expatriate missionaries on the team would understand and feel the tension, powerlessness and embarrassment of the national. And, in sympathizing with the national's frustration, that they would become more open to changing. Because of the various dynamics of the group (quieter personalities, more reserved cultures, lack of fluency in expressing oneself in a second language, minority representation of one's culture in the group), the group was encouraged to make every attempt to understand the other, not to be too quick to make judgments or excuses. Those who tended to be more direct were asked to look at the other person to see how they respond to one's words as well as how they express themselves; and those more reserved were asked to take courage and say what they really thought - in love. The premise was: It's better to know what they think than to try to guess. The fictitious case study was as follows:[277]

> The continental headquarters of your mission is in Macon, Georgia. From here the ministry in North, Central and South America is led. There are no national field missionaries in Macon however. In nearby Atlanta there are some national missionaries who work with students and some teams, comprised mostly of nationals, who work in cooperation with churches there.

---

[277] This story is entirely the product of my imagination. None of the people are real and the choice of nationalities is no reflection of real situations or feelings towards them. In order to make the point, though, I had to choose two nationalities which were not culturally closely related to the North American culture. No offense of any group, nationality or individual was intended.

You work in Macon and you are the only U.S. American. The ministry coordinators at the HQ in your office are all Korean. The continental director is a Mexican. Most of these missionaries have had cross-cultural training before coming to the field and have served here two to four years. Some of the Koreans and Mexicans can speak English relatively well. Others, not so well. Some think they can get along okay without learning English.

Because the Korean missionaries are in the majority their actions are particularly noticeable to other missionaries and especially to the community. Most of them live in the larger homes in the area and drive Cadillacs (in order not to be considered inferior as foreigners). The missionary wives don't go out much; they have their maids and babysitters, who take care of the household and children and shop. The wives are not present at team meetings or most retreats either and speak little English. On January 16 they celebrate their national holiday together, a big party with lots of kimchee.[278]

Some of the Korean men have tried to apply their "Soon" strategy[279] *in Macon. They spent a whole weekend with the deacons of one church in a cave in the mountains fasting and praying. The church members thought it a little strange and are not quite sure how to proceed with the other ministry offers of the Koreans. There are rumors that these Korean missionaries are actually Moonies.*[280] *Other pastors in the area are very skeptical and are not sure how to respond to these foreigners. Some of the foreigners have even started house churches, using songs they have translated from Korean.*

You, the American missionary in the office, have offered to give some cross-cultural training, so that the Koreans and Mexicans can learn how to work better with the American community around them, especially on a spiritual level. But only five of the thirty-five were inter-

---

[278] Kimchee is a tasty Korean specialty made from cabbage with lots of garlic, spices and vinegar, stored in large ceramic pots.

[279] The "Soon" is a small group of Christians with an intensive discipleship commitment to one another. They meet often, share meals, study the Bible, and have extended prayer and fasting retreats for days and nights in the mountains together.

[280] Moonies are followers of the sect started by the Korean Sun Myung Moon. Born in 1920, Moon claims to have had a vision at age 16 in which he was told to finish the work that Christ began. He founded the Holy Spirit Association for the Unification of World Christianity, referred to as the Unification Church. His followers strongly imply that he is the Messiah, the Lord of the Second Advent. His revelation superseding the Bible, is called "The Divine Principle." Josh McDowell and Don Stewart, *Handbook of Today's Religions*(San Bernardino: Here's Life, 1983), Chapter 11.

ested. They said they had gotten enough orientation and training at home in Seoul.[281]

The identification process set in motion by this case study succeeded in raising awareness - to a certain extent anyway. There was a fiery response first to the situation and then to the assumption that the case study might even be distantly descriptive of the "real situation!" But all in all, several things became clear: cultural awareness, awareness of the dominant role the majority culture was playing, and the dominance of all expatriates over the host culture with its minority representation on the team. There were excuses given, but one was surprised at the sound of one's own words and how far the team had to go, how unclear the direction of the team actually was, not spiritually, but culturally, if one can really separate the two.

One thing is clear; a multicultural team is far more complex than a monocultural team. And it's not fair to the team members to operate the team under certain one-sided cultural assumptions. A few of the assumptions which have caused problems are: 1) the majority culture or the culture of the team leader rule the team culturally, 2) English is the team language, 3) only men do the leading, 4) only the wives carry the responsibility for the family and household, 5) the salaries are fixed in the home country without respect to the host country, 6) leadership is from the top down. Such assumptions as these are initially cultural blind spots but, if

---

[281] Lianne Roembke, unpublished. The following are questions for discussion of the case study:
1. Putting yourself in the place of the U.S. *American* missionary in this case study, how would you feel in his situation?
2. As a *European [national]* missionary, how do you feel in our present situation?
3. What is adaptation? How would you describe adapting to another culture?
4. In what areas have you changed to identify with the people of our host culture since you arrived?
5. What areas of your life have changed because of the other (expatriate) staff with whom you work?
6. What kind of dynamic equivalents of your home culture have you found in your host culture in the following areas: use of money, sports, health, food, eating habits, clothes and fashion, personal property, room temperature, personal relationships, friendships, hospitality, clubs and interest groups, group leading, authority, personal Bible study, prayer, service.
7. What cultural barriers could easily be removed in our situation? How?
8. In which areas do you have difficulties with changing? Can you pinpoint the reason for your internal resistance?

insisted upon, can cause deep rifts in the lives of individuals and the team as a whole.

It may be a rude awakening to some joining a multicultural team, naively assuming the dialogue of cultural exchange is only a two-way street between their culture and the host culture. It is indeed much more complex. The mix between the host culture and the home cultures of the various team members is most interesting, even exciting, as well as a source of conflicts, some gapingly major and some naggingly minor. One experienced missionary would have it no other way; for her a monocultural team spelled boredom. A multicultural team is "enriching," "a wonderful opportunity for growth," "keeps one flexible and sensitive," "adds spark, flair" and is "fun." Foremost, it is a "positive example in the host country" and "helpful in reaching the people."[282]

But, to be realistic, many surveyed acknowledged that there is pain in the adjustments to be made. The pain many experienced was due, by their admission, in part to their own sinfulness. It represented a struggle between doing what, or reacting as, one is accustomed to, *without having to think of the other and consciously act for his benefit.* That is the seed of sin. When cultural values (not biblical values, perhaps even neutral values) are imposed upon the team or a team member because the others on the team are insensitive or blind to their attempts to elevate their own value as the norm, this too is cultural imperialism. Self-centeredness is at its core. It is the subtle assumption that "my way is the right way." This superiority needs to be exposed for that which it is, in reality, and dealt with honestly, in a culturally appropriate way.

So, in essence, a multicultural team is a hothouse in which spiritual growth is accelerated. It is accelerated in the sense that one is confronted more often with the negative effects of one's own culture on others. But the intensity of confrontation should be carefully portioned out and it should be endurable for the missionaries, new and old alike. Team dynamics (or member care) is an important responsibility of the leadership which implies that a team be so constructed so as to avoid foment or self-destruction. There is a delicate balance between internal team functions, which should not become an end in itself, and ministry to the community. In a real sense, both are ministries, and both are vitally necessary. Westerners, in particular, tend to evaluate their productivity in terms of outward ministry, however, and may see team functions as less important (until they reach a crisis level

> A multicultural team is a hothouse in which spiritual growth is accelerated.

---

[282] Roembke, surveys and interviews.

and consume "an inordinate" amount of time). On the other hand a team (or any sub-unit of the team, e.g. family or individuals) dare not consume all the resources of the missionary team. The responsibility of the mission or church leadership in the formation of teams is not to be treated lightly.[283] In this chapter a number of areas affecting the life of a multicultural team are dealt with practically.

Cultural Norms in Team Life

In addition to true biblical values[284] exemplified in our Lord Jesus Christ, the only other culture that is allowed to play the secondary normative role is that of the host culture because it is to this culture that the gospel message is being communicated. This is self-evident, though not in all cases viewed this way. Some missionaries have as a primary focus auxiliary ministries, such as administrative, medical aid or schooling of missionary children. But no missionaries should be oblivious to those people around them, being able to communicate the gospel with them through their lives and words. Although the majority culture in a multicultural team, through the force of its very "weight" of opinion, unconsciously or consciously will attempt to take a leading role in forming the values and habits of team life, they cannot claim this role as their right to establish the norm. Nor can the culture of the team leader, if it is not that of the host culture, be allowed to become the normative culture for the team. Even the culture of the "mother" mission organization may not impose its cultural values upon a multicultural team serving in another country.

The majority culture and the culture of the leadership are powerful influences and it often feels like swimming against the current to resist these cultural influences. Those in the place of power should be especially sensitive to curtail their culture's influence on the other teammates. One not only increases the stress but can also injure those from other cultures on the team. This is not only unfair it is not respecting the other in the spirit of Christ. The leadership and those of the majority culture especially should solicit

> *The majority culture and the culture of the leadership are powerful influences on the team.*

---

[283] See the section in this chapter on teams, Team Formation" in chapter 5 and "Team Talks" in chapter 7.

[284] Biblical values were discussed under "Cultural Values and Norms" in chapter 1.

feedback from time to time to see if they are unconsciously putting others under pressure to conform culturally. Power of any kind is only good if it is held in check and within reasonable boundaries.

But even the host culture should not be viewed uncritically. It must be filtered through the biblical values. In the survey I conducted with over 140 national and expatriate missionaries, some were careful to delineate certain values they found in the host culture which they felt were in opposition to the norms of Scripture (not just clashing with their own culture) with which they would not want to identify, for example bribery.

A belief in the validity of other cultures does not obligate one to approve of such customs as cannibalism, widow burning, infanticide, premarital sex, polygamy, and the like. But it does insist that *one take such customs seriously within the cultural context in which they occur* and attempt to appreciate the importance of their function within that context.[285]

The concept of "mutual respect"[286] applies to relationships in the host culture as well as to team relations. Traditionalists rely on things as they were and "should be," respecting only their own culture, rejecting all others. The concept of "mutual respect" leaves the missionary free, yet it requires him to respect his own culture while at the same time respecting

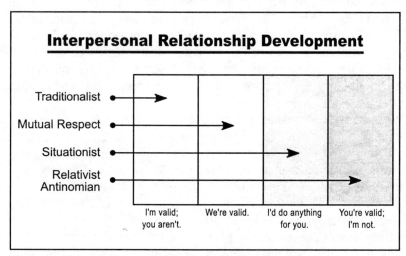

Figure 9: Ways Interpersonal Relationships Develop (adapted from Mayers, *Christianity Confronts Culture*, Zondervan: 1974, 69)

---

[285] Kraft, *Christianity in Culture*, 50; his emphasis.

the host culture. In contrast, apart from the mutual respect and traditionalist models, the other two models force expatriates to negate, deny or devalue their own cultures. The traditionalist model emphasizes the preserving of form versus meaning and forces others to abandon their culture. The situationalist model (Joseph Fletcher's situational ethics) forces one to sacrifice one's principle, thus injuring one's own conscience. There is no guarantee that the next decision will not be a reversal, thus undermining trust. Relativists abandon all that they are to cater to the other. This is the extreme of cultural adaptation, "going native." This causes a serious loss of self-respect and eventually loss of respect for others.

The principle of mutual respect is very important because it leaves both the missionary and the national securely "intact" as valid persons and as products of their own culture. It sets the stage for reciprocal relationships between equals, which is the foundation for trust. It communicates what God communicates, acceptance of the person. It does not judge one cultural pattern or value better than the other; but it does allow the question to be posed - in this given context, what is more credible, expedient, advisable, productive?

When, out of *agape* love, a decision is made by the missionary that change on his or her part is prudent, the loss is hardly noticed. One need only observe those "in love" or with a deep love to see to what extremes one will go to express that love. It is understandable, then, that some nationals question the reality of Christian love when the reality of Christian love when missionaries continually dwell on their "losses." It is quite

> *When, out of agape love, a decision is made by the missionary that change his or her part is prudent, the loss is hardly noticed.*

normal that expatriate missionaries would miss their families and friends at home and this can be properly expressed. But if they dwell on the losses and do not mention the gains, for example, the valuable new relationships, a negative message is being sent. This was born out in the survey by rating such items as the following as necessary for credibility or adds to credibility: "doesn't emphasize what s/he misses from home," "eats national foods," "has 'fun' the way national staff do," and "is aware of culturally offensive things and tries to change."[287] In fact, to speak too often of "loss" or "sacrifice" may well be interpreted as: "I don't like it here." Or one step further, "I don't like the people." One national, after hearing this message too often said, "Well, why don't they just go

---

[286] Mayers, *Christianity Confronts Culture*, 68f.
[287] Roembke, survey, see Appendix A, note especially the "C" items.

home." An insensitive reaction to a missionary floundering in culture shock? Or insensitive remarks to a national who, like most of us, loves his people and culture? In such a phase as this, it helps the missionaries to concentrate on the benefits they have gained in exchanging some of their values for new ones. In any case, they should hear their own thoughts through the ears of a national missionary before they express them to see how they might be interpreted. Jesus said, "for those who want to save their life will lose it, and those who lose their life for my sake will save it."[288]

The foundation for this willingness to change is found in allowing God to fill us with His love and in sharing this love unconditionally. No one is perfect; no one is able to demonstrate 1 Corinthians 13-type love all day, every day. But if His Spirit is working in us, this will be our desire. And His Spirit will give discernment on the what, when and how of change. Neither are we free to judge one another as missionaries. God may direct us differently in different contexts, at different times for different reasons. In acknowledging the blind spots that we have to unfamiliar cultural issues and perceptions, however, soliciting feedback from nationals is imperative. No one missionary or group of missionaries can claim to know through their own perceptions what is correct and appropriate for a new situation. That would be the ultimate in pride. One may well be surprised at the "little" things they recommend be changed and the "big" things the expatriate might think need to changing whereas the nationals deem neither expedient nor desirable. The process of inviting this feedback will build such a foundation of trust. "Acceptance is primary and prior to all feelings and emotions extended towards others and is rooted in trust."[289] Because this inviting of feedback will not be perceived as a mere academic inquiry, but rather as integral to relationship-building, it is incumbent upon the querying missionaries to be prepared to respond according to the recommendation of the national or to explain why not. It is possible, for example, that their observation was not yet validated by other nationals or that it's not possible for the missionary at this time, etc.

If the whole issue of soliciting, receiving and giving feedback is important in the interplay between two cultures, it is ever more crucial to a multicultural team. Several points have already been made as to the necessity of receiving feedback and the importance of a cultural guide.[290]

---

[288] Luke 9:24.

[289] Mayers, *Christianity Confronts Culture*, 61.

[290] A list of specific guidelines is in found in chapter 6: "Soliciting and Giving Feedback."

Communication

One can perhaps best see the conflicts in inner team communication when one observes a practical example. Let's say the multicultural team has agreed on the need for a large evangelistic event to draw the attention of non-believers to Jesus, to give the Christians new courage in witnessing and to provide a means of filtering out people whose hearts are more responsive at this point in time to the message for further discussion. But the agreement stops there. When this event is discussed in detail, it seems that even the introduction of the speaker presents a problem. Elaborate introductions, for example, including titles, accomplishments and degrees, common in the USA, are embarrassing and reek of pride to Germans. The precision of timing in the program expected by North Americans with keen sensitivity to the quality of the mass media, will feel coldly professional and look "showy" to most others, European, Asian, African and Latin American alike.

Even during the planning of the event, the non-verbal communication comes into play. The proximity of the members of the group may well affect the emotional climate. Do they sit close together where they can touch one another as they express their opinions? Or do they sit a "safe" distance from one another? Can they each see all the others, or are they all positioned to look at the leader? Do they look directly at one another when talking or avoid eye contact? These non-verbal modes of communication are very important in setting the underlying tones of trust, unity, collegiality and vulnerability. There is a magnetic effect, for example, when two persons from Latin-influenced cultures are standing and talking - they "huddle" closely, touch each other on the arms or back a lot. But if one approaches Europeans or North Americans of European descent in this manner, they automatically back away. One has stepped into their "intimate circle" and it becomes so uncomfortable for them that they unconsciously back away to keep the distance (about one meter). These are, as it were, the same poles of the magnet repelling each other. And what feels overbearing to the Northerner, indeed feels like rejection to the Latin. Someone has labeled such a conversation (getting in close, pulling back, etc.) between a North American and a Latin American as "the dance of the Americas." This enculturated sense of the limits of the intimate sphere is, although unconscious, very real, and the "abuse" of this sense by others communicates a powerful message of either rejection or intrusion.

The way the team prays together for this event may tend to be more divisive than unifying because, especially in the spiritual realm, one tends to judge differences as lacking spirituality. The first exposure of many of my European colleagues to the group prayer of the Koreans in 1974 was very confusing to them. "How can I concentrate on worshipping God when all others around me are praying aloud? It sounds like a beehive!" Some, however, grew to like this method and brought it home. The reactions at home were even more drastic.

Such tensions in the communication of the team need to be discussed and resolved as they come up, otherwise tensions will build up that become unbearable. For the team, developing common patterns and methods of communication as closely as possible to the host culture, which all begin to grow to cherish, is a key to good team relations. Almost all teammates will be giving up something from their own culture that they value, but it should be their choice and no one should feel like it is being imposed upon him or her. It is wise to remind oneself during the process that there is a sense of sacrifice for the privilege of being a missionary in that culture and a sense of giving up something for the good of the group as a whole. Dwelling on the sacrifice alone as a loss will distort the perspective and rob the missionaries (and their coworkers) of joy.

> Dwelling on the sacrifice alone as a loss will distort the perspective and rob the missionaries of joy.

There is no way or method of communicating that is the only right way. The moral issue is how we react to others when they act differently than we do.[291] When one considers Mayers' pairs of basic values, most of us have definite tendencies one way or another.[292] Those of opposite extremes may cite their differences to reject others. "The who rejects and maligns a fellow worker because of personal flaws or even sins, whether thinking dichotomistically or holistically, is taking the matter of judgment into his or her own hands. Such a critical and judgmental attitude is a divisive and destructive force in any community."[293] The categorization of missionaries into these tendencies serves as an explanation of behavior, not an excuse for it. But as to our temperaments, our growth in Christ will tend to weaken our weaknesses and to strengthen our strengths. Contrary to the opinions of some who feel "stuck" in their type or temperament or too comfortable with themselves to change, change is desirable, it is a sign of growth, and it is not impossible.

Another important question asked in the context of communication is: What if I feel I've destroyed my credibility by insisting on my cultural ways of communication already? Can I make amends? Although human

---

[291] Lingenfelter and Mayers, *Ministering Cross-Culturally*, 57.

[292] Mayers, *Christianity Confronts Culture*, 147-70. See discussion on "Cultural values and Norms" in chapter 1, and the matrices in Appendix C.

[293] Mayers, *Christianity Confronts Culture*, 147-70.

nature has a tendency to continue to judge a person by past experience, with negative experiences being the last to be erased from the memory, forgiveness is a basic tenant of the Christian faith and, hopefully, of the Christian community. One can begin communication by admitting past mistakes, sincerely inviting feedback and acting on it in correcting one's patterns of communication. This will be viewed positively and the missionary can gradually win back the right to be heard. This was substantiated in the survey; the response to the item "profits from own mistakes" was rated extremely high in the credibility scale.[294]

Conflict resolution resulting from the clashing of norms is a crucial part of communication in any multicultural team. Based on the desire Christ has for us as His body, we should try every means possible to preserve this unity.[295] Without proper examples of good resolution of conflicts, most of us develop patterns of communication that affect resolution adversely. Such mechanisms include, for example, polarized thinking, in which both parties think they are right and are unwilling to discuss the issue, or the "splinter-beam" thinking, where one party admits partial guilt for the conflict but pushes the majority of the blame on the other party. Such mechanisms are destructive to communication.

Some basic principles which are helpful in resolving conflicts include: repeating in your words what the other has said. He or she can then confirm the accuracy of what you heard or correct the impression. Another principle is to preface the discussion with true statements about your relationship and motivation for wanting to resolve the conflict (e.g., "You mean so much to me . . ." or "Because I want to understand you and don't want to hurt you . . ."). One should be careful in phrasing statements so that the blame is not placed on the other; the statements should rather be a description of the other's behavior or speech and an expression of how it affects you ("When you did/said . . . it made me feel . . .). Use "I" messages, not "you" messages. One should create a climate of trust for the discussion by making oneself vulnerable without taking advantage of the vulnerability of the other. One makes oneself vulnerable by expressing feelings, hurts, positive emotions towards the other person. One accepts what the other is saying and supports him/her.

> Use "I" messages, not "you" messages.

---

[294] Appendix A, item G.20. "Necessary for credibility" and "adds to credibility" were rated together at 93 percent. (The 10 percent differential indicating "necessary for credibility" between expatriates and nationals might have been due to the misunderstanding of the term "profits" in the phrasing. "Learns" would have been a better choice of words.)

[295] See section on "Conflict resolution" in chapter 1.

To actually go about solving the conflict one must first isolate the issue. Each person should express what they think is the real conflict and then express their opinion on the issue. Often when the problem is named (and this is sometimes no easy task), the problem is half solved. Each person then discusses what is unacceptable to him/her about the other's behavior, being as specific as possible. Together try to trace the statement or action that precipitated the problem. At this juncture, one will begin to discover cultural or personal values

> One should create a climate of trust for the discussion by making oneself vulnerable without taking advantage of the vulnerability of the other.

that differ. There may be flashbacks to one's childhood and how one was (mis)treated by one's parents which may have triggered a reaction. Avoid hardening the fronts by generalizing and using terms such as "always" or "never"; describe rather specific events. Be careful about presupposing motives; we can't begin to really know why people do what they do; give them the benefit of doubt. Explore all the alternatives that are suggested to arrive at a solution you want to try together. If it doesn't work, come back to other solutions and try them. In love, persist together with the expectation that the Holy Spirit will give creative alternatives.

It is not possible to outline every area of conflict which has surfaced or may arise. The principles mentioned above serve as guidelines in team communication. Compromises will be necessary. No team situation is ideal. Sensitivity to persons and awareness of typical areas in which problems may catch the missionary off guard will help.

Language

In discussing the area of language I will be referring primarily to the multicultural teams that are involved directly with ministry to nationals, not necessarily the administrative and support teams. The level to which the language should be learned depends on the job assignment the missionaries have and the longevity of their stay (not disproportionate to the length of time on the field). I do believe, however, that all missionaries should learn some of the national language and be continually growing in their knowledge of the language.

In the multicultural teams of today, most on the team will probably speak English, either as their mother tongue or as a second language. This is because most of the training courses for such teams are offered in English. A pioneer team, with perhaps less than a majority of nationals, will probably, therefore, be tempted to do their internal (as well as international) business in English. This automatically, however, raises the requirements for all missionaries of such teams by requiring one big factor - a good working knowledge of English. This often puts a double burden on those missionaries who don't have English as a mother tongue. In actuality, the time and efforts of these teammates, probably already struggling emotionally with being less understood and appreciated as a minority, should be invested in learning the local language rather than learning or improving their English. This is not to say there is no value for non-native English speaking missionaries with potential for leadership on an international level to give attention to learning English. But this should not be a requirement for "full membership" in a multicultural team, as such. It also limits the full and profitable use of multicultural teams and promotes subcultures of missionary activity. North Americans will be less likely to work with a group of French missionaries or Koreans with Americans unless the team language is the language of the host country. We have faced this problem in our mission and it is not an easy problem to overcome.[296]

To avoid such situations, one can take a number of preventative measures: 1) having a national as the team leader helps guard against this; 2) a majority of the team well-versed in the language of the host culture tends to encourage the others who are just learning to express themselves in the new language; 3) not expecting the new missionaries to participate in the "business part" of team meetings (but of course including them in the social-spiritual life of the team which is motivation for language learning) during their "initial" language learning phase; 4) not overloading the team with a number of new English-speaking missionaries all at once, and 5) limiting the amount of short-termers in any one team who don't know the national language and won't be emphasizing language learning.

Sometimes one just doesn't have the choice, however, and using the national language exclusively becomes a game if most are new language speakers and trying to communicate in the local language, reinforcing each others' bad pronunciation, when communication could be done easily in English. In such a case, where *all* team members speak English,

---

[296] There were Korean missionaries who knew no English who joined a team in Hungary composed of primarily Americans and Hungarians before the team language was Hungarian. East German missionaries, whose knowledge of English is presently limited, are working in Russia but some have to serve in cities separate from the teams that use English as a team language. Granted, it seems easier and more beneficial at the outset to get started quickly by using English but it does limit the participation of other missionaries if the national language is not used as the team language.

one might compromise for a time. But it is also wise to set a target date to switch over to the local language. This is not as easy as it sounds. If a predominant cultural value is efficiency, English will be resorted to and once a relationship has been begun in one language, it's very difficult to switch to another in which one is less fluent. Such a compromise is *not* an option if *all* of the team members do not speak English (or the common language) well. It limits the participation of those teammates in everything from strategizing, to recreation, to prayer, and hinders the team from profiting from their experiences, wisdom, spiritual lives and humor. This is sacrificing a lot as a team, not to mention the unnecessary personal sacrifice being asked of these team members.

One of the highest credibility ratings in my survey was given to the items: "learned the language well" and "continues to grow in language ability."[297] In addition to high expectations from national missionaries, this area was often enhanced by comments in interviews and in answer to the question of what missionaries desire in teammates. Smalley has observed that: "the world language hierarchy reflects language role relationships, but it also creates relationships and symbolizes them."[298] When one language is used it may connote casual acquaintance whereas another language may communicate close friendship. Contrary to what one might expect, English connotes impersonalness (when it is not the mother tongue) because it is used internationally and for higher learning. "To speak a local language instead is to say, 'I want to talk to you where you live, the way you are, where your feelings are. I want to be allowed into your life.' "[299]

One would be hard pressed to find a better way of communicating the incarnate love of the Living God than in learning the language of those people with whom one lives. There are missionaries who have been greatly loved and clearly effective despite their lack of a local language. They communicated love in other ways. But lest one be deceived, "they are not the norm, and we can easily deceive ourselves when we think we can be like them." Subtle and nearly insurmountable barriers are created by selecting the wrong language for the kind of relationship we seek.[300]

---

[297] Appendix A, items C.4 and C.6.

[298] William A. Smalley, "Missionary Language Learning in a World Hierarchy," *Evangelical Missions Quarterly,* October, 1994, 484. The world hierarchy of languages lists the languages in the order they want to be learned. "The language hierarchy is defined by language aspirations, but it also influences them. Once hierarchy is established, it tends to feed itself, helping to define which languages people want to learn." Smalley, ibid., 482.

[299] Smalley, ibid., 484.

[300] Smalley, ibid.

But the language is not usually the real problem. There is a set of underlying cultural assumptions that most native English speakers share including: others must adapt towards us; speakers of other languages are "below" us in some ways; the international mission language is English; everybody speaks English; it's more prestigious to speak English etc. He then exposes the resistance for that which it really is: colonial, elitist, and paternalistic! "Instead of servanthood, we signal authority. Instead of identification, we signal alienation. Instead of solidarity, we signal condescension. Instead of warmth, we signal coolness and distance. Instead of incarnation, we signal incursion."[301] In a multicultural team we signal this to the nationals on our team as well. This hardly creates a good foundation for mutuality and partnership. Smalley pleads for a "cultural conversion of the language learner" in what he unfortunately sees as a losing battle. "We need to demonstrate our own reconciliation to people through use of their local language(s) as we seek reconciliation between them and God."[302]

A wonderful example of this is a missionary couple, who had been in a Middle-Eastern country six weeks and wanted to entertain guests. They invited a handful of nationals they had gotten to know in that short time, cooked national dishes, served in their humble home and attempted to

---

[301] Smalley, ibid., 485-87. Smalley's list of 12 assumptions bears noting: 1. We assume that other peoples should adapt to our communication needs. 2. We assume that Anglo North Americans do not learn (are not good at) other languages. 3. We assume that the exception among us, the people who do learn another language, are therefore abnormal . . . strange . . . extra smart, forgetting that millions of people in India speak several languages and think little of it. 4. We assume that native speakers of languages other than English are "below" us in some ways. 5. We assume that the mission language of an international mission must be English. 6. We often assume we should learn the highest one [of the languages in the hierarchy] in that country even when only a minority of the people we want to talk to use it. 7. We assume that if we succeed in learning one language that language is certainly all we can be expected to manage. 8. The benefits we want to bring to other peoples include English . . . we assume we should talk to such people in English. 9. The shorter time we plan to spend as missionaries, the less likely we are even to try to learn a little of the language. 10. The more prestigious we conceive our position to be in a non-English speaking country, the more we assume our work needs to be done in English. 11. The more high-tech or large scale we see our work to be in a non-English speaking country, the less we assume our own need for a local language. Our public ministry is more important to us than our relationship to people. 12. The more we promote national leadership, the less we feel a need for a language other than English.
[302] Smalley, ibid., 487.

speak in their language the whole evening. The nationals reported to another missionary later, "You can bring all the missionaries here you want like these!" This missionary revealed in an interview that they are the only missionary couple who have nationals as friends.[303]

In conclusion, the answer to the question of what "deserves" to be the norm for multicultural teams, presumes that this question be posed in the first place. What comes naturally to the team leader or the team majority should not necessarily become the normative language. In almost all team situations, it is unjustified to allow any other norm than that of the host culture to dictate the normative patterns.[304] It can bring ill-repute through its feeling of foreignness in the community and produce an even more resistant climate to the Gospel. Why create more barriers to the Gospel than need be? And for such trivial matters? Adaptation is removing these barriers for the sake of clear communication of the Good News.

> *In almost all team situations it is unjustified to allow any other norm than that of the host culture dictate the normative team patterns.*

Trust Factors

In a multicultural team there are many opportunities for misunderstandings. These misunderstandings are time bombs of tension ticking away, undermining the basis of trust, waiting to explode. Every relationship needs a foundation of trust, which needs to be reinforced by regular, positive trust-evoking experiences. For example, team members will want to be faithful in giving positive feedback to one another often. In the area of conscience, K. Müller indicates that the Holy Spirit plays a significant role in helping missionaries filter through their intellect, emo-

> *Misunderstandings are time bombs of tension ticking away, undermining the basis of trust, waiting to explode.*

---

[303] L. Roembke, interview with a missionary in the Middle East.

[304] Notable exceptions are: a (sub-)continental office needing to use a regional language primarily for communication among all the countries they serve, an international office, and teams (long- or short-term) in a pioneering phase before nationals can be added to them. The latter should be for a limited time only. This refers to the team language. The language of ministry should be the local language.

tion and will to arrive at a conscience which is biblical.[305] Priest comments, "Although obedience to the Spirit and the Word 'sanctify' the conscience, the consciences of the godly will still diverge, rightly so." [306] If one missionary is continually offending the consciences of his or her teammates this usually results in judgments on their part (e.g., relating to his or her spirituality). A hot issue among some North American Christians (not exclusively, however) is the consumption of alcohol. Though absolutely forbidden in some denominations, it is considered an integral part of others. It is commonly agreed among Christians that there is no biblical justification for the misuse of alcohol. Neither is its use explicitly forbidden. One Spanish missionary commented to a North American missionary that he was glad she had accepted the custom of drinking wine with her meals. He felt it made her more a part of the fellowship. Other missionaries, who prayerfully reconsider and try to filter out their cultural prejudices, still cannot drink wine, for example, because of their personal conscience or health reasons. They have learned to refuse politely, in their hearts not judging their brothers and sisters in the Lord. They ask instead for a culturally appropriate substitution (usually mineral water). Those who insist on Coke or tap water, however, stand out as strange in a European context. On the other hand, European missionaries, for example, who cannot decline alcoholic beverages when they know it hurts their fellow teammates, are equally guilty of offending.

In Romans 14, the Apostle Paul advises us that the right to offend our brothers and sisters is not a part of our Christian liberty. Liberty is the ability to not hold on to rights; Christian liberty is to not offend. Again, unless the Bible specifically prohibits certain practices of the host culture, it is to be normative for the multicultural team. Exceptions to the norm can be made where they are unobtrusive and do not create a barrier to the Gospel. No one is to try to make the other into his own image. There is "a deep humility which recognizes that, as a cultural expatriate, one is not in a good position to authoritatively and unilaterally declare how biblical principles should be applied to culture particu-

> *The right to offend our brothers and sisters is not part of our Christian liberty.*

---

[305] "Missionaries must, with great care and thoroughness, think their way into the form, function and orientation of the conscience of the people, those they want to help in the knowledge and application of biblical and spiritual values." Klaus Müller, "Elentik: Gewissen im Kontext," *Festschrift zum 80. Geburtstag von George W. Peters,* (Lahr: Johannis VLM, 1988), 437-44, transl. Lianne Roembke.

[306] Priest, "Missionary Elenctics," 313.

lars."[307] Even when one is respected as an authority he or she should be humble enough to refuse an inappropriate scope of authority. This is the priesthood of *all* believers at work. If this principle of deferring to one another out of love is at work, trust will be built up. If not, suspicion and mistrust will eat away at the foundations of trust. If, among the team members, other practices are found to be offensive, they should be discussed and a decision, or decisions, should be made in love and out of deference to one another. Having a different cultural heritage or holding to different practices for conscience's sake, is not necessarily the same as being offended. But to continue to disregard the differences and not discuss them in love can readily lead to a breach of trust.

Mayers gives an important guideline in evaluating actions and attitudes. Posing this question focuses on the others in communication, their perception, their reactions to the message being communicated verbally and non-verbally. "Even as language differs from society to society, verbal and non-verbal cues also differ and must be learned."[308] Mayers calls it the prior question of trust: *"Is what I am doing, thinking or saying building trust or is it undermining trust?"*[309]

The question could be asked of such things as house size. "Were the missionaries to have too large a home, trust would be undermined. It would also be undermined were they to have too small and simple a home."[310] In this par-

> *Is what I am doing, thinking or saying building trust or is it undermining trust?*

ticular case, the decision was made in consultation with national Christians, who then found they could be comfortable in the home of the missionaries. One caution is in order: Overuse of the prior question of trust may communicate subtle manipulation, whereas underuse of the question may be misconstrued as insensitivity. Not all aspects of every area of life are affected by the issue of trust. Some are neutral. This "prior question of trust" is a good check for teammates where they notice tension with another team member, "Is what I am doing, thinking, or saying building trust or is it undermining trust?" Mayers takes this to another degree, "Is what I am doing, thinking, or saying *potential* for building trust or *potential* for undermining trust?"[311] This is not just a question for those oversensitive ones who are afraid to offend; it is a question which is asked out of respect for the other. Posing this question in and of itself

---

[307] Priest, ibid., 314.

[308] Marvin K. Mayers, *Christianity Confronts Culture,* 40.

[309] Mayers, ibid., 32.

[310] Mayers, ibid., 37.

[311] Mayers, ibid., 32.

opens channels of communication and sets the stage for building trust, even when the outcome of the discussion is uncertain.

Good powers of observation are helpful to detect whether a misunderstanding has been created. Good speakers are trained to "read" their audience, to observe non-verbal communication, to see how they are communicating. If yawns, fidgeting, or whispering increase or eyes close and bodies slouch, this indicates that the attention is wandering - in North American cultures, for example. If, in a team meeting, eyes wander, conversation is sparse, the posture is such that the people face away from the person to whom they speak, arms and legs are crossed, there is no direct eye contact, tardiness occurs, in certain cultural contexts it would be time for the team leader, at least, to wake up! The rules of the new culture must be learned as well. In most cases it is appreciated by other teammates if one picks up on verbal and nonverbal cues and asks what they mean. This must be done, however, in a culturally appropriate, non-threatening way. It is far better to ask than assume. Even for those teammates from countries culturally close to one another, there can be surprises. If love is truly "believing the best" about someone else and his or her motives (1 Corinthians 13), then love will also ask in order to clear up the misunderstandings which may lead to a breakdown in trust. This is true in all relationships, not just cross-cultural ones.

How is trust broken? Misunderstandings, in almost any area, if left unclear, can lead to a breach of trust which will only further widen with more misunderstandings which are inevitable in a multicultural team. For example, consider the team member who shared his problem with his team leader, who, in turn, at the next team meeting voiced it as a prayer request. The team member was dumbfounded. "I thought he was my friend. I told this about myself and then he printed it in his prayer letter and he brought it up in a prayer meeting as a prayer request."[312] On the one hand, what was interpreted as a clear betrayal of confidence, can, on the other hand, also be interpreted as a clear desire to help. Such misunderstandings can be avoided if these issues are talked about beforehand. In any case, it is good to ask before one shares anything, even with a spouse, even for prayer. One can ask, "I would like to share this with our team/my wife/my husband, so when we pray together we can pray for you. Is that okay with you?" No pressure should be exerted to push him beyond the level of confidentiality with which he is comfortable. His circle of confidence will probably grow as trust grows in other relationships. And to be sure he is correctly understood, the team member sharing should indicate beforehand, "I would prefer you keep this confiden-

---

[312] Lehtinen, "Through the Prism," 8.

tial; please don't mention it even to your husband/wife/the team/the director," indicating the circle of confidentiality with which he feels comfortable. If the issue is such that the team leader feels inadequate to handle it *or* he feels it needs to come to the attention of the leadership, he should also tell the team member that *before* he communicates it further. A betrayed confidence tears down much hard-earned trust.

Sometimes it is not what is said or done but what is left unsaid or undone that creates a breach of trust. Unmet needs and unfulfilled expectations can well cause a breakdown of trust. In crucial areas that concern all team members, expectations should be talked about initially, before problems and confusion arise, to avoid disappointment and injury. It may seem unjust but trust can be destroyed momentarily, whereas it takes much effort to build it and even more time and effort to rebuild it.

> *It may seem unjust but trust can be destroyed momentarily, whereas it takes much effort to build it and even more time and effort to rebuild it.*

Learning to "speak the truth in love," in a way so as not to hurt the other unintentionally, is part of the second greatest commandment Jesus gave to us. Trust is built in stages, always preceded by communication, verbal or non-verbal. This is cyclical, however. Without trust, there is usually no communication, and without communication, trust cannot be built.

When suspicion or hurt is there, who, then, can break into the cycle of mistrust? Actually the Bible gives both parties the permission and the responsibility to initiate communication which will lead to trust. "If anyone offends you, go to him . . . and if he doesn't listen, take someone with you to begin to communicate, clear up the offense and begin to (re)build a relationship based on trust."[313] And, "if you have offended someone, set aside your plans even as important as worshipping God, and go to him and make it right."[314] One can surmise that the awareness of such a problem is most often felt by the more sensitive types, so, logically, the initiative to deal with such problems will fall primarily on them. This is a hard lot. Sensitive types don't usually like to rock the boat. And others can be quick to equate an awareness of problems with being negatively critical, hypersensitive, or even with creating the problems. This reputation is unfair. Awareness and spiritual sensitivity are gifts and responsibilities from God. In a team context, it would be most helpful to the sensitive persons among them to support each other in the necessity to talk about such issues, even if that is not a "felt need" by all. (For example saying, "If John or Mary feels we should talk about it I

---

[313] Matthew 18:15-20, free translation.
[314] Matthew 5:23-24, free translation.

think we should discuss it.") If an offense is sensed, though unintended, it should be cleared up in deference to the offended. Relationships are not static; they are either growing or being actively destroyed or passively eroded.

A preventative approach to building trust in multicultural teams is to let every team member start with a clean slate. With expectations of true partnership in the team, many potential enemies of team unity are defeated.[315] Destroying stereotypes that may have unconsciously crept into one's thinking and accepting the person as he or she is are key to maintaining trust. Many impressions of the missionary's home country have preceded him to the field; some true, some not; some flattering, most not. "The standard images - Americans are immature or childish, the Japanese are devious, the Germans are ruthless - need to be confronted because they subtly damage good relations." [316] But this implies an awareness of how one's country is perceived in the eyes of the world. For example, Americans are particularly visible in the world and "as long as American Christians are blind to the way that American political and economic power operates in the world, their well-intentioned efforts in global communication will only reinforce false perceptions of Christians and Christianity in our non-Christian societies."[317] These prevalent attitudes are difficult to overlook, even among team members. But Americans, for example, (as with anyone combating a negative image) are grateful for the opportunity to be judged by their own person and not according to a stereotype of an American. This privilege should be afforded every team member. The community, as such, will probably hold to their stereotyped

---

[315] Ted Ward proposes ten guidelines for such relationships:
1. Both partners must want to work together.
2. Both partners must identify and profess their own motives.
3. Both partners must honestly confess their own needs and vulnerabilities.
4. Both partners must respect and share their resources.
5. Each partner must put concern for the other above self-concern.
6. Each partner must carefully avoid making the other dependent.
7. Both partners must respect each other's capability as a helper.
8. Each partner must be willing to be helped.
9. Each partner must value the worth of community effort above the worth of individual effort.
10. Each partner must experience growth through giving while receiving.
Ward, *Living Overseas*, 220-21.
[316] Brian Butler, "Tensions in an International Mission," *Evangelical Missions Quarterly*, October, 1993, 416.
[317] Vinoth Ramachandra, "The Honor of Listening: Indispensable for Missionaries," *Evangelical Missions Quarterly*, October, 1994, 407.

> *Destroying stereotypes and accepting the person as he or she is, are key to maintaining trust.*

impressions, which means, in some cases, the missionary will have to start with a negative score and improve it by acting and speaking in such a way as to be positively perceived. The greatest gift of love missionaries can give their teammates is to accept each other unconditionally, irrespective of each country's past or even their own personal past. This is God's grace, which none of us has earned, in action. And we have the privilege of extending it to one another.

Ward gives a word of caution in relating to the community, "It pays not to be too free with one's trust."[318] Although it may initially sound contradictory, he is referring to the fact that the unscrupulous will take advantage of the gullible. Keeping one's guard up in such situations is necessary. But among friends and teammates "it is far better to take a leap of faith and run the risks. Vulnerability has always been the price of true friendship."[319]

Lehtinen offers some good points relating to trust in what he calls "building bridges":

1. *Awareness* - growing in awareness of the cultural differences and not being surprised or offended.
2. *Willingness* - not ignoring but using awareness to deepen understanding of the other, putting yourself in his shoes, to feel with and listen to him; taking time to ask for clarity and hear his heart; not getting stuck in a mode of polarization.
3. *Accepting* the differences without a feeling of superiority or inferiority; seeing God's unity as differences complementing one another.
4. *Clear objectives and clear structures* - these should be defined before methods are discussed and kept in the forefront.
5. *Love* - "Love is communication on the conditions of the other person."
6. *Revival* - keeps us from getting bogged down in nitty-gritty issues because our focus is on Him.[320]

His latter point bears emphasizing. As crucial as sensitivity to cultural differences is, the unity and trust relationships in the team will be duly strengthened by keeping the focus on the Lord clear and emphasizing the unifying factors often. But the divisive factors should neither be repressed nor glossed over. If real issues are left to simmer under the sur-

---

[318] Ward, *Living Overseas,* 138.
[319] Ward, ibid.
[320] Lehtinen, "Through the Prism," 12-15.

face, some team members will not only be unable to work together but also unable to pray with others and the enemy will have gained a foothold.

According to my survey, missionaries who are "faithful" and "forgiving" are valued highly by their teammates.[321] Given the occurrence of misunderstandings, a multicultural team must live from forgiveness. Forgiveness is not just necessary when one has evil intentions toward another, but also when offenses are caused by insensitivity and oversight. Just as Christians need forgiveness and cleansing in their relationship to God, their relationships with others need this continually, too. Hopefully, with developing sensitivity towards others and learning from past mistakes, asking for forgiveness will not need to occur as often. It should not be neglected, however. Trust is a fragile thing; it is more easily destroyed than built. Time and attention given to building trust among teammates is time well-invested. It places value on people.

Team Concept and Functions

Often during my survey/interview process the issue of teams, as such, was discussed. From an historical point of view, it can be said that most missionaries have been assigned to work in teams (some just in pairs) in a given location. Whether they really function *as a team* was fairly often called into question. This is a research topic in and of itself but needs to be addressed here insofar as it affects the functioning of multicultural teams. Missionaries often vented their disappointments, even bitterness, when asked to reflect on their team situations. Such comments and emotions demonstrate that the concept of team may be both culturally and personally defined and indicate that there are a host of expectations connected to the concept of team. It doesn't really matter how *Webster's Dictionary* defines "team,"[322] it's how one's team leader (not exclusively, but primarily) perceives it and lives it out. One missionary wrote recently that the team felt their leader thought the team functioned well when there were no conflicts and the ministry was running well. They, however, indicated that there were real needs under the surface left unmet and the leader was oblivious to them.

Some team leader personality types see the function of the team as loosely coordinating ministry efforts, occasionally reporting results, with

---

[321] See Appendix A: items F.2 and F.6 (95-96 percent).
[322] Refer to more details on "teams" in chapter 2.

voluntary social, spiritual commitments to one another. The position at the other end of the spectrum sees the team as a substitute family-and-ministry (and sometimes church) all rolled into one. If the team members themselves don't agree on the functions among each other, there is bound to be excess stress. Arriving at a consensus is not an easy task. Even the selection of the team leader plays an important role - is he or she appointed or elected? How often and under what conditions is leadership changed? Each mission will, no doubt, have written as well as unwritten tasks for the team/team leader. Those written tasks may be reviewed from time to time and changed to meet needs. But they, along with the unwritten tasks and the expectations, should be thoroughly discussed by the team. All personal needs and expectations cannot be met, even in an ideal situation. People are just different. Agreeing on which needs the team itself can meet is good reality therapy. And it is applying excellent Christian theology on the body of Christ. Included in this discussion are such questions as: What needs should the local church(es) meet (if there are local churches)? What needs are better met within nuclear families? How will singles' needs be met? What kind of extended family situations are there for singles and families? What role do personal friendships play? Only when these support structures are defined *for each team member* can the discussion about the function of the team, as such, really begin.

> Only when the support structures are defined for each team member can the discussion about the function of the team really begin.

There will be overlap. Missionary husbands, for example, whose wives and families provide an intensive support structure, are notoriously oblivious to the others' lack of support structures. Sometimes they see the needs but their lives are so full they feel helpless to meet them. Which social functions will the team as a whole want to plan and do together (being careful of celebrations of non-host culture national holidays unless all can participate and all nations represented have a chance to celebrate their holidays)? Somewhere along the continuum of possible team definitions, each team will reach a workable consensus. Presumably, the team will not just want to limit their team life to "ministry functions" exclusively (i.e., common goals, strategies and programs) but will include some functions that meet personal and group needs as well. This is obligatory, in my opinion, for a "mission" team. There is no getting around the fact that the team, as a microcosm of the body of Christ, should demonstrate in its corporate life that "we need each other" and "we are gifted by the Holy Spirit to complement one another." Even to the goal-oriented person, this is justification enough for the time and energy put into the team.

The most complex team I have ever experienced personally was a multicultural, multifunctional European continental headquarters team located in a small town in Southern Germany. Included in the team were expatriate, administrative personal who raised their own support; national, salaried administrative personnel; and national field personnel and expatriate, continental leadership who also raised their own support. These were all long-termers, some "oldies," with a constant stream of newcomers. In addition, there were expatriate and national short-termers, neither of whom spoke each others' languages. The ages ranged from 20-60 years old. Team expectations ran the full gamut. Many solutions were tried over the years to meet the needs of this heterogeneous team. Most effective were a combination of departmental teams or other sub-teams with whole team programs. But in reality it was too large (varied from 20-40) and too complex to manage as a whole. The dangers of becoming ingrown, completely absorbed in team life to the exclusion of the church and community, or the temptation to dissociate oneself from most of the team and seek refuge in the "real world" of the community or the church were ever-present. The sense of "needing each other" was hardly a felt need. One needed a few significant others, but the team was too big and complex with too many needs to get one's arms around. We often asked ourselves: How could these varied groups and individuals ever function together as a real team? That was not to say: How could these people become the same, share all the same interests or deny their cultural back-

> To enable good group dynamics, a reasonably sized team should have five to eight members.

grounds? It did mean: How could those relatively minor things which seemed to divide the team become insignificant enough so that the major things that united us could be cherished? A good place to start is with a reasonable size. The principles of a small group apply aptly to a team situation; the group needs to have an intimate knowledge of one another to be supportive. Most suggest that five to eight, at the most ten, members are about the limit if one is to have emotional energy for outward ministry as well. Jesus had no more than twelve in His most intimate circle of disciples. The missionaries need to estimate their capacities accurately.

Another example of team life stands in contrast to the above, in which a team of two served in an isolated environment in which no church or other Christian support systems were available. This was a worst case scenario - they may have a high felt need for another person but not for *that* person. It seemed that either team selection was not democratic enough or a relationship had been allowed to sour. Two may be enough for an initial pioneering situation, but others, especially national coworkers, should be added as soon as possible for the team dynamic to be healthy.

The question begs to be asked - is teamwork or work in teams a Western cultural value? How much does the Western value of "democracy" influence our expectations in team decision-making? The value of the group over against the individual has the potential of producing better team work among those of non-Western cultures. In fact, most non-Westerners need the structure and emotional support of a team for their own well-being as well as maximum performance.[323] In this sense, teamwork is not an invention of Western culture, but can also be seen as an extension of the family. The collective feeling exerts a strong sense of team identity, whereas some from Western cultures are strong individualists and give the impression, at least, that they are self-sufficient. It is fair enough to conclude that there is no set of givens and that each item on the team agenda, each value that influences team life must be discussed thoroughly by the team. And each new team member should be brought on board as they join, if misunderstandings are to be avoided and an atmosphere of trust preserved.

> *How much does the Western value of democracy influence our expectations in team decision-making?*

A good percentage of team problems are related to personality factors present when any diverse combination of human beings come together. But these problems are not just added to, they are multiplied by the complexity of cultures in the team. It is, therefore, essential that problems in team relationships be dealt with early and thoroughly. Indications that relationships are not in order, unusual silence or aggression, non-verbals such as sloppy posture or persistent tardiness on the part of some, should be investigated. It is no secret that interpersonal problems are the source of most missionaries returning early or leaving mission work. This comes as no surprise to the experienced missionary. Nor does the advice, "teamwork needs

> *Teamwork needs to be modeled from the top down.*

to be taught from the top down, even in the schools back home."[324] Better yet, it needs to be modeled from the top down. One retains more of what is "caught" by example than taught, says Christian Education expert Dr. Lois LeBar. Modeling is powerful influencing. The individualistic ten-

---

[323] Elbers, *Protestantische Missionare aus Indonesien*, unpublished, 1995, 115-119.
[324] Ward, *Living Overseas,* 41-42.

dencies of most Western missionaries need to be curbed a bit by a sense of team responsibility. Supporting this was the rating that the item "is spiritually accountable to someone"[325] received on the survey. The ratings were all high, but it was rated 12 percent higher by nationals. And most expatriates who questioned this came from "highly individualistic" cultures in which personal freedom is of higher value than the vulnerability that accountability would require. This point of accountability was perceived as a way to hold power in check, to limit what was felt to be extremes in individualism. It reflects the fact that the desire for a group is a high cultural value. This presents an obvious conflict with Western values, particularly in the postwar West German culture, which educated its youth to have strong opinions and resist being swayed by the group at all costs in an exerted effort to compensate for Hitler's sins of using group persuasion. Missionaries with such strong norms fight with new values at the outset because they are aware of the historical dangers. Knowing this and other facts that are shared by the team members, the team is then in a better position to grow together, without threatening each other.

Discontinuity in teams caused, in part, by home leaves, attrition, crisis or illness seems to be a major problem. A smaller team size (between five and eight adult members) could help alleviate some negative effects of this disruption. The careful scheduling of home leaves so as to take into account the ministry of the team to the team, not just the work, is advisable, as is the general consideration of the rhythm of home assignment versus field assignment. New modes of transportation (plane rather than ship), the schooling of the children and support needs have been, to date, the major dictating factors in interfacing with the ministry. Maybe more thought needs to be given to revising this pattern with the advent of home schooling,[326] faster and cheaper flights, family needs in the home country (the missionaries' parents and/or adult children) and team needs, in addition to ministry needs. The options are as varied as the imagination. Perhaps the ministry is in a phase when all expatriates could take home leave simultaneously and the nationals would be more challenged if they had to take over the majority of responsibilities in their absence. Or is the fear too great that the gap would close? National missionaries

---

[325] Appendix A: item A.5.

[326] Home-schooling is a movement that grew out of a concern on the part of Christian parents as a result of a decline in the quality of public schools in the USA The movement has been highly developed, including sophisticated school curricula, recognized by state authorities, and support groups for parents, who do the schooling. With this available to missionary parents in remote areas, the opportunity is given to keep families together.

have a more readily accessible supporter group and don't need or want long "furloughs." Most expatriates find they and their children do better if they can make visits to the home country more often, preferably in the summer, so that neither the children's schooling nor the work flow is greatly disrupted. One, of course, doesn't try to visit all of the supporters each time. And a longer home leave can be arranged at an appropriate time, for example, at the end of an assignment, before reforming a team, upon returning home to enroll a child in college, or even when one must go for

> *Team factors are very important in home leave decisions because they are crucial to the well-being of the missionaries as a whole.*

medical reasons. The point is that team factors are very important in such decisions because they are crucial to the well-being of the missionaries as a whole.

Methods of solving team problems in a multicultural team are also very influenced by culture.[327] An Asian team member in a European country was distressed that her team leader was not clear in stating and motivating towards goals but she was reluctant to approach the leader directly and would certainly not talk to the team leader's supervisor about the issue. The first step recommended was to pray about the situation, asking for God's wisdom on the person and the cultural background and how to overcome the misunderstandings, secondly, to formulate her thoughts to be able to express them and thirdly, look for an appropriate time, perhaps make an appointment to begin to discuss the issue little by little. Because of the cultural context, the Asian missionary was prepared to overcome her reluctance to communicate directly. After having taken the first two steps, but before an appointment could be made however, the team leader asked the missionary for her input on leadership in the team and she was, happily, prepared to answer.

Imagine Western missionaries as team leaders in Asia, armed with good management training, confronting team problems directly, democratically asking each member to voice his or her opinion on a matter. They mean well, but the cultural forces of indirect communication, so inbred from childhood in the Asian missionaries, shout, "Be polite, be polite!" and they remain silent.

> *The cultural forces of indirect communication, so inbred from childhood in the Asian missionaries, shout "Be polite, be polite!" and they remain silent.*

Criticism is then leveled at them that they are not "team players" when they might already be reeling from opinions expressed directly against

---

[327] See discussion on culture in chapter 1.

them from teammates who say they love and care about them. Indonesians, for example, have neither learned to express themselves verbally and directly at home nor in school. They hope their teammates will read their non-verbal communication.[328] They feel very misunderstood; the Westerners think they are uncooperative, even unspiritual, and the breech in team relationships is widened.

What worsens the matter is when one begins "justifying" one's own culture as representing *the* biblical way to do it. This is a not-too-subtle form of ethnocentrism. In the above example the Westerners might claim, "The Bible says let your 'yes' be 'yes' and your 'no' be 'no,' " insisting on integrity and clarity on their terms. But the Bible is not speaking here about mere two- or three-letter words; the passage is asking for clear statements and no wishy-washiness. The issue is, clear statements *on whose terms*? The Asian didn't feel he was being unclear. He felt he was being responsible *and* polite when he asked his teammate to explain his situation to the team leader after the meeting. To him, impatient, confrontive communication is one of the greatest offenses that can be made and a mediator is very appropriate. Multicultural teams have the additional responsibility of working to understand one another's cultures as well as learning to operate together in a new cultural context. Such factors as: "avoids overgeneralizing characteristics of nationals or culture" or stereotyping, "is aware of culturally offensive things and tries to change," and "has a cultural guide (friend) and listens to feedback" all rated over 90 percent in necessary for credibility and adds to credibility in the survey.[329] Some even expanded the list with the category "listens" rated as necessary for credibility.

> *Multicultural teams have the additional responsibility of working to understand one another's cultures as well as learning to operate together in a new cultural context.*

The deeper values (for example "clarity" illustrated above) are very similar from culture to culture, but the *culturally appropriate expression* of these values may be as different as night and day. One must ask each team member - how is clarity arrived at in your culture? One will then learn much about the thinking and communicating processes of the teammates, understand and appreciate them and their team contributions. A good place to start for the team would be to pose the question, "How is love (1 Corinthians 13 *agape* love) expressed in your culture in a team context?"

---

[328] Elbers, *Protestantische Missionare aus Indonesien*, 120-22.
[329] Appendix A. Items C.11, C.12, F.14.

Often a function of team leadership has been to solve interpersonal problems on the team. But this is not always the case. What is to be done when all has been tried and a problem seems unresolvable? Or if the problem involves the team leader himself/herself? Former missionary and psychiatrist Dr. Marjory Foyle says, "Missionaries need access to an impartial third party in case of complaints against the administration [or leadership] . . . Many missionaries carry a heavy load of frustration because there is no one to whom they can turn."[330] Those who would argue

> *In case of complaints against leadership, missionaries need access to an impartial third party.*

that the missionaries can appeal their case "up the chain of command" disregard the fact that the leadership structure, though not maliciously intended, in all likelihood, has an established bond which does not allow for an impartial or unprejudiced hearing and judgment. A neutral third party, such as member care specialist, who is trusted by the others, who guards confidentiality and who is listened to by all, is needed to give a fair hearing.

Understanding one another is a long, but enriching process. How many husbands and wives, with their lifetime commitment to a relationship, need to really work on understanding each other? If they have to work on it so long, so must team members. Understanding a person is not static, but rather a dynamic process because the missionaries are continually changing and coming to new discoveries about themselves and their culture. While understanding is one step in the procedure, it is not the last step, by any means. Appreciation must follow, giving their teammates right to be "different, but not wrong." But to begin to work together as a team, certain procedures will have to be agreed upon. The team norms must be discussed and agreed upon by all.[331]

Meeting Personal Needs

What does a person need to live? What does a person need to live a fulfilled life? What is needed to minister effectively? Lists of basic needs in life differ from society to society. For example, fellowship, a house or shelter, rice, water, salt were the elements listed by a Malaysian to fulfill

---

[330] Foyle, *Honourably Wounded*, 118-19.
[331] For further discussion on norms refer back to "cultural norms" in chapters 1 and 4 and to "Team talks" in chapter 6.

basic needs.[332] The various lists one might find reflect cultural values and the effect of materialism upon them. Maslow's model, however, generalizes all human needs, fitting them into a hierarchy of needs. It is based on the assumption that until the basic needs at the bottom of the pyramid are met, one is not free to move on to meeting higher needs. That is, until the needs of hunger, thirst, sex, oxygen and sleep are met, people will be exclusively preoccupied with meeting these needs first.[333] This has great implications for missionaries living in another culture and especially those working on multicultural teams. These needs, along with the need for a safe, stable environment, Maslow maintains, are human deficits which the person will attempt to meet motivated by self- preservation (D-motives). The other needs are basically B-motives, needs of being, necessary for the ego-identity, the inner continuity of a person. The higher order of needs are less tangible, less urgent (therefore more easily repressed), and less selfish. The easiest way to release a person from the lower order of needs to move on is to satisfy them.[334] To these five levels Howard J. Clinebell, Jr. adds a sixth and overriding dimension which takes into account the *imago Dei*: spiritual need.[335] One recognizes the tension, then, into which the missionaries are plunged, pulled out of their former context in which most of these needs were being met successfully, now in a situation where their deficits are predominating. If there is a sense of scrambling, a feeling of urgency to put his world in order, it is justified.

"It must not be assumed that candidates and missionaries, no matter how resilient they seem, are self-sufficient people. Adequate doses of member care are needed to keep them healthy and effective."[336] There is the responsibility of the home mission, the field representatives, the team

---

[332] This is the norm for Rungus in Sabah, Malaysia. Source: missionary and professor Karl Rennstich.

[333] Sex is defined differently by Christian psychologists. Rather than being an animalistic drive, it is seen as a God-given gift, much broader than genital sex. In this sense, the fulfillment of needs in the area of sex for an unmarried person, or person away from their spouse, can be well within the boundaries outlined in the Bible and exemplified by Jesus Himself. Jesus was a single man, with healthy contacts to men and women. We have every reason to believe that He was a man of integrity, living in conformity to what He taught, e.g., in the area of the sanctity of marriage.

[334] Abraham H. Maslow, *Motivation and Personality,* (New York: Harper and Row, 1970), 28-30, 131-148, 229-239.

[335] Howard J. Clinebell, Jr., *Growth Counseling Hope-Centered Methods for Actualizing Human Wholeness* (Nashville: Abingdon, 1979), 84.

[336] LeRoy Johnston, "Core Issues in Missionary Life," 38.

Figure 10: Hierarchy of Personal Needs

leader and members, as well the missionaries' responsibility to themselves, to begin to rise above these lower needs and begin to function on an altruistic level.

One of the saddest things I have observed is missionaries "stuck," so to speak, on these lower levels of satisfying their needs, unable to feel productive, unable to give to others. And it was indeed more tragic that no one observed this and tried to offer help. Granted, this was partially due to a lack of vulnerability, but cues were there if one had been watching. The incidents involving illicit sex are

> *More missionaries are caught in the cycle of satisfying psychological needs, trying to increase their self-esteem and worth, a preoccupation which keeps them from being free to minister as whole persons to others.*

not nearly as rare as they used to be, unfortunately. But, in my observation, more missionaries are caught in the cycle of satisfying psychological needs, trying to increase their self-esteem and worth, a preoccupation which keeps them from being free to minister as whole persons to others.[337]

Assuming adequate provision has been made for food and shelter and general safety, interpersonal relationships will be the most significant area of felt need. Friendship, of course, provides a base of personal support necessary for missionaries, either among their missionary colleagues or in the host culture, preferably both. The missionary cannot afford to be alienated from either. The book of Proverbs is full of wisdom on friendship, for example, "One who forgives an affront fosters friendship, but one who dwells on disputes will alienate a friend" (17:9) and "A friend loves at all times." (17:17). Despite the fact that a married couple or family goes to the field together or, more unusual, that friends are sent to the same field, the first inner drive is to make friends. This may occur unconsciously, but is nevertheless a positive force to be reckoned with, motivating the missionary to develop relationships in the community and among teammates. People are different. Not all relationships will grow into friendships, and they should not be forced. Force spells death to a friendship. Expectations from a friend vary. Whereas some work toward having a large circle of good acquaintants, others are looking for a few good friends.[338] On the other hand, because friendships are based on common interests, care should be taken to be inclusive of those teammates, who, for example, are the only ones from a given culture.

Mutual understanding, essential to friendship, requires a degree of vulnerability and openness. This opens the door for appreciation. Such vulnerability may not be a value in some cultures represented on the team. This needs to be respected. The process of making friends may be slower but hardly less valuable. Tasteful, tactful self-revelation will help open the doors of the most reserved cultures. Status may play a role, too. The team leader may feel s/he has to support a certain image of non-vulnerability, so it may take longer to get to know him/her. Although vulnerability should not be forced, a safe climate for being vulnerable can be created. To have someone who listens and tries to understand, especially during the initial phases of adjustment, is the greatest gift of friendship. The experienced missionaries can do a wonderful service of

---

[337] For the area of self-esteem I refer to: M. Wagner, *The Sensation of Being Somebody* (Grand Rapids: Zondervan, 1975); H. Cloud and J. Townsend, *Boundaries* (Grand Rapids: Zondervan, 1992) and J. McDowell, *His Image My Image* (San Bernardino: Here's Life, 1984).
[338] Veronika Elbers points out that Indonesian missionaries prefer a large circle of friends to a few, close ones as the Germans, for example. *Protestantische Missionare aus Indonesien*, 113.

> *Experienced missionaries can do a wonderful service of love for their teammates by offering their ears, their hearts and their prayers.*

love for their teammates by offering their ears, their hearts and their prayers. A word of sincere encouragement about the progress in language, the attempt to cook a meal from local ingredients, an invitation to drop in for a cup of coffee, tea or whatever, and talk about how it's going, spurs on even the most discouraged newcomer.

The interviews and surveys indicated that many factors have the potential of creating distance in the team. Surprisingly, the elements of social interaction, for example, visiting one another spontaneously in their homes, celebrating together, playing together, when missed, created distance. Where a strict Puritan influence has invaded the value system in some Western missionaries, play needs to be relearned. People are for play; children learn the serious things of life through their play and adults can learn a new culture with less stress if they take on the light-heartedness of play as well. Play is not as childish and unattached to reality as one might think. There are rules, there is concentration of energy towards goals and it takes place in social interaction with others. There is the relaxing element involved that has a healing effect, a compensation for concentrated work. Play is symbolic and reveals the true character. The secret is to find means of social interaction that are inclusive. Distance was created by such things as inside jokes, using a "secret language" (the mother tongue, which only a few understood), or slang. Viewing imported sport videos and not showing an interest in national sports were also offensive. Giving exclusive attention to home and family so that others were left out, entertaining only one's countrymen, not dropping in to visit (if that was what was culturally expected), and not taking the initiative to get to know others created barriers. Not praying together, not attempting to change offensive ways that have been pointed out were perceived as superficiality. A lack of interest in history and culture, and in the politics of the host country, was offensive. Pride, boasting, and misjudging cultural inappropriateness as lack of spirituality created obstacles to good relationships.[339]

> *Financial inequities cause hard feelings and create classes of missionaries within the team.*

Some divisive factors are due to financial inequities, according to my survey results.[340] Not all missionaries were in a position to afford eating out, for example, although an invitation by other missionaries to join them was

---

[339] See Appendix A.
[340] See sections on finances and lifestyle in chapters 1 and 4.

well-intentioned. This, over a period of time, can cause hard feelings and create classes of missionaries within the team. Again and again the role of informal hospitality was emphasized as important. The New Testament encourages hospitality as a Christian virtue. A quality looked for in the leaders of the churches was hospitality. The writer of Hebrews says that we are not to neglect showing hospitality to strangers.[341] Sensitive observation and inclusive hospitality will not go unappreciated.

Other divisive factors centered around single-married issues. Whereas most families take their "support system" with them, singles are dependent on forming new relationships. It is false to assume, however, that families, in themselves, form a complete support system. Each individual, too, needs new relationships. There are advantages and disadvantages to both statuses. Singles tend to get closer to nationals. This is especially true if they arrive alone. They are thrust into new relationships out of sheer personal need and necessity in beginning to order their new life. If they have been properly oriented towards bonding with the people of the new culture, it is most natural that relationships with nationals are formed quickly. The couples and families have each other to interact with and are not "forced out" of the nest as quickly as singles. But in most societies, families as a whole have a more natural place in the culture and a natural entrée and network of contacts through the children.[342] These natural inroads should be used without hesitation while the effects of initial curiosity are present. Singles may have more expectations from the team as a substitute family. Missionary children need substitute aunts and uncles, grandmothers and grandfathers. As team expectations are discussed, honesty is required so that all of these needs can be taken into consideration.

Many singles approach their first term on the field with the hope it will be their last - as a single. They neither feel "called" to this status of life nor do they prefer it. They are to be commended for being willing to go to another culture at this time in their lives, leaving the "shopping center for appropriate Christian mates" that their own culture probably provides. This is indeed a sacrifice for them. It is an area they will trust God with again and again. Some will experience a growing conviction that the advantages of singleness outweigh the disadvantages in their particular ministry. Others will have a growing desire for marriage and

---

[341] Hebrews 13:2; Romans 12:13; 1 Timothy 3:2; Titus 1:8; 1 Peter 4:9.
[342] This is true of preschoolers and children who attend national schools. Children who attend missionary or private schools and who later live/study in the home country serve to pull the parents away from the host culture. Intermarriage of the children with those of the host culture pulls the missionaries towards the host culture.

some of them may be extremely frustrated at not being able to begin friendships with the opposite sex in a manner to which they are accustomed. Dating is a practice pretty much confined to the North American cultures, a form of which is seen in some European cultures. It is rarely culturally appropriate in most other cultures and is therefore considered a "no-no" by most missions for missionaries away from their home culture. There are countless stories which could be related to support the fact that the practice of dating, even with great discretion, is almost always misunderstood and has led to discrediting the missionaries and their message. This is especially true of relationships between nationals and expatriates. Expatriates may rely too much on the cultural sensitivity of their national friend and ignore the warning signals coming to them from the observations of other nationals. Because love is blind, love sometimes does things it would not normally do with proper reflection. Keeping in close contact and heeding feedback from a cultural guide at this point is indispensable. These issues are not easy ones; many singles struggle greatly with this perceived loss of casual interaction with potential partners of the opposite sex.[343]

Two aspects of the desire for dating are important to consider. First, sometimes the desire to date is in reality a desire for a meaningful relationship with a member of the opposite sex, clearly differentiating biological sex from creative sex. A single woman conditioned by a dating culture, for example, has come to expect her needs for healthy male attention, appreciation, help and opinions to be met exclusively by a single, marriageable male in a casual or dating relationship. She must be reconditioned to appreciate all of the males on her team, in her church, in the mission, as part of God's provision for her life as friends, outside the exclusive dating relationship and, of course, if they are married, without threatening their spouses. In this way, she is learning not to limit God in the way she prays for God to meet her needs and the way He chooses to answer her prayers. God is bigger than the culturally confined dating relationship and can meet those needs very creatively and adequately.

> *Offenses in the area of opposite sex relationships are nearly impossible to unravel.*

A man from a North American culture, with similar expectations, for example, is probably used to taking the initiative in such relationships. He must carefully filter these practices, soliciting feedback from nationals as to the appropriate way of relating to or interacting with women. One date may mean he is engaged, and if he tries to break it, he, his ministry and the team may well be in disrepute! In many cultures all in-

---

[343] See also the sections on "Women" in chapters 1 and 4.

teraction of this sort is in groups, and even in modern Muslim countries, to be seen in public with a woman to whom he is not related is discreditable.

Second, sometimes the dating relationship is the expressed desire to have a relationship leading to marriage. In this case, this desire, as with all other perceived rights, must be recognized and consciously put under the lordship of Christ. God will either confirm it or allow it to be changed, but it is under His jurisdiction and is not being demanded from Him. Dating then, as a pre-condition for marriage, must be considered as any other part of the cultural baggage the missionaries bring with them. They need to look for the dynamic equivalent and avoid giving offense by imposing their culture on the host culture. In most cases this will mean that dating is "out"; group gatherings are "in." And sometimes the group gatherings will be under the supervision of older married couples. What may seem like a juvenile measure should not be taken as a personal offense, but observed out of respect for the host culture, or culture of other team members affected. No one's conscience should be hurt, nor should such practices bring the team into ill-repute. The same principle holds for overnight guests of the opposite sex. Offenses of this nature are nearly impossible to unravel. One cannot overstate the need to be cautious in this area before appropriate research has been done and validated.

Some missionaries have been very strict in their conduct in the area of the country in which they serve, but feel freer to conduct themselves according to Western values in the cities or tourist areas of the host country. Again, others are more cautious even here because one can never be assured of anonymity in such situations and a lot is at stake. Even at missionary conferences, where one might want to be comfortable and resort to one's own cultural values, in deference to other members of the multicultural team it is wise not to disregard the values of the host country.[344] One of the most difficult situations encountered is when the two worlds of the missionary clash with one another because there are visitors from the homeland, who neither fully understand the culture nor are understood by the people there. When I was confronted with such a situation involving offering alcohol in Germany where it is appropriate and even expected, I decided to explain to the visitor, my father, what was culturally appropriate. He was graciously understanding of the culture and participated as far as he could in good conscience without embarrassing either my host family or me. There are no easy answers, however.

---

[344] An example of this would be mixed swimming in some parts of Asia and Africa.

Assumptions of the mission or the team regarding housing for singles can cause offense. "Single missionary accommodation raises the blood pressure of too many victims of traditional missionary housing patterns. Some of these encourage a feeling of second-class citizenship in single women."[345] Singles deserve to have a

> *Singles deserve to have a household and to choose with whom they want to live.*

household and to choose with whom they want to live. "Living with strangers is a major stress factor for some single missionaries. Married couples have at least said 'yes' to their future living companion, but singles have to move in with some one they may never have seen before."[346] And this tends to be repeated over and over with every change of team personnel, with every home leave, and with every mission conference or team retreat. It would be doing a great courtesy to singles to let them select their living companions, even their roommates at conferences, or to choose to live alone. A psychologist, who was also a missionary, writes, "There is no harm in living alone if it suits your personality better, and provided it does not clash with the values of the local culture. But be careful not to become a recluse."[347] To chose not to live alone can also raise eyebrows in some cultures. There is a lot to say for the give-and-take and flexibility one learns to exercise in a good living situation, but constant changing of roommates, with the resulting readjustments, requires much energy, siphoning it off from the ministry. Our mission has developed a tool that is helpful for determining the compatibility of future living companions.[348]

The issue of culturally-mixed marriages also has a bearing on multicultural teams. I have known of marriages to experience a great deal of stress, requiring professional help, others ending in divorce, because the partners were personally immature and because their marriage had not stood the test of time. Because of the cultural complexity of the situation it is hardly advisable, at least until the marriage has stood the test of time, to place a couple from two different cultures in a third host culture to live. In such cases the stress factors on the individuals, the couple and the team are multiplied. The God-given inclination of the couple is to grow together. This usually means they consciously or unconsciously sort through and filter out cultural values of both of their heritages and arrive

---

[345] Foyle, *Honourably Wounded,* 30.

[346] Foyle, ibid., 30-31.

[347] Foyle, ibid., 31.

[348] Our mission uses the Roommate Questionnaire, with a related Bible study, with questions for discussion on almost every topic that a common household could encounter from finances to orderliness. This can be used with roommates or potential roommates. See Appendix E.

at a third culture combination for their marriage. If placed into another culture too soon, the process of adaptation begins again and the added stress, which brings up personal unresolved issues may well be too much. The chances of resolving the conflict under the stress of a three-way pull are not as good as when they are only adapting in two ways, provided the couple is personally mature. If their activity is focused internally, there is great loss in their adaptation to the host culture, to say nothing of the multicultural team. Most couples from different cultures who have adapted happily to one another in the context of one or the other's culture find that stressful enough. I have observed successful mixed marriages and those with ministries in a multicultural team in a third culture. It seems to work best in cases in which both are spiritually and emotionally mature and/or when they have come to the team/new country as singles and adapted on that level successfully first, seeing each other in that context. I have also observed that mixed marriages in a multicultural team in a host country to which one of the marriage partners belongs have a good prognosis for marriage and ministry because the expatriate partner is usually highly motivated to adapt.

For some, sports seem to belong to that inner circle[349] of their personality which cannot be changed (or at least that has never even been considered as a possibility). If, indeed, one finds one cannot live without it, serious consideration should be given to learning how to include, but not force, others of different national backgrounds in the excitement. Rather than being spectators of videos, being participants and coaches proved to be a good alternative for one missionary team. American missionaries began training neighbor-

> *In sports the issue is: How can others be included in the activities?*

hood children in the skills of baseball, and got an official team together, much to the surprise and joy of the village! Another missionary has been an invaluable resource to a professional basketball team and is now their assistant coach and chaplain. He and his summer project team from the USA offer evangelistic basketball camps in the summer - a great avenue for reaching the youth. This is *not* to say that relaxing with a football video is wrong, the issue is rather: how can such an activity be used to include others. If it is inclusive only for expatriate countrymen, care should be taken that it doesn't consume an inordinate amount of time, sapping energy that could be used for inclusive activities.

National holidays fall into the same category. If the holidays are so important that they have to be celebrated, one can use them as a bridge to help others get to know the missionaries and their countries better. I per-

---

[349] See Figure 7 "Values Categorized in Concentric Circles."

sonally have an easier time explaining the American heritage with some holidays (Thanksgiving) than with others (Halloween). Again, hospitality and inclusiveness are key. But this kind of hospitality has many different faces. If the fun centers around word games in English, for example, that presents a disadvantage for non-native English speakers. Thoughtful hosts and hostesses will create opportunity for more than superficial interaction. Active involvement of all, playing and laughing together is very wholesome for the team. Coming together only to eat, for example, with superficial conversation is less satisfying. Care should be taken that the preparations and clean-up are evenly distributed. Often the bulk of the work falls to the women, who, living in another culture especially, are the ones overloaded.

> The celebration of national holidays can be used as a bridge to help others get to know the missionaries and their countries better.

If teammates remain on a superficial level with one another or if some tend to take offense at cultural differences, it may mean that the personal needs of the missionaries are not being met. Perhaps some team members are being discriminated against. Maybe a team member, a lone representative of a culture, has not been consulted on important items, or is not a part of the "inner circle" and feels left out. Perhaps women, in general, are not being taken seriously in the team or feel relegated to the menial tasks as far as ministry is concerned. Many wives are offended if sufficient thought has not been given to their job descriptions as well as their husband's. It may be that gift-oriented ministry has been overlooked as a whole, creating a stiffness in the team atmosphere. The team atmosphere is a good thermometer in measuring the health of the team. Do all feel free to pray? One Christian worker once commented how little Christians talk about the Lord unless they are "required" to. This is usually a sign of a lack of openness or difficulties in the team, or personal spiritual dryness. This does not mean one has to make a prayer meeting out of every gathering. It does usually mean that if every gathering does not have the potential atmosphere (openness, warmth, care and spiritual discernment) of becoming a prayer meeting, the team as a whole, or individuals affected, need to work on it. Are the contributions of all to the discussion equally long? Are all being listened to equally attentively?[350] This may

---

[350] In a Time Management Seminar (North American context) the leader once explained that in order for one's contribution in a meeting to be listened to, one had to state one's point in no more than five minutes. He verified that for women that time frame was cut in half. Women are not generally listened to with the same intensity and expectation that men are. I, too, have observed this to be true. Women are cut off more in the middle of a sentence in meetings also. And

be difficult with the different levels of language fluency, but patience and politeness to hear one another out, not cut in or finish sentences exhibit respect and love.

In some cases problems may occur in the team that are not caused by the team, as such, but affect the team. As referred to earlier, the stress of a cross-cultural situation and a multicultural team[351] will cause areas of immaturity to surface in individuals. "The attached negative emotions are reactivated. The emotions then become fastened onto other adults, for no apparent reason, and interpersonal relationship problems develop."[352] Dr. Foyle goes on to explain that these "are stress-induced revivals of old problems that had long been buried in the mind." Although the missionaries pray and pray over their problems there is no apparent result. "The reason there is no benefit is that the emotions they are experiencing have nothing at all to do with 'today.' Yesterday's problems have emerged, and it is these that need to be healed up."[353] As soon as it becomes clear to a teammate that he is not the source of the problem, but rather a factor that provokes a reaction in the team member, he should not withdraw and abdicate himself of all responsibility. Dr. Foyle goes on to say that this knowledge should lead us to compassionate understanding and not reproach for the teammate. Symptoms which can be observed on an over-stressed missionary are: "difficulty in trusting anyone, boastfulness and over-dogmatism, over-dramatization of events, persistent exaggeration, persistent negative emotions to a marked degree, and over-dependency on colleagues, family or friends."[354] All of us are affected by these occasionally, but over-reaction is a sign of immaturity. Dr. Foyle suggests four steps in dealing with the recurrence of such problems:

1. Do not brood about the matter. God is keen to help you and will remind you of anything you need to know that will help in getting rid of them.
2. Write a list of people who have aroused negative emotion within you . . . Describe all the occasions on which you were

---

sometimes they are not listened to at all. I was once asked to explain certain elements of the training of missionaries to a colleague who refused to listen on the grounds that I was a woman and shouldn't be teaching him. His director, who had requested that I do this, forced him into a seat and said he'd better listen.

[351] See Figure 3, a table of stress factors, which can precipitate problems that affect the team.

[352] Foyle, *Honourably Wounded,* 127.

[353] Foyle, ibid., 127.

[354] Foyle, ibid., 128.

troubled. The description should be detailed, itemizing all the circumstances. At the same time, study the Scriptures relating to this negative emotion, so that you know what you are aiming at.

3. Try to understand why they behaved the way they did . . . Such understanding adds an element of compassion to your thinking, which is enormously healing.

4. Make a definite act of forgiveness of those who hurt you. This is never easy, but the power of our forgiving God is available to help . . . When we forgive others we are forgiving their debt to us . . . Forgiving such a debt is healing for it is voluntary - we choose to forgive. This makes us masters of the situation and not victims. This in turn leads to increasing maturity in our damaged personalities.[355]

The purpose of such an intensive exercise is to be free from the "crippling emotion that makes you and others unhappy."[356] We know that the Holy Spirit is then free to work through us and is not quenched by such negative emotions. This is God's desire for all Christians. God has not promised all roses for the missionary team, as some naively expect. Dr. Foyle wisely advises, "We can use interpersonal relationship problems as a means of learning something new, rather than as an irritant leading to despair."[357]

One hears the term "burnout" rather often in connection with missionaries (hardly exclusively, though). According to psychologist, Christina Maslach, burnout is defined as, "a syndrome of emotional exhaustion, depersonalization, and reduced personal accomplishment that can occur among individuals who do 'people work' of some kind."[358] To

---

[355] Foyle, ibid., 128-29.
[356] Foyle, ibid., 129.
[357] Foyle, ibid., 111.
[358] Christina Maslach, *Burnout--The Cost of Caring* (Englewood: Prentice Hall, 1982), 3.

Burnout is recognized by such warning signals as: exhaustion, detachment, boredom and cynicism, increased impatience and irritability, a sense of omnipotence ("Only I can do this job well."), feelings of being unappreciated, change of work style, paranoia, disorientation, psychosomatic complaints, depression, and suicidal thinking. *Mental* burnout shows up in disillusionment or failure, helplessness and self-doubt, depression, guilt, apathy, lack of concentration, decreased self-esteem, feelings of disenchantment, disillusionment, disorientation, or confusion. *Physical* warning signals are often psychosomatic: backaches, neck aches, headaches, migraines, insomnia, loss of appetite (or a never-satisfied appetite), ulcers, high blood pressure, constant colds, digestive problems, allergies, or heart attacks and strokes. People can experience *spiritual*

counteract the effects of burnout the author offers a "Taking Care of Yourself" Test: 1. Have you laughed several times today? 2. What percentage of your self-talk was positive today? 3. What amount of time this past week did you spend living in the present? 4. Did you do something three times this week for relaxation and recreation?[359] More and more missionaries and clergy are taking this sort of pacing seriously. The well-known pastor of Willow Creek Community Church, Bill Hybels, takes a study break for two months each summer to refresh himself personally in the Word and listen to the Lord for a concentrated period of time.[360]

Most psychologists and psychiatrists point to extreme imbalance in the lifestyle of the missionary as the source of burnout. One needs a balance between stimulation and relaxation, says Dr. June Morgan. Stress (pulling apart or pushing together) produces the temptation to sin.[361] Certain points in the life of the missionary seem to be predictably vulnerable to burnout - entry to the field, after intensive preparations, language learning when combined with other responsibilities, relationship problems at home or in the team, phasing out of job responsibilities without a new challenging assignment, living beyond means or support needs, re-entry into the home culture and other crises.[362]

During these times in particular, but also generally, mental health experts advise pacing oneself, planning in such a way that time for the essentials in spiritual, mental and physical health is allotted. The observance of the Sabbath, one day off a week, is a God-given principle for maintaining freshness in our relationship to Him and physical and mental resilience. This is not to be in an attitude of legalism, but in a discipline of obedience to the One who knows us and our needs better than we do. Dr. Foyle encourages this in the concept of maintaining "the integrity of your own person . . . body,

> The observance of the Sabbath is a God-given principle for maintaining freshness in our relationship to Him

mind and spirit."[363] She also wisely advises, "Take all the holiday your mission rules allow . . . there is nothing unspiritual in spending a little

---

burnout, too. Exhaustion, loss of perspective, failure to recognize own limits, and an increasing feeling that God is powerless accompany spiritual burnout. Flournoy, Hawkins, Meier and Minirth, *How to Beat Burnout*, (Chicago: Moody, 1986), 19-26.

[359] Maslach, *Burnout-The Cost of Caring,* 111-12.

[360] Interview at Willow Creek Community Church, June 1996.

[361] June Morgan, unpublished lecture, April 22, 1988 in Müllheim, Germany.

[362] See Figure 3, a list of stress factors as a result of life changes, which, when combined, can lead to burnout.

[363] Foyle, *Honourably Wounded,* 123.

money on a holiday."[364] Dr. June Morgan underscores this by saying we need physical as well as spiritual renewal "time to be with God and time to recognize our own idols."[365] Therein lies deep wisdom; it is so subtle and so easy to allow things to replace our Creator in our lives. To neglect recognizing them and being cleansed from them early on is the beginning of the slide into burnout.

> Without realizing what they are doing, they refuse - consciously or unconsciously - to rely on God's power and try to play God themselves. They may drop times of personal spiritual meditation and Bible reading, only to feel as if they are in a spiritual vacuum where nothing or no one appears to be able to help. Then, as time passes, they realize that their own power and energies are not enough either. They become disillusioned or feel like giving up, believing that others, including God, have given up on them.[366]

To avoid such extremes, as has been mentioned, good planning is necessary, time to pull back, daily, weekly and periodically. Dr. Morgan encourages one to treat one's calendar/diary as a friend and a tool, not an enemy, and when the week is full, including the appointments with God, write over it, "Take on no more engagements." The principle is good; almost every missionary from every culture will agree to this. The question remains - how does one learn to say "No" in a culturally non-offensive way.[367] Often it means avoiding the word "No," as such. This may communicate rejection of the person. It is better to kindly think through with the person asking a favor and suggesting other alternatives to avoid these feelings of rejection or abandonment. Or, if the new activity does indeed have priority, it requires eliminating a lower priority item.

Other planning tips include a daily break as well. Dr. Morgan, for example worked from 9 a.m. to 10 p.m., but she took off two hours mid-afternoon and "switched off completely." Families may prefer to have several evenings per week off. "All need time to think, not just do," she encourages, perhaps a block of one-half day per week. Time for the family and building close relationships should not be neglected, as well as doing other things one *likes* to do. Not allowing enough time for this can contribute to broken relationships.

---

[364] Foyle, ibid.

[365] June Morgan, unpublished.

[366] Flournoy, Hawkins, Meier, Minirth, *How to Beat Burnout,* 20.

[367] Saying "No" in a culturally appropriate way, as well as managing other conflicts is one of the subject of the workbook, *Managing Conflict Creatively, A Guide for Missionaries and Christian Workers*, Donald C. Palmer and *Cross-Cultural Conflicts* by Duane Elmer.

Many do not plan in enough time for essentials, such as household. If a home is to be hospitable it takes time to keep it in order and prepare for guests. This is no little task, but it is one of the most appreciated gifts of love in every culture. This is as important for singles as it is for married missionaries, for men as well as women. They need to have and make time for such important Christian ministry.

It bears repeating that eating and sleeping need adequate time allotment as well. Some new missionaries have difficulty changing their diets to the products available in the host country. Thought needs to be given to maintaining a balanced diet primarily out of products available locally, not importing much, if anything. Culturally appropriate exercise, especially for women, is the next challenge. There may be few places she can go jogging but she may be able to ride a bike or take brisk walks. These can be wonderful doors of opportunity for language learning and friendship.

Recognizing that some teammates function better in the mornings and others in the evenings, some at the beginning of the week, others at the end, should lead not just to understanding and sensitivity, but also to setting the team meeting mid-week, Dr. Foyle says.[368] Physical patterns and make-up should never be used as an excuse for laziness, but as a way of learning to give deference to one another, she continues.

> *Stress is often caused by not adapting to the new culture.*

Stress is often caused by not adapting to the new culture. Hanging on to things from the home culture under the presupposition that one would lose one's identity raises the stress and creates a barrier to trying new things. Developing new areas of creativity in the host culture can be exciting for the new missionary or missionary families. New forms of folk dancing, exploring the landscape or photography can be enjoyed with the team as well as those of the host culture.

An amazingly successful way to reduce stress is by talking it out. One expresses how one feels in the situation, learns how it affects others, and comes to possible conclusions about what could be changed: 1) in the culture, 2) in the team/mission, 3) in oneself or 4) by learning to laugh earlier. This is not the same as criticizing teammates or speaking disparagingly of the host culture. The Scriptural injunction to: "let no unwholesome word come out of your mouths" is still the safeguard to avoid destroying people and relationships. The passage continues, " . . . but only what is useful for building up"[369] indicating there is a way to vent

---

[368] Foyle, *Honourably Wounded,* 113.
[369] Ephesians 4:29.

frustrations without being destructive.[370] Talking assumes someone is listening; each teammate will need to learn to do both.

Feeling threatened by people different from us or judging or being judged according to stereotypes (cultural or otherwise) causes a rise in "team stress." One very important area related to mental health dare not be overlooked. Dr. Morgan calls it "the discipline of appreciation." "Learn to accept it and give it!" she encourages. Honest, healthy, loving affirmation gives the necessary boon to team relationships. A note, verbal affirmation, a look and a smile speak worlds of love and acceptance.

In summary, attention must be given to personal needs of missionaries. "Missionary care" is not a luxury; it's a God-given responsibility to those missionaries entrusted to a mission. This is not to put missionaries into a consumer-mode; many of their needs they must attend to themselves. But in the body of Christ we are called to care for one another, too. Burnout is a very real danger for people in helping professions and the symptoms should be observed carefully. Many needs of missionaries are differentiated according to status and cultural background. Attention should be given especially to those without built-in support groups, i.e., to those in the minority culturally and singles.[371]

> Missionary care is not a luxury; it's a God-given responsibility to those missionaries entrusted to the mission.

Leadership Styles, Authority and Decision-Making

If the spectrum of human expectations weren't varied enough, the backgrounds and expectations of a multicultural team would make leading such a team complicated. And if a significant number of missionaries I surveyed requested personal and spiritual maturity in their team members, how much more so for their team leaders. Expectations from team leadership are indeed great in such a complex team. It is a job for the spiritually mature and culturally aware, who are continually growing in

---

[370] The suggestion made earlier applies here: "When you (or so-and-so) says/does that, I feel . . . " Say it without accusing or assigning guilt. Describe your feelings: Not: "You make me . . . (e.g., angry)," use rather sentences in "I" terms.

[371] See sections in this chapter on "Women missionaries" and "Non-Western missionaries."

their skills and awareness by observing, listening to, and learning from others. In this section the practical aspects of cultural norms for styles of leadership, authority, as well as the transition of leadership to nationals, and the relation of patterns of logic to decision-making will be dealt with.

Which way of leading is *right* in a multicultural team? This is the *wrong* question to ask, but it wells up within in a team. The host culture should play the most significant role in forming the leadership style of the team. In practice, however, this is not always self-evident. In the discussion on cultural values and norms[372] the case was made for the host culture to provide the primary direction (apart from the unquestionable primary role of biblical values) for the team's adapting. Sometimes this issue of the culturalness

> *Leadership is a job for the spiritually mature and culturally aware, who are continually growing in their skills and awareness by observing, listening to, and learning from others.*

of leadership style is never even considered. In most cases leadership style would be placed in one of the inner concentric circles of values[373] (i.e., hard to change). There will be resistance to this if the team leader is from another culture and tends to impose his/her cultural values in leadership. This would be reason enough to have a national as team leader as soon as possible. There will be even more resistance - consciously or unconsciously - if the majority of the team is from another culture. And if *both* the majority and the team leader are from the same culture, it will be an uphill battle, even with all good intentions and sensitivity. But the endeavor to hold to the principle of deferring to the host culture, at least not offending the host culture, should not be abandoned. If it is a matter of principle, it is more a matter of empathy. "In the research of criteria relevant to overseas experience, empathy has been found in all studies to be an important quality for both adjustment and success. Ethnocentrism and empathy are opposites."[374] Moran is speaking strictly from a management perspective. Walking in the shoes of others, learning to see the world as they do and feel it as they do, perceive oneself as they do, is empathy. This combination of integrity and empathy in the items, "lives as best as s/he can according to what s/he knows of the Bible," "is compassionate" and "knows what it means to be a friend in host culture" in the survey and interviews, were all perceived to be crucial to credibility in communicating the gospel.[375]

---

[372] See the discussion on this topic in chapters 1 and 4.
[373] See "Values Categorized in Concentric Circles" in chapter 3.
[374] Robert T. Moran, *International Management,* March, 1988.
[375] Appendix A: items A.3, B.1, F.5.

Other factors in the decision-making process relate to styles of leadership and the exercise of authority. Top-down authority structures (sometimes called "chain of command") centralize decision-making and implementation. Linear logic lends itself to this authority structure, but not exclusively. These types of leaders may incorporate "democratic" elements into their decision-making process, such as soliciting the opinions of some of the group on specific items, but in the end they alone make the decision and the team lives with it. This method carries with it the disadvantage of then having to convince the dissenters of the benefits of their decision, or the team is abused by the team leader's insistence on unconditional submission (sometimes with specific Scripture references). If this authoritarian method is commonly used in a culture in which leaders cannot be directly confronted and the team members are unaware of the procedure of getting information back to the leaders, there will be no little discomfort in the team and attrition is pre-programmed until the lines of communication become clear. The satisfaction with this, as with any style of leadership, lies in the expectations of the team members. These expectations have been culturally conditioned. European missionaries, in particular, have been offended by some African, Asian and American team leaders in this way because their expectations for participating in the decision-making process as a team is very high. The expectations of North Americans are moving more in this direction, too.

On the other end of the continuum is the democratic leader who makes all decisions with the group. For teammates who are not used to this, the process may seem very tedious. They sit in meetings and wonder why the leader is incapable of making the majority of the "trite" decisions himself/herself so they can "get on with the ministry." They feel bogged down with details they would rather be free of to do the ministry. The leader's qualifications are subconsciously called into question, some teammates are frustrated and others bored in the process. Some Africans, Asians and Americans have little tolerance for this leadership style.

One does well to recognize that leadership functions, such as planning, motivating, creating momentum, advising, shepherding, summarizing, leading, training, problem solving, administrating, innovating and making decisions, are all culturally conditioned. Some cultures go so far as to say that all of these functions belong to the group as a whole; the leader only coordinates them. If the team expectations from the leader and from the team as a whole are different (as they most likely will be), functions and processes will have to be discussed and agreed upon by all. This may be fraught with complications because the process of how agreement is reached is also culturally conditioned. Commitment to being patient with one another and trying to understand each team member is of utmost importance. If impasse results, it may be necessary to call in a cultural expert from the outside, one respected by all parties involved, to mediate the situation.

Another important issue in leadership is: "Who is allowed to lead?" In some cultures there are hard and fast rules, albeit mostly unwritten, relating to the status or class of a (potential) leader. Some cultures automatically exclude certain groups of people from leadership, e.g. the working class, those without formal education, the women. For the German or Finnish culture, for example, not to consider a woman for leadership just because she is a woman is unthinkable. For other cultures in the team of which I was a part for many years, women in leadership was unheard of. Initially deferring to the mores of the host culture may be wise. But uncritical acceptance of them, though it presents the path of least resistance, is unjust and unbiblical.[376] There is no getting around working through these issues together as a team with the Bible in hand. But, as egalitarian as one might claim to be, no one is entirely free of prejudice on this issue. Precedence for leadership and developing in leader-ship responsibilities should be given to nationals, but not just one person or group of nationals. A reservoir of representative national leadership should be developed, including all groups, women and men alike.

Transition of leadership is one of the most difficult processes there is. The identity of the leader may be closely tied to the position and the effects of the "loss" are then great. Turning over the leadership is one of the hardest tasks there is because the missionaries are too often "more impressed with their own work than

> *A reservoir of representative national leadership should be developed, including all groups, women and men alike.*

with the development of the church" and determining the point of national maturity is subjective and difficult.[377] Tied in with leadership and authority issues, especially in transition, is the area of the use of money.[378] The control of finances may indeed be the hardest to release. It is the last bastion of power.

Education and experience also mean power. Those "in the know" have the power, even beyond their knowledge sometimes, to motivate, to convince, even to manipulate. The dynamics of such "information power" play a subtle but significant role in multicultural teams. It is the privilege of most expatriates, for example, to be connected to an interna-

---

[376] See the section on "Women" in chapter 1.

[377] H. Wilbert Norton, "He Got a Second Chance," An Interview by Jim Reapsome, *Evangelical Missions Quarterly,* April, 1984, 148-149.

[378] See the section on "Money" in 1. and the section on "Finances and lifestyle" in chapter 4.

tional home office, to other missionaries and organizations, to periodicals and to a wealth of resources in the world through the Internet, which provide them with a rather extensive network of contacts and information equal to, but most often superseding, that of the nationals. This can be lorded over the other teammates in many ways, e.g. by surprising them with announcements of changes or preempting them with their knowledge. Better is when the "wealth" of information is shared, giving others the same benefits. Often the advantage of being fluent in English is enough to create a hierarchy of the privileged and the underprivileged in access to information. Sometimes the kindest gesture on the part of expatriates is to enable some non-native English speaking missionaries to learn English in order to have access to the various sources of information and to be able to interact with them and exert international influence directly. The least expatriates should do is to be a friend and advocate to

> *To have mutual partnership in ministry demands that expatriates give nationals equal chance to hear and be heard.*

these missionaries without this access, translating for them in important international meetings, representing their standpoint and explaining their cultural context, and this in both directions. Often the expatriates need to explain how the international organization works both, functionally and culturally, to the missionaries not from the country of the home mission; they also need to explain the cultural inner workings of these missionaries to the international leadership for both to be properly understood.[379] This advocacy role is especially critical for the nationals, the ones usually with the least amount of power and influence, at least in the pioneer stage of missionary work. To have mutual partnership in ministry demands that expatriates give nationals equal chance to hear and be heard. This kind of mutuality has a high value and is an explicit goal in missions.

I certainly have not been without fault in my missionary experience, but I was persistent about wanting to turn over my responsibility of Coordinator of Staff Development and Training in Western Europe. Though an advisory leadership position, it still represented a platform for influence and I felt it best to be transferred to the hands of a European after the national ministries had developed. If too much time elapsed, I reasoned, the experience gap would only become wider putting nationals more at a disadvantage. But the practice was not as easy as the principle. Although I had trained a group of very competent nationals in this area, most of them saw their place of greatest effectiveness in their own coun-

---

[379] In our mission, this is a role Jim Green fulfilled well. See "Green, Jim"

tries and were reluctant to move to another country into a position on the continental level. The only solution seemed to be for me to terminate, so I gave two years notice. Only after the vacancy neared was the move taken seriously and a European was chosen. Because, in the opinion of some, the difference in experience might have created subtle tensions or hindered development of the new coordinator, I pioneered in another area within the same language group (traveling/training ministry into the then-closed East Germany) and remained available for consultation as requested by the new coordinator. This proved to be a very satisfactory solution for providing a smooth transition.

A special word about Western leadership in a non-Western world: In today's scene, the reputation of the West has preceded expatriate missionaries from the West to most fields creating a rather unjust burden of proof for them. They are, as it were, guilty until proven innocent. This international metaculture produced by technology and the television and film industry exerts an incredible force towards global acculturation. These media values of the Western culture are being adopted by an increasing number of the rising socioeconomic strata of many countries, which aspires to speak English and conform to such Western values. The minority in any given culture which adapts to this metaculture carries much influence, and that not just on the level of music, clothes or material well-being, rather it includes such things as Western ideas about the definitions of success. A backlash against the spread of Western culture is already occurring in the Islamic world and there is likely to be increasing opposition to the popularization of Western culture. In all probability this will come to be resented in more than just the Middle East.[380] Through media exposure, Westerners are generally thought of as exploiting, money- and sex-driven, criminal, violent, impersonal, painfully direct, etc. These values, though mostly half-truths in the minds of the people, are hardly conducive to creating credibility for the message of Christ. And this is less than a good prospect for Westerners launching out to bring the good news of a loving God to a people who may already be quite skeptical of the messenger. But complaining about the unjustness of it all will not change the situation that Western expatriates have inherited from history, tourist reputations and media. So, guilty or not, the Western expatriates do not come with a clean slate. The burden of proof lies with them to correct this image.[381] These assumed values may

---

[380] Larry Keyes and Larry Pate, "Two-Thirds World Missions: The Next 100 Years," *Missiology* Vol. XXI, 189-206.

[381] U.S. Americans are particularly pre-judged because the country is large and the political reputation well-publicized. Colonializing nations are also affected

loom high in the minds of the members of a multicultural team as they meet their Western team leaders. All it will take are certain "normal" (from a Western standpoint) exercises of leadership and "being themselves" for the non-Western nationals to subconsciously associate them with this image.

Some qualities less easy to detect for the Westerner perhaps, are perceived as negative by other cultures - an "exaggerated emphasis on the

> Some Western qualities are perceived as negative by other cultures: punctuality, preoccupation with things, and megalomania.

virtue of punctuality, which so much of the rest of the world regards with wonder and unabashed contempt," or a "preoccupation with things, in contrast to concern for people . . . concerned about people primarily in terms of what the people in question think about us. We are also addicted to a kind of megalomania - we insist that everything must get bigger. Quantitative growth seems often to push qualitative performance into the background."[382] The American propensity for numbers is almost despised in Europe. And Western, particularly American, team leaders stand out as more visible representatives of many of these values. According to the missionaries surveyed, the qualities of time-consciousness and result-orientation, along with goal-orientation, were rated lower, with a significant number of participants rating them as actually "hindering the credibility" of the gospel message.[383] This is a potential source of conflict with the leadership in almost every multicultural team. Nida, speaking for Westerners, hits the nail on the head:

> If we carefully examine the whole range of cultures throughout the world, we soon discover that our Western modern culture is actually the aberrant one. We are the ones who are so vastly different, with our highly involved technology, specialized division of labor, impersonal systems of communication, and unprecedented mobility (geographical, social, occupational and ideological).[384]

Westerners may subtly think, "The rest of the world will catch up," and some will indeed become acculturated to Western values, primarily for career purposes. But, as others have predicted, the backlash will come and Westerners will be despised. Wanting to communicate the most crucial, the most life-changing message in the world as effectively as possible, Westerners cannot afford to have that negatively perceived cultural

---

by a bad image, as is Germany, particularly because of the atrocities of World War II.

[382] Nida, *Message and Mission,* 170.
[383] Appendix A, items: G-5, G-7, G-9.
[384] Nida, *Message and Mission,* 49.

baggage. And most Western leaders, by virtue of what is respected in the West in leaders, have many of these perceived ignominious qualities. Hanging on to such despised qualities will not engender respect in teammates. Leaders have, then, a special

> *Leaders have a special responsibility to be sensitive to the host culture, as well as other cultures in the team.*

responsibility to be sensitive to the host culture, in particular, as well as other cultures in the team.

As a result, crises in team leadership can result from many Westerners equating their own worth with achievement. And the absence of visible achievements as perks may cause them to begin to question themselves. Every prayer letter, every report, every furlough has the potential of bringing up the painful lack of achievements so necessary to reinforce their ego. Learning to adapt in this area might be one of the healthiest spiritual exercises the expatriate goes through.

Differences in expectations on reports is also an area which is very culturally defined, affecting the leadership of multicultural teams. A good percentage of the reports of international missions are geared towards the cultural understandings of the supporters in the homeland. Lehtinen encountered it this way:

> During the first years I gave a *report*, and they [the other continental directors and international leadership] felt that we had failed badly in Europe. But, for me, a report meant that I shared what happened - the good things and the problems. After my reports ended, they prayed that God would free us from problem-orientation and that someday something would happen in Europe. I was always surprised at how fantastic every other continent was until it finally clicked, and I realized that we come from different cultures. When they asked for a report, according to my vocabulary, they actually were asking for an advertisement. . . I had to adopt their communication codes because they felt that sharing negative information was a lack of vision, but I felt that not covering the problems was a lack of honesty.[385]

This "clicked" because Lehtinen reflected on the cultural values that were playing a significant role. The American culture, he reasoned, "has been contaminated by generations of advertisements." One has to choose the vocabulary from American advertising language to make an impact on the audience. He concluded that, as one filters advertising down to the

---

[385] Lehtinen, "Through the Prism," 6.

basic message, he must conversely take others' reports "at 50 percent value" in order not to be misled.[386]

Written reports have a way of being misunderstood because they reflect both personal and cultural values. What is requested on the report form is what is important to the leadership, but not necessarily what the missionaries feel is important in their ministry. As a result, there is a subtle "devaluing" of the missionaries' work when they are truly unable to reflect what they value (how they use their time) on a report form. This process is aggravated even more if their supervisor does not respond to their report. Report forms, to be fair, should reflect not only the international mission's goals and cultural values, but those ministry and personal goals and cultural values of the missionaries themselves. Again, the misunderstandings are greater in a culturally mixed team.

Words have a way of misleading when the cultural context is not taken into consideration. Cultures change and words take on new meanings - even lose their meaning. One summer on home leave I was surprised to hear the term "awesome" in every other sentence. It was not that the youth of America had experienced revival, unfortunately, but that this word had now been "devalued" to include almost anything over which one could wonder, including pop stars and ice cream flavors. It was no longer just reserved for God and His creation. I was embarrassed in having to translate the new use of the word for my German teammate.

Someone has said that a true test of the missionaries' identification with the people is being able to serve under national leadership. With nationals in leadership positions, many of the Western qualities that expatriates have come to value in leaders will not be present, provided, of course, the national is not conforming unduly to Western values. "Koreans tend to be strong top-down leaders, which may be a problem when they move into leadership. Other Asians, such as the Chinese, are more consensus-oriented in making decisions. Australians have strongly anti-authoritarian strands in their culture," explains Brian Butler (England).[387] This doesn't mean that the nationals as leaders don't need correction, but it does imply that expatriates must filter their comments and suggestions to them very carefully. "Am I just trying to replicate what I think of as good leadership in my culture? Do I desire change so I feel more comfortable following this national leader? How do other *nationals* respond to their

> *The true test of the missionaries' identification with the people is being able to serve under national leadership.*

---

[386] Lehtinen, ibid.

[387] Brian Butler, "Tensions in an International Mission," 414.

leadership? Are the national leaders behaving consistent with scriptural principles of leadership and with their culture?"

In his article "Breaking the Power Habit: Imperatives for Multinational Mission," Peter Hamm challenges missions to make a periodic, conscious analysis of structures. "Do our present structures clarify roles and facilitate brotherhood?" "Do our structures imply a unilateral relationship, or are they in fact bilateral or multilateral?" He concludes: "The test of the change in our assumptions will be demonstrated in our willingness to let go of obsolete structures."[388]

> *"Are women proportionately represented at the mission's highest level?"*

Brian Butler adds another crucial dimension of leadership by posing the question, "Are women proportionately represented at the mission's highest levels?" [389] These are good power checks for the leadership to use in evaluating the balance of power.

It is generally agreed that the expatriate leadership is too slow to hand over responsibilities to national leadership. This is a difficult process indeed and takes much preparation. Perhaps part of the reason lies in planning only the "entrance" of new leadership and not the "exit" of the former leadership. I have heard quipped more than once, "If these missionaries are really worth their stuff they will find a new responsibility. Or maybe it's just time for them to go home." This attitude hardly reflects good partnership. Good transitions must be prayerfully planned, both transitioning *to* and transitioning *from* leadership positions. The experienced missionaries would feel complimented to have a number of opportunities offered by their national brothers and sisters who have a vision for them, such as where they could fit into the changing structures, *even if* the missionaries, for one reason or other, plan to return home. Lack of this kind of forethought can communicate a feeling of "being used." The missionaries came, gave the strength of their youth and the wisdom of their age, perhaps buried family in their adopted country, and are now being tossed aside like a worn out shoe. Although missionaries should not expect it, a worthy conclusion honoring them and their service would, in most cases, honor the Lord. "Give honor to whom honor is due." This the multicultural team should be aware of as well as the new leader.

All too often it is assumed that missionaries should "disappear" when leadership has been turned over. Many factors such as the personalities

---

[388] Peter Hamm, "Breaking the Power Habit: Imperatives for Multinational Mission," *Evangelical Missions Quarterly,* July, 1983, 181-82.
[389] Butler, "Tensions," 414.

and working relationship of the new and old leaders play a role in this decision, but there are non-threatening "mentor" positions which can be created to help new leadership indirectly. It is of great advantage to the new leaders to have on hand a trusted colleague who knows the cultural, unwritten inner workings of the international organization and who also can interpret it to them. And can interpret them to the international leaders. But the authority and the decision-making power needs to be vested in the new leadership completely. These mentor positions are only advisory. And, frankly, not every missionary is willing to be in an advisory position. It takes a good measure of humility. One of my former directors, Jim Green, did just this. After some years in a continental leadership position in East Africa, he learned French and moved to West Africa to mentor the new mission leadership there. For years he served in an advisory capacity, interpreting in all the international meetings for the West African leader, Kassoum Keita. Today, although living in the USA he uses his spheres of influence (contact with international leadership, raising of funds for projects, recruiting personnel for long and short term work in West Africa), to benefit the ministry, visiting there himself several times a year. He is a great example of a humble leader who is more concerned about cultural relevance and nationals being trained to lead than about his own career.

Is there a proper time to transition to national leadership? This is *the question* uppermost in the minds of leadership. Not too early, not too late. The Apostle Paul transferred leadership in each new city as fast as possible, moved on, but did not break off contact. He appointed men and women as elders, of high moral quality, not necessarily well-educated or young, to lead the church and he took younger men along with him to give them further supervised training. There is no evidence that Paul returned to appoint a second time. The next generation of leaders must have grown up under those leaders to be appointed by them.[390] Leadership must be trained in order not to fail. The higher the lack of vulnerability in a culture, the longer the training period. This can boomerang, however, because in the time it takes to train thoroughly, the expatriate leadership could have become either experts or entrenched. In both cases, they are hard to replace. Entrenched leadership takes reason or revolution to unseat. But if the expatriate leaders have done a good job, the team(s) have come to love and respect them, the national leader

> The expatriate leaders need to see their responsibility as transitional from the very beginning and be training national leaders concurrently.

---

[390] Roland Allen, *Missionary Methods, St. Paul's or Ours?*, 101-05.

who replaces them will inevitably be compared to them. A risk is involved in any case, but if the choice is made by electing rather than appointing, the chances are better. The indication of support from all of the team will carry through many a rough time. The expatriate leaders need to see their responsibility as transitional from the very beginning and be training leaders concurrently.

On occasion a time for transition to national leadership cannot be chosen, it is forced upon the missionaries by the change in political winds. This was indeed the case with China. *The* question being asked in the wake of the Cultural Revolution (1966-1976) was: Will the church survive? Missionaries were labeled as imperialistic, "having misused religion for their own purposes to poison the thoughts of the people," accused Chou En-Lai.[391] Even the Three-Self Churches (self-governing, self-supporting, and self-propagating) were closed. All Western imperialistic influence was to be rooted out. Today, though little is known statistically of the growth of the church in China, the church is a vital, witnessing, spiritual church that has been purged by the blood of martyrs. The Christians, estimated somewhere between 10-50 million, are not split by denominationalism, their leaders seem spiritually, not materially minded, though possessing little in property or formal education.[392]

Very pertinent to the topics of decision-making and leadership are the different patterns of logic. If not understood, this can create confusion and frustration. As my former director, Kalevi Lehtinen, describes:

When an African talks about an issue, he paints a picture. Everything is included. He does not need to have a central point. Contextual logic is also very common in Southern Europe. People paint a picture with their words. When they discuss, it's a long discussion. They talk and talk and talk and talk. And a person who comes from a linear culture asks, 'When will they get to the main point?' . . . The whole discussion is the answer to the question. At a certain time, they start to agree, they reach a consensus, and then they finally all agree, 'Yes, yes, now I see the whole picture.'[393]

Those with linear logic, of course, will claim that "painting pictures" is no logic at all, the assumption being that only their pattern of reasoning is "logical." But that reflects circular as well as ethnocentric reasoning, the assumption being: What is logical is that which fits *my* pattern of

---

[391] Karl Rennstich, *Die zwei Symbole des Kreuzes,* 235.

[392] See, for example, the description of a lay preacher in a House Church in China in Karl Rennstich's article "Christliche Mission heute" in *Bis an die Enden der Erde,* Ruth A. Tucker, Karl W. Rennstich, ed., (Metzingen: Franz, 1996), 444f.

[393] Lehtinen, "Through the Prism," 10.

thinking. Logical patterns for most Africans and those from Latin cultures is contextual logic. And for Germans and some other central and northern European cultures the dialectical form is logical. An opinion is stated (thesis) backed up by lots of facts, a counter opinion (antithesis) is given, supported by more facts and back and forth it goes, each side apparently trying to persuade the other to change 180 degrees, or so it seems. Then, suddenly, a compromise will be made (synthesis), surprising the naive observer who doubted that such a thing would be possible in that heated discussion! Lehtinen isolated a fourth kind of logic that he feels represents his native country of Finland, as well as Scandinavia and France (among others) - existential logic. This pattern of logic is not linear, adding fact to fact to reach a conclusion; it is "an experimental leap of faith to the new truth." You grasp something which is not yet there. You are intuitive.[394] Because facts and quotes are not convincing for him, the existential thinker or "feeler" (not necessarily related to existential philosophy) tries to create the same emotional response in the heart of his hearers to enable them to grasp his truth also. Lehtinen observes that Jesus used all these forms of logic in His ministry, depending upon His audience and the nature of His message.[395]

The misunderstandings and false judgments that arise out of not recognizing and respecting the fact that different patterns exist are legion. As I alluded to from my previous experience in the German culture, the heated discussions sometimes sounded and "felt" sinful to me! That leaves the door open for all kinds of accusations - lovelessness, being unspiritual or negatively critical. The contextual and existential forms of logic don't seem to get to the point quickly enough by dealing with seemingly extraneous bits of information. They are accused (perhaps only inwardly, but nevertheless accused) of wasting time by their frustrated goal-oriented, linear logic teammates. These teammates, in turn, are categorized as being paper- or project-oriented and not at all interested in people. And on it goes, accusation upon feeling, verbalized or not, until the bubbling cauldron boils over. Anticipating the fact that not all people think as one does, foreseeing that adjustments will probably have to be made, alerts one to shift into "patience-and-understanding" gear. All (hopefully) are not nearly as quick to assume that their culture will dominate and they can proceed without sec-

> *The misunderstandings and false judgments that arise out of not recognizing and respecting the fact that different patterns of logic exist are legion.*

---

[394] Lehtinen, ibid., 11.
[395] Lehtinen, ibid., 12.

ond thought. They do have to take the extra effort of being sensitive to their teammates, who may be very puzzled or hurt over the process or whom they may not at all understand at this juncture.

Applying these patterns of logic to the decision-making process one can observe a number of methods, not just those taught in management seminars. Contrasted with the linear process of gathering information, evaluating alternatives and choosing the best alternative, the other processes may seem laborious, indirect and somewhat superfluous. But one needs only to look beneath the surface to see some of the benefits of other methods. European leaders tend to reach a decision by consensus. The issues are discussed very thoroughly before they arrive at a decision. Lehtinen adds, "They make few decisions and it takes a long time and can be a painful process to make a decision. But in the same package with the decision, there is already the motivation because the whole discussion has created goal-ownership." Europeans also tend to live with the tension of lack of resolution longer. "American leaders want fast solutions and it's difficult for them to live with unsolved problems."[396]

The benefit of goal-ownership is incorporated into the process. And, at least in a German context, there is almost a moral obligation to hear an opinion from everyone (even if that opinion has already been voiced by someone in the group). Although laborious to the observer this has the advantage of reinforcing the person's value in the group. Everyone gains a hearing and no one's opinion is overlooked when a decision is finally made. Ignorant of these expectations, team leaders could cause personal injury to team members, who might assume the leaders think their opinion is not worth voicing. To the uninitiated, however, the persistent asking of the question, "Why?" makes them wonder why this teammate is so critical and rebellious, never accepting what the other person says.[397] Though *seemingly* abused, the "Why?" questions serve to sharpen the issue, focus the thoughts and give good background reasons. They are well-intentioned and not to be viewed as negative, though this fact needs to be stated again and again in the team. When consensus has been found, the decision will be indisputable.

Consensus, by the way, needs to be carefully distinguished from compromise. No one sacrifices his/her values or viewpoints. Consensus

---

[396] Lehtinen, ibid., 7.

[397] Understanding the background of such questioning gives depth to the relationship as well. In West Germany after World War II the school system, and parental training to a lesser degree, challenged the children to understand why they did what they did and to be able to verbally defend it. This was an obvious reaction to producing a generation of "blind followers." Critical thinkers, who would painstakingly question *everything* were now called for in the new society.

is "a new invention, a higher level of truth that satisfies the prerequisites and the axioms of both thesis and antithesis."[398] For those with a tendency towards dichotomist thinking, this process, unless personally experienced will seem virtually impossible. A study of the New Testament Church, however, reveals a history of decision-making by consensus, through prayer.[399] One may need to withhold judgment on the method of consensus until experience proves the better teacher.

Much more could be pursued in the area of leadership by the team itself, keeping their unique situation and the general principles for all multicultural teams in mind. My director once commented that there are two types of expatriates - those who are willing to adapt when they come into a new culture and those, who by the very force of their personalities, change everything around them. In the latter case (sounding more than a little like a bull in a china shop) they may say they mean no harm, that they are just being themselves. This is an indication that they are oblivious to blind spots in their cultural observation and basically insensitive to people. Such leaders need to hear from their teams, and not too subtly. "Left unchecked, or ignored, problems will fester and become a hindrance to spiritual vitality and to the work. However, the attitudes that underlie cultural insensitivity and relational problems are identifiable and curable."[400]

To summarize, in the areas of leadership, authority and decision-making one is dealing with the use or abuse of power. Position is power. Money is power. Education, experience and networking all spell power. The use of the English language in an international setting is power. It is how this power is used that matters. Sometimes power is used for self-exaltation and the destruction of others, even without knowing it. This is a deeply theological problem. Growth in self-awareness and maintaining checks and balances are necessary to combat destructive uses of power.

---

[398] Lehtinen, "Through the Prism," 10.

[399] See Lawrence O. Richards, *A New Face for the Church* (Grand Rapids: Zondervan, 1970), 122f and 188f in which he discusses the history of the church and the nature of the church as reasons for making decisions based on consensus. Consider how often the church is described as acting as one body in their decisions of discipline (1 Corinthians 6), of judging a dispute between believers (1 Corinthians 6), to give an offering to meet the needs of others (2 Corinthians 8 and 9) and to settle doctrinal issues (Acts 15). When Peter and John were put under pressure not to speak of Christ, they went back and reported it to the church, which came together to pray and seek God's will. God met them, they were filled with the Holy Spirit and spoke the word fearlessly (Acts 4 and 5). The church acted "by common consent" (Acts 5:12).

[400] Butler, "Tensions," 418.

> Growth in self-aware-
> ness and maintaining
> checks and balances are
> necessary to combat
> destructive uses of
> power.

A well-functioning multicultural team, in which all members have the freedom to express their opinion, form decisions and share the weight of responsibility is also a good check against the misuse of power. Leaders who are aware of the various cultural patterns of logic, the needs and values of the team members, especially the values of the host culture, and who are servant-leaders modeled after Jesus and sensitive to the work of God's Spirit, will not be as prone to abuse the power they exercise.

Finances and Lifestyle

One of the most critical areas of adjustment, visible to the new community and open to judgment according to the missionaries cultural standards, is the area of their use of finances and their lifestyle. Their lifestyle, as reflected in their use of money or material resources, such as houses, buildings, property, cars, machines, technical instruments and the like, either greatly contributes or erects a great barrier to credibility in communicating the Gospel. It is a high visibility issue and, as such, has the potential of being a great stumbling block in team life, too. Lotje Pelealu, an Indonesian nurse serving on a multicultural team in Gambia, reflected on her inner struggles as a missionary from a poorer country than her Western teammates. Although she enjoyed the advantage of not being sought after by nationals because of her money (she had little), she admitted it did get under her skin that she couldn't afford as much as her colleagues. She had to pray and wait longer for the motorcycle for her ministry while they were able to buy a car immediately.[401]

One of those missionaries who responded to the Pietist founder Philip J. Spener's challenge to missions was Dr. Hermann Mögling of the *Basler Mission* in India. After he was influenced by Blumhardt and joined the Pietists, he decided to "follow the Lord in everything . . . with the logical consequences of poverty, identification with and service for the poor." He moved out of his "mission palace" and lived in the huts of his students, sold all the mission property and threw the proceeds with the mission's cash in the well! Later it became clear to him that the self-

---

[401] Veronika Elbers, "Dritte Welt Missionare - Ein Interview mit Lotje Pelealu, Indonesische Missionsgemeinschaft," *Evangelikale Missiologie*, 2/1992, 48.

denial and going down to the level of the Indians also needed a "bringing them up to us" element too.[402]

The issue of the use of money and goods (lifestyle) is a central one to the Christian faith; it is a question of truly following our Lord. Roger Greenway describes his most embarrassing moment as a missionary as the day his family's shipment arrived in Sri Lanka, after they had lived well for four months without it. Under the observation of the neighbors who had gathered, he and his wife unpacked what 15 oxcarts had delivered.

> But then, suddenly, we were discovered to be what some probably suspected we were all along - filthy rich Americans. . . A thousand sermons could not undo the damage done that day. It would have been better for our ministry if the ship had dropped our barrels and crates in the Indian Ocean.[403]

In light of the many things they had learned to live without, the Greenways' embarrassment on that day increasingly grew to discomfort, forming a conviction about the detrimental effect of so many things. Hindsight is better than foresight. Decisions that are made based on the negative experiences of others may help missionaries today avoid mistakes that are hard to undo. Decisions about what to take and what to leave are often based on antiquated information and perhaps values of a different generation of missionaries. If the process of adaptation means in essence, "removing the barriers that are a hindrance to the communication of the gospel," then each missionary must carefully scrutinize his values in this area. Greenway defines lifestyle as including, "the way missionaries use money, the kind of housing they choose for themselves, the type of vehicles they drive, and the kind of entertainment and recreation they spend money on. Missionary lifestyle includes everything about us that local people observe."[404] All these things have the potential of affecting the reception of the gospel negatively or positively. All these things also have the potential of affecting team relationships positively or negatively.

The Brewsters have advised those who, wishing to bond with the people of the new culture when they first arrive, to meet four conditions, all of which communicate a picture of the missionary's willingness to simplify his lifestyle:

1. Be willing to live with a local family
2. Limit personal belongings to 20 kilos

---

[402] As quoted in Rennstich, "Mission und Geld," 22.

[403] Roger S. Greenway, "Eighteen Barrels and Two Big Crates," *Evangelical Missions Quarterly*, April, 1992, 126-27.

[404] Greenway, ibid., 127.

3. Use only public transportation
4. Expect to carry out language learning in the context of relationships that the learner himself is responsible to develop and maintain.[405]

After this initial bonding period (about three months), the missionaries are in a much better position to judge what should belong to their lifestyle and what could indeed prove a hindrance. "Happiness is belonging, not belongings."[406] Are the two mutually exclusive in the new culture of the missionary? After careful

> After the initial bonding period, the missionaries are in a much better position to judge what should belong to their lifestyle and what could indeed prove a hindrance.

observation, he must decide, hopefully before he is a "marked man," and has lost credibility that will be very hard to regain.

Ron Ornsby changed the class of people he worked with in Hong Kong and purposefully scaled down to an appropriate lifestyle in order to increase his identity with the people and become more approachable.[407] He arrived at his conclusions by studying anew the passages of Jesus' relating to people and applying them. Where some missionaries have contested their ability to "identify" with the people (and therefore questioned how realistic it is)[408] others have tried it for themselves, not just to experiment but out of pure motivations, and done well. Identification lies foremostly in the attitude of the missionary, a genuine *agape* love that would not want to do anything to offend, but that would instead remove barriers of misunderstanding. It is this attitude that allows missionaries to give up their right to the familiar, the comfortable, even the healthy things in their previous lifestyle. This is not natural and, in some cases requires a deep working of God's Spirit. The extent of this identification should neither be defined nor enforced legalistically - it is a spiritual and cultural process between the host culture, missionaries and their Lord. If the changes are induced from a desire to conform or prove their dedication, they are bound to put a heavy load of guilt on the missionaries. Asking themselves why they resist changing might reveal the source of their struggle.[409] Often looking back on such inward battles the mission-

---

[405] Brewster and Brewster, "Bonding and the Missionary Task," 458.
[406] Brewsters, ibid., 461.
[407] Ron Ornsby, "How to Be Downwardly Mobile," *Evangelical Missions Quarterly*, October, 1993, 392-399.
[408] Harriet Hill, "Incarnational Ministry: A Critical Examination," *Evangelical Missions Quarterly*, April, 1990, 196-201 and "Lifting the Fog on Incarnational Ministry," *Evangelical Missions Quarterly*, July, 1993, 262-69.
[409] See Figure 7, "Concentric Circles of Values".

aries are in a better position to see that it was just part of the process of becoming more mature as a person and as a Christian.

"Nobody is perfect!," it's true. Idealism would put the missionary under this kind of pressure, however. But one of the most credible characteristics mentioned again and again in the qualities that missionaries most like in team members is "personal maturity."[410] Growth takes time and much grace and forgiveness of one another. The

> *The attitude of genuine love, that would not want to do anything to offend, allows missionaries to give up their right to the familiar, the comfortable, even the healthy things in their previous lifestyle.*

missionaries would do well to heed input from others, but it should be their decision as their mind, heart and conscience are enlightened and the Lord deepens their convictions. In the multicultural team, the missionaries will change in different ways and at different rates of speed. Mabel Williamson, missionary in China and Indonesia since 1934, reflects, "My experience on the foreign field leads me to the conclusion that it takes a good deal more grace to live happily with one's fellow workers on the foreign field than at home."[411] This is perhaps due to the fact that missionaries are strong-minded, tend to live very close together and are not able to select fellow workers, she comments. Perhaps the last two factors can be modified so the refining fire of the crucible is not in the team itself but in the "battle." Comparing the teammates to one another is devastating and may even eliminate the last hope or desire to change on the part of a struggling missionary. Vulnerability on the missionary's part should call forth sensitivity on the part of the teammates. Only the secure missionaries who know they are loved and accepted (by God foremostly, but also by their teammates) will be in a position to change and grow. All missionaries need patience, insight and love, as well. This is not to say that missionaries do not need to challenge one another on issues of lifestyle. But the decision must be one borne out of personal conviction.

In referring to lifestyle differences, one national missionary I surveyed commented, "They [the expatriate missionaries] build a cultural barrier in their home that nationals cannot cross." Jonathan Bonk examines the consequences of such disparity in his book, *Missions and Money: Affluence as a Western Missionary Problem*. He writes, " . . . in the exchange for the various comforts and securities of personal affluence, Western missionaries must sacrifice a measure of apostolic effectiveness and credibility." But this is nothing compared to the price of

---

[410] Appendix A, item G.1.

[411] Williamson, *Have We No Rights?* 84-85.

personal integrity that the "rich missionary" must pay. The contrast of Christ, who so loved the world that He became poor and gave His life for it, and the "rich missionary, who so loves this world that he cannot give it up for the sake of Christ and for the gospel," leaves a huge credibility gap.[412]

It is indeed difficult for missionaries, even Western missionaries, on a meager living allowance, to imagine themselves wealthy. They inevitably compare themselves to their peers in their home country, and conclude they *are* living sacrificially. They are certainly not living on the level of those in the homeland. This is especially true of those missionaries in faith missions who are responsible for raising their own support. But, for the sensitive missionary, it doesn't take long

> To arrive then, without all the trappings, only with the necessities, will be most beneficial.

in the new host country and in a multicultural team to realize the uncomfortable feeling of living way above the norm. To arrive then, without all the trappings, only with necessities, will be most beneficial. One gains perspective and knows the right nationals to ask for input. The new missionaries in a Middle Eastern country who arrived with few clothes and no home furnishings, "committed to picking up on things," won the respect of the nationals. They won their hearts as well when they opened their humble, rented home and spoke their language as best they could after a few weeks. They stand out in contrast to some other missionaries in that country who are suspected of working for the CIA. They couldn't have earned that much money otherwise, the nationals felt forced to conclude.

As I mentioned earlier I have moved relatively recently into a new cultural context, the former German Democratic Republic,[413] where the living standard is not (yet) what it is in the West. Nearly six years after the currency unification, the salaries in the East are just 71 percent of those in the West, not to mention the negative effects of higher unemployment on the economy. Although this move had been preceded with several years of traveling into this then "closed country," the process of observing and soliciting feedback to discover what kind of housing would be appropriate began anew. The housing market was extremely tight but meanwhile, a "free housing market" had begun to develop with, of course, astronomical prices.[414] Doris, my East German colleague, was

---

[412] Bonk, *Missions and Money,* 44.

[413] See pages on "East Germany."

[414] Initially, when we began looking for housing, this market was not available because, with the unification of the two Germanys, pre-World War II property

in the process of raising her support for the ministry (required by the mission) which created a "ceiling" on the level of housing we could consider. In Germany, the popular opinion of the Christian community and the supporters, is that missionaries should only live in very modest housing. Prayer support and help in looking were solicited. This gave additional information as to what kind of housing would be appropriate and created expectations in those who prayed over the two years as to what God would provide. In the end, the rental apartment allocated from the city was "better" than imagined, since it had been privileged housing for party loyals prior to the fall of the Berlin Wall. The temptation was resisted, in a time of great need, to "go over our heads" and do what few in this society could afford - buy or build. Even if mission policy allowed it, it would have been greatly misunderstood by the Christian population struggling to keep their jobs and supporting missionaries they never had to (or had the opportunity to) support before. All are astounded at what God provided because it would have been humanly impossible to "make this deal" and see the benefits for the ministry. Their prayer support and opportunity to give input in the process and our willingness to take what we got were important in determining the appropriateness. The fact is that most of our friends benefit directly or indirectly from the apartment as a "center of ministry." Furnishings included almost all "used" items. The list had been put together with Doris' careful filtering. Wallpaper and paneling were donated and many were involved in the renovation. No major purchase was made without consulting national friends.

It may feel like an "inordinate" amount of time is used in making such lifestyle decisions when the drive to get settled is so strong, but in reality, the missionaries are accomplishing just exactly what they came to do, if they evaluate it consciously. They are establishing rapport with the people, gaining their trust, hearing their viewpoints and "gut-level" impressions, learning the language (certainly enlarging their vocabulary), and they are positing themselves as learners, which is generally perceived very favorably, as long as help is requested and not demanded. Goal-oriented missionaries need not fear that they are "wasting time just getting things set up." If these tasks are approached correctly, they are gaining much more than they would coming into a ready-made situation (or trying to get set up quickly and efficiently without outside help) and then attempting to

> *Goal-oriented missionaries need not fear that they are "wasting time just getting things set up."*

---

rights were being disputed and no one could purchase property to build houses for rent or for sale.

"minister." God's timing in these things is part of His goodness and sovereignty.

Some ambiguity may be perceived from nationals about things relating to lifestyle. The surveys showed that such factors do affect credibility,[415] however some nationals interviewed indicated they expected the Western missionaries to live above their standard of living. This was also Nida's observation, "If these Europeans know how to live better than we [Africans] do, why don't they? We would, if we could!"[416] There is a tension here. Having and hoarding is not credible, but having and sharing is desired, being careful not to attract nationals as "rice Christians." This is a very delicate tightrope to walk, calling for wisdom, discretion, generosity and a modest lifestyle.

Defining the extent of "personal property" plays a role in understanding values of the host culture. What belongs to whom (which person or group)? It begins with a vehicle. Does it belong to the missionary? The mission? Who has access to it and under what circumstances? What are the mission's policies regarding purchasing and maintaining vehicles, office equipment, housing, land, etc.? What are the rules and conditions for borrowing? Anthropologists have researched these concepts of property and ownership extensively. The responsibility lies with all team members to try to understand the others on the team, give feedback on their own cultures and expectations, and to learn to behave appropriately in the host culture. This is indeed difficult because even within the same culture, personal and family values play a strong role here, as most married people have discovered! The point again is to be "non-offensive," not perceived as pretentious. Even with appropriate feedback, this will take time to discover. It is, of course, better to first discover the limits theoretically (without the "barrels") rather than having to work against an impression created.

The issue of property ownership, along with setting salary levels, has been the Pandora's box of many a mission with multicultural teams. Our European leadership spent years trying to arrive at equitable solutions for all involved, and the missionaries on this team were all from the West. Sometimes wonderfully equitable policies did not fit under the tax laws of the country in which we lived or the countries from which all the different missionaries were paid and we had to start to think again.

Establishing a salary level was the initial problem, for example. In our mission the international guidelines state that the "living allowance"

---

[415] See Appendix A: items: "wise use of money" (C.9) and "culturally appropriate standard of living" (C.10) rated "necessary for -" plus "adds to credibility" at 86 percent.

[416] Nida, *Message and Mission,* 162.

must be set according to the number and age of family members (a couple together receives more than a single, a family with older children more than one with younger children, etc., and older missionaries receive a bit more). The rule of thumb was to find an equivalent occupation in the culture (teacher, pastor) offering a modest salary to use as a means of comparison. In one country represented on the team, the level of a teacher's salary was modest and used as the standard. In the countries of other teammates, the teachers were paid very well, as was the clergy, so those standards were inappropriate. In other countries clergy were underpaid and had to have outside employment. Some team members had access to salary supplements from the government for housing or children; others didn't. Finally a level was agreed upon, valid for all full-time missionaries in this location, regardless of country of origin. (It still was higher than others in the national ministry in Germany, however.)

But taking a second look, eyebrows were raised. These levels had been set for net salaries; state and church taxes, pension and hospitalization plans were not yet included. When some of the team began to add on these amounts to arrive at the sum they had to raise personally, they began to protest. Added to this hardship was the "Christian climate" factor of each given country - some home countries of the missionaries have a larger Christian population than others. In those countries, however, not all of the Christians are used to "faith missions," supporting missions or missionaries individually. Although the salary level looked equitable, with the additions and subtractions the governments imposed, the "opportunities" were not equal to get the support.[417] In our situation, a solution was finally reached in establishing an upper *and* lower basic salary level[418] to try to be sensitive to host cultural expectations and the opportunities of the different teammates in raising personal support. (In this case there were no housing regulations as most lived in

> *The issue of finances is difficult even with good intentions and cultural sensitivity.*

rental properties, as is common, and tried not to spent more than 30-40 percent of their income for housing. The issue of purchasing houses later complicated the issue.) This illustrates how difficult such a problem can be even with good intentions, "relatively" close cultures and cultural sen-

---

[417] Our Polish missionaries, for example, calculated that they have to approach 11 times more people than their American teammates do in their home country to get the same amount of support to live side by side in Poland.

[418] Establishing an upper level guards against abuse or greed on the one hand and setting a lower level guards against laziness in support raising or an inappropriate poverty mindset, equating this with greater spirituality. If one finds the salary is still "too high" one is free to give it to others who have special needs.

sitivity. Such decisions need much prayer and wisdom, and policies need to be reevaluated from time to time, as the culture changes, also the constituency of the team. Hardly any area can cause as much misunderstanding and hard feelings in a team as the area of finances. All those affected (at least representatives from each group - each culture, male, female, single, married, parents) should, therefore, be drawn into the decision-making process.

At the time of this writing, the constituency of the larger national team of which I am a part includes missionaries from Taiwan and the Philippines, as well as various European countries and U.S. Americans. In addition to the difficulty of transferring the money from the home country to the missionary, the costs of living modestly in Germany seem astronomical to those back home in America and especially in Asia. Efforts are being made to supplement the finances by raising them in Germany; but that's not yet the best final solution.

For decisions relating to lifestyle (purchases, entertainment, recreation) to be "non-offensive," missionaries need to be more and more in tune with the host culture soliciting input and listening to feedback. The addition of every piece of "necessary" equipment may begin to drive a wedge. "Since biblical faith is, above all, a relational faith, it is not only sad, but sinful, when personal possessions and privileges prevent, distort, or destroy the relationships of Christ's followers with the poor," comments Bonk but adds, "But this appears to be an almost inevitable consequence of personal affluence."[419] If there is financial inequity among teammates, the enemy of our souls has his foot in the door already. "Between families of widely disparate means and standards of living, friendship is extremely unlikely. With whom does a missionary naturally choose to spend leisure time?"[420] Some of the African missionaries I interviewed felt rejected by their expatriate colleagues because of the lifestyle difference, primarily the way money was used in recreation. The African missionaries were quick to say they did not feel this was an intentional exclusion, but the reality of being excluded was nevertheless there. There is a direct relationship between lifestyle and genuine fellowship, this *koinonia* to which Jesus has called us all. And if missionaries are not choosing to spend leisure time together, they are sending a message of rejection to their teammates, and probably to those of the host

---

[419] Jonathan Bonk, "Missions and Mammon: Six Theses," *International Bulletin of Missionary Research,* October, 1989, 176. Bonk's book deserves to be read and digested by every missionary. If it hasn't been read before going to the field, the multicultural team would do well to read and discuss it together. See also "Money" in chapter 1.

[420] Bonk, ibid.

culture, as well. "The staggeringly high relational price that Western missionaries must pay for their affluence could perhaps be overlooked, or at least endured, were it not for its insidious effects upon the communication process. . . Missionaries are above all Way-showers, whose lives must be imitable by their converts."[421] Bonk aims his comments at Western missionaries, who are, no doubt the greatest offenders, but interviews have revealed that they are not alone. Some Korean missionaries have been known to move to the field with their video recorders and other equipment. No missionary, regardless of origin, can point the finger at another. Each must take personal responsibility before God to "remove the log from his own eye."

> *No amount of words can explain away the impression of "greed" or "serving mammon instead of God" which is conjured up in the minds of the have-nots.*

Granted, part of the problem lies in the perception of the observers, but perceptions still form the basis of conclusions and they are hard to counter. No amount of words can explain away the impression of "greed" and "serving mammon instead of God" which is conjured up in the minds of the have-nots.

> Both the motives and the message of affluent missionaries are suspect, and biblical teaching on wealth and poverty, the rich and the poor, must necessarily be truncated when conveyed via an affluent channel. Missionaries cannot challenge converts to a way of life that they themselves are unwilling to live.[422]

Nor can such lack of credibility create much respect in the life of a multicultural team. Such issues must be discussed together openly and prayerfully.

Where can one start to make meaningful changes? The North American continent is full of books on simplifying the lifestyle. And there are many others on sacrificial giving. While one cannot begin to do everything simultaneously, one can begin to change some thing(s) in one's own personal lifestyle. Exposure to how most of the world really lives, which new missionaries will get, will do a great deal to alert their conscience, if they don't allow their hearts to be hardened. Observations and feedback will sharpen their view even more. This, followed by a rigorous evaluation before the Lord and with their families, they will come to a conclusion of what they really need to do. The children most certainly need to be a part of this decision-making as their lives are directly affected by it. It needs to be their choice, too.

---

[421] Bonk, ibid., 177.
[422] Bonk, ibid., 178.

"We yearn for 'structural change,' which will make personal change easier."[423] Ah, the bluff has been called! No one is immune to the subtleties of material accumulations and their imposition on our lifestyle. While home on leave, this time with my East German colleague (Doris' first trip to America), I was taken aback at how complicated life had become. Just the energy used to make choices in the rows and rows of cereals on the shelf, not to mention comparing all the sale items from the great many stores from which one can choose, was overwhelming. How much time really needs to be spent in such "commercial" activity? And how much money? The issue is not, trying to make missionaries unattractive when they return home periodically. One can be brought on board and made "presentable" for visits pretty quickly and with very little investment. It's a matter of making the gospel attractive to those who desperately need it. It's good to practice the lordship of Christ in the area of possessions, purchasing them prayerfully and holding them loosely. A number of years ago the Lord moved me to designate a certain percentage of income to give away. And to make sure the challenge to live simply and trust the Lord consciously would always be there, this percentage was to increase each year. Sometimes the temptation comes indirectly - "Does this, too, belong to the percent to be calculated, Lord?" But there is great joy in becoming increasingly free of being possessed by things.

When Ron Ornsby mentions that his room is above a certain Chinese restaurant, there is instant identification. "Some of the strangeness surrounding me as a *gweilo* [foreign devil] is removed. I now have at least one point in common with their world that they can relate to easily."[424] What makes it possible for him to make these changes? He relates candidly, "Living here has forced me to redefine my 'comfort zone.' I have learned to develop a sense of contentment that is not based on a clean, attractive environment, but on a heart that is focused on Jesus." And this newly developed sense of contentment is not as otherworldly as it may sound, "Often as I negotiate the stairway, I simply pray, 'Lord, help me look beyond the trash. Help me rejoice in you.' After such a prayer, the trash and dirt remain, but they no longer affect my attitude."[425] And there are similar feelings, reactions among team members.

No doubt, Ornsby's credibility has increased. But this was not an automatic process with him; it was a result of deep spiritual reflection on the concept of the poor and how Jesus related to the poor. He consciously raised his awareness of the poor and needy. "To give attention to the

---

[423] Bonk, ibid.
[424] Ornsby, "How to Be Downwardly Mobile," 397.
[425] Ornsby, ibid.

> *This was not an automatic process; it was a result of deep spiritual reflection on the concept of the poor and how Jesus related to the poor.*

poor, I must overcome the hardness of my heart. I become indifferent to the poor when I exaggerate my own needs without considering the needs of others."[426] He claims his change is through no merit of his own. "Study, reflection, and models can clear away fog, but only the Spirit of God can make us both willing and able."[427]

What about the issue of missionaries from non-Western countries raising personal support? Is not even raising a percentage of it in their home countries expecting too much? The issue of where support is raised and by whom touches on two important financial issues: the redistribution of wealth for Christ's Kingdom and the exercise of faith. To accept contributions "anonymously" without establishing some kind of empathetic connection between the donor and the cause, the missionary or the mission project and the people whom it benefits, is to circumvent the biblical intention of giving. The New Testament recounts money and goods given in the context of relationships and responding to needs. Giving is not to soothe the guilty conscience of the donor, which is what anonymous giving affords. For both the giver and the receiver to be blessed of God some kind of relationship must be there, primarily one supported with prayer. Then the receiver can be assured of the heart-support behind the gift and can pray with the Apostle Paul that God will meet the giver's needs as well: "Not that I seek the gift, but I seek the profit that accumulates to your account. . . . My God will fully satisfy every need of yours according to his riches in glory in Christ Jesus."[428]

Giving and receiving is reciprocal and cyclical. It is reciprocal in that both the giver receives and the receiver gives; both receive benefits. And it is cyclical in that the giver gives ultimately to God, who uses it to meet the needs of others, and the giver and the receiver are both blessed by the redistribution of God's resources, and He gets the praise.[429] Faith is the reliance on God to meet these needs. All missionaries should be challenged to trust God for their needs, not just to meet financial needs, of course, yet they are very concrete. Dr. Bill Bright, founder and president of Campus Crusade for Christ, which is now the largest evangelistic

---

[426] Ornsby, ibid.

[427] Ornsby, ibid., 399.

[428] Philippians 4:17;19.

[429] Faith missions have a structural advantage in relating missionaries to donors and keeping the contact personal, especially those faith missions who require the missionaries to secure at least a percentage of their personal support and maintain the contact to those supporters themselves.

movement in the USA with affiliates in 180 plus countries, speaks of how God stretched his faith in the financial area by allowing him to trust God to meet his needs as a fledgling movement. With a staff of two and needing only a few thousand dollars a year, he learned to trust Him for more staff and the conference center, Arrowhead Springs, as well as for the present needs of the ministry worldwide which amount to several hundred million dollars a year. One of the earliest innovations which Bill Bright feels was God-given, was the principle that all full-time staff members are responsible for seeking out a group of Christians and churches with whom they communicate directly and regularly, who give to support their ministry and their modest living allowance. This has enabled the ministry to expand even in poorer countries and has insured that a network of friends stand behind the missionaries in prayer. It is a unique relationship for which I myself can look back with gratitude on twenty-seven years of God's faithfulness through these dear people. It has not always been without problems, times of need, times when the living allowance could not be paid or ministry purchases, thought crucial, could not be made because the money was not there. But it has fostered a deep trust in God as the Giver of all good and perfect gifts and has encouraged a large circle of Christians to be directly involved in missionary giving.

Brad Walz laments that many Latin countries have an unhealthy dependence on North America as the provider of their needs which he calls a "spirit of poverty and inferiority." This spirit paralyzes them into a comparison of themselves with richer countries and a dependence on them instead of saying, "We can do all things through Christ!" Walz continues, "However the potential is there, waiting to be unleashed."[430] God expects each church, each missionary to trust Him directly to meet their needs. Veronika Elbers writes about Indonesian colleagues, "Missionaries and missions must find new ways to be financed better in the future. Of course, this does not mean that the principle of faith missions should be eliminated."[431] She includes the concept of expanding the circle of supporting friends in the home country, avoiding dependence on the West, with the caution of keeping the living allowance modest so as not to put distance between the missionaries and the people.

John Pobee sees this financial over-dependence as inhibiting growth, keeping "imperialized Christianity" and paternalism in place. "The Peter

---

[430] Brad Walz, "The hard road to missions vision in national churches," *Evangelical Missions Quarterly*, October, 1994, 416.
[431] Veronika Elbers, *Protestantische Missionare aus Indonesien*, 187-188.

Financial over-dependence inhibits growth, keeping imperialized Christianity and paternalism in place.

Pan syndrome[432] and paternalism have been manifested in the areas of financial support and church structures. The historic churches have been self-governing in the sense of having African or Asian leaders. But not infrequently that gain is mortgaged because of an unnecessary material over-dependence on churches of the North and a burdensome wasteful un-contextualized church structure."[433]

It is a step of faith for non-Western as well as Western missionaries to trust the Lord for support and provide an opportunity for the Lord to confirm His leading in their lives. Psychologist Dr. Henry Cloud, is a proponent of the method of each missionary being responsible for raising support for his/her/the family's living allowance and ministry expenses. He finds it psychologically very healthy for a missionary to take personal responsibility in this area, as with all other areas of life. Even when the non-Western missionaries are not able to raise full support from their own countries, they can still be responsible for seeking out Christians who stand behind them in prayer and personal support. The situation of Polish missionaries was alluded to before. In our mission, before the political revolution, they were subsidized by monies raised in the West, primarily in the USA. Afterwards, however, many more Christians were able to respond to God's call to serve full time and a graduated subsidy system was devised to support them (with an annually decreasing subsidy) until they had their full support team. Questions were more numerous than answers then and now. If the addition of new supporters did not cover the loss of subsidy each year, attrition was preprogrammed. This was often the case in Southern Europe. As soon as the subsidy was gone, if the missionaries hadn't been able to get enough new supporters, sad to say, they left. Sometimes they were "bought off" by other mission groups willing to finance them.

This was not a case of inequity in levels of living allowance, but perhaps a miscalculated, unrealistic subsidy scale or failure on the part of the missionary to faithfully look for new supporters. Each country needs to be considered as a separate entity, taking into consideration such criteria as: per capita income, the Christian population, history of missionary giving of that Christian population, advantageous tax laws for gifts, relation of missionaries to the church (their home churches) and outside

---

[432] The Peter Pan of James Barrie's imagination refused to grow up. Such a syndrome, then, holds one in a child-parent symbiosis indefinitely.

[433] Pobee, "Christian Mission towards the Third Millennium," 9.

source of gifts (partner relationships in the international community), just to mention a few. Some individual non-Western missionaries, through marriage, acquaintance with short-term missionaries, relatives, etc., had ties to the USA and other Western countries, a privileged status. Such contacts were generally encouraged, with some cautionary restrictions. For example, special permission needed to be obtained to travel to the West to raise support. Correspondence was encouraged, but not with a "begging" mentality. In light of the limited resources and the desire to have every Christian who is qualified and called to be able to minister full time, it seems wise to continue such a course. Being free from just receiving "hand-outs" means that a good degree of personal responsibility must be taken by the national as well as the expatriate missionaries. There is then no subtle creating of categories or classes of missionaries.

> *Being free from just receiving "hand-outs" means that a good degree of personal responsibility must be taken by the national as well as the expatriate missionaries.*

Although our mission channels a certain percentage of the finances that the Western missionaries raise for their personal support to the non-Western missionaries[434] (in addition to raising money to subsidize their living and ministry allowances), this is not enough. A plan was devised to encourage more support through personal contact (as personal as it could be with language barriers). In this plan, called "Two-of-a-Kind," the USA missionaries designate and raise a certain amount per month for the non-Western missionary they choose. If they have not had any international experience, they choose the country and are paired up with the missionary of that country.

But this was still not getting enough funds to the non-Western missionaries. I have experimented personally with building more bridges. As a "known entity" (in contrast to the national missionary) in my home country, with an albeit limited sphere of influence, and having the trust of a team of supporters and churches for several decades, an attempt has been made to try to channel that trust to national missionaries I have trained who have relevant and credible ministries. Though still in the embryonic stage, this seems to have met with good response in my supporters who have a heart to support nationals and are glad to have a recommendation from someone who is much closer to the situation. It is a great source of satisfaction, too, to be used of God not only to give but

---

[434] In Campus Crusade for Christ, USA 5 percent of what each individual missionary raises goes into international ministries. In Campus für Christus, Deutschland, 3 percent is allocated.

also to help others give and see partnerships established. There is a relationship created between the national staff and new supporters which is then strengthened by communication, such as prayer letters, and prayer. Most national staff have access to someone who can translate a letter for them occasionally. In addition, I mention these nationals by name in my letters regularly so information for prayer is current. This plan probably works well because it encourages national involvement in their sphere of influence without undue dependence on the West, not any more than most Western missionaries have. It only stands to reason that if there are funds to be used for missions and they are primarily in the West, they should certainly be distributed more evenly. But this is difficult without the personal relationship and the trust involved. Caution must still be taken in maintaining non-paternalistic and impartial relationships.

The ministry budget is another area in which there are large discrepancies. There are tensions if money is available for equipment only if the Western missionary is there to supervise and control it. Further, there are also tensions created by status-conscious super modern mission offices in poorer countries, the assumption being that university educated national missionaries deserve this. There is even financial competition between different missions and churches for qualified nationals. Often misunderstanding is created when there is enough to buy new office equipment but not enough to help augment national missionaries' living allowances. It is not unusual that an empire of complicated systems and machinery has been created which take special training to maintain in addition to the money and access to repair parts. "What happens when the [Western] missionary leaves and takes his 'treasure chest' of funds with him, his effective transportation and the volumes of materials and literature?"[435] Cultural sensitivity is needed to know how to equip a local office efficiently without being presumptuous, giving the wrong impression to the community. And resources should not be connected to people, per se. National missionaries can learn to work with computers and other equipment as well. The question is: What does the ministry really need in the way of equipment that can be repaired locally? "Power, more often than not, is directly associated with resources."[436] Power is not bad, it just needs to be curbed and kept in check.[437] A good personal check is to renounce power, refuse to wield it,

> *What equipment does the ministry really need that can be repaired locally?*

---

[435] Myron S. Harrison, *Developing Multinational Teams* (Singapore: Overseas Missionary Fellowship, 1984), 158.

[436] Harrison, ibid., 159.

[437] See "Power" in chapter 1.

and to delegate it. Does accruement of expensive equipment really accomplish our purposes or does it just increase our status and divide us from the very ones we want to reach? In the final analysis, do we spend more time with people or with things? Can local means of transportation not be used rather than expensive vehicles? "The result will undoubtedly be fewer outreaches and possibly fewer programs, but this may be good if it means the work is more indigenous and able to be carried on by the national when the expatriate leaves. Furthermore, using local transport gives numerous occasions for direct contact with the people which a closed vehicle will never provide."[438]

Important cultural values attached to giving and receiving must be considered in the host culture. Giving too freely may create flashbacks to the colonial era. "Understanding colonialism is essential for the expatriate. It is so easy for the outsider to set in place again the very processes that have enslaved people before." This is hardly maliciously intended; it is usually inadvertent, perhaps even well-intentioned generosity. "But underneath all these humane person-to-person motives are some powerful economic forces . . . Colonialism's tendency to degrade both the colonized and the colonizers is still the great tragedy of social exploitation." [439]

Some nationals are deeply hurt by the flaunting of wealth. They conclude that to a great extent the wealth was attained by colonialization, plundering the South. In this sense, it is indeed appropriate to think of missions as paying retribution for these evils. If retribution is being paid, then the power and the money must be released - no strings attached. "If that is achieved, it will be the most critical illustration of the message which the Christian message brings, namely that life in its abundance, which God desires for his creation, is possible only in self-emptying ourselves of power in its manifold forms. To that extent a de-imperialized mission is a 'kenosis.' "[440]

In the Yap culture, for example, to receive is humiliating, because of the fear that one cannot repay in kind. But "missionaries feel pressured by nationals to give goods and money to them."[441] The obligation for reciprocity, responsibility to pay back in kind, is created by giving. It is therefore humiliating in some cultures to create a situation in which repayment would be impossible. "The giver occupies a position of superiority and power over the receiver. The only way that one can restore the

---

[438] Harrison, *Developing Multinational Teams,* 159.

[439] Ward, *Living Overseas,* 232-33.

[440] Pobee, "Christian Mission towards the Third Millennium," 9.

[441] Lingenfelter, *Transforming Culture,* 96; 100.

balance in the relationship is to repay the debt." Refusal or inability to pay creates shame and an avoidance pattern.[442]

A knowledge of the worth of things and maintaining a careful balance is imperative. Neither the feeling of exploitation nor the feeling of humiliation are comfortable in a relationship. Virtually no assumptions can be made about similarities between cultures in this area. There were such misunderstandings created by giving and receiving among Germans from the two Germanys (which grew apart inside only 40 years). Understanding what and how much, is appreciated is crucial to establishing mutual relationships. Giving too much can create feelings of inferiority if reciprocity is not possible. I remember inadvertently surprising East Germans more than once with what seemed to them to be lavish gifts. To put things into perspective, among friends it became necessary to tell the price paid. And it was imperative to receive what they so graciously lavished on us as their guests when we visited, even when we were thoroughly embarrassed by the sacrifice that represented. Embarrassed? It's difficult to describe how we felt. Their having to stand in lines, asking favors of friends and paying extremely high prices just to entertain us seemed exorbitant. The next day, shopping in the grocery at home in the West, we paid one-fourth of the price for coffee and we shook our heads at the inequities, our hearts went out to them and we again became angry at a system that repressed their people in such a way. And they were not poor. East Germany was the envy of most socialist countries. Only by comparison to their cousins in the West did they feel "taken in" by their government. With those really poor, one dares not flaunt "wealth." It must be shared in such a way as to not hurt their person and make them feel inferior.

Such inequities may seem easy to resolve on the surface, but they affect relationships deeply. Mistakes will surely be unavoidable but an attitude of love, trust and understanding will pave the way and cover a multitude of sins. Love will ask for advice and feedback discreetly. The multicultural team should, in time, provide the secure environment needed to discuss these issues openly and learn from one another. The non-Western missionaries, after they recover from their shock of exposure to the consumerism and wealth of the Western world in the form of cultural baggage brought by the Western missionaries, may be gracious and kind enough to realize that the Western missionaries need time to process their impressions and make changes in their lifestyle.

There is, however, hardly an excuse today to exclude such sensitizing experiences from the training phase of missionaries. More and more, the

---

[442] Lingenfelter, ibid., 87.

decision must be made by the missionaries before they leave the home shore, and before their reputation needs to be repaired. Participating in a mission project in the Two-Thirds World is a sobering conditioning factor. Doing a Bible study,[443] a personal evaluation and a family evaluation in conjunction with the mission project, will enable one to plan for the future more realistically. In the preparation phase one can consciously start scaling down in "expensive" possessions and entertainment. Indeed, a "conversion experience" is needed for every Western missionary in relation to lifestyle and finances. Light must be shed on this blind spot in most missionaries' consciences. It is never too late to learn. The following are suggested, by way of summary, to aide in this conversion experience, in developing a new conscience in regard to lifestyle and finances: Ask God for compassion and the ability to see people as Jesus did. The study Jonathan Bonk gives in his book would be very appropriate.[444] When exposed to poverty, don't repress it, don't harden your heart. Decide as a family how to remove this huge barrier to communicating love. Remember Jesus said, "where your treasure is there your heart will be also."[445] Purposefully choose/agree to enter the culture through the simplicity of the bonding process[446] to sensitize you to the culture before you make grave errors. Gain input and feedback from trusted nationals as to what is offensive and how to simplify your lifestyle. Learn to give and receive in culturally relevant ways. Ask for input from your national colleagues before making major purchases. Consider how you use your discretionary income. Does it create a dividing line between you and your national colleagues, your children and theirs? This kind of feedback is often not volunteered but it should be solicited and an evaluation should be made. Ask God to keep your heart compassionate and sensitive to the (potential) damage that financial injustices produce. Help your non-Western colleagues by channeling funds from your home country to them. Represent them to your supporters as trustworthy recipients, helping others back home learn to give in a culturally relevant way.

> *Ask God to keep your heart compassionate and sensitive to the potential damage that financial injustices produce.*

> *A "conversion experience" is needed for every Western missionary in relation to lifestyle and finances. Light must be shed on this blind spot.*

---

[443] See Jonathan Bonk's study in *Missions and Money*, 86-107.

[444] Bonk, *Missions and Money*, 85f.

[445] Luke 12:32-34.

[446] See Brewster in *Perspectives on the World Christian Movement*, 452f.

Removing barriers to the credibility of the gospel in the areas of finance and lifestyle is a major undertaking; it is a spiritual venture. To ease tensions, eliminate misunderstandings and experience real *koinonia* missionaries must remove the inequities in the multicultural team.

Women Missionaries

Certain subdivisions of the multicultural team have uniqueness or needs warranting special attention. Each nationality deserves special attention, different age groups, families, singles, men and women. Each team itself will want to look into these. But two sub-groups of multicultural teams warrant a bit more explanation because of their unknown or overlooked uniqueness: the non-Western (*Two-Thirds* or *Three-Fourths* world)[447] missionaries and women missionaries.

For every North American man there are two American women on the mission field.[448] In the last decade of the twentieth century it is indeed rare to find a woman on the mission field who herself has not been called to missionary work. Most mission agencies have learned from the mistakes of mission history that the work of a husband can be greatly hindered, if not sabotaged, by a wife who is not suited to the rigors of the mission field, is not herself called or fights her husband's call at every turn.[449] Such hardships are hardly conceivable these days because of many factors: most missions wisely require wives, as well as husbands, to go through the personnel process, checking to see that both are qualified for missionary service. Faster transportation means that couples don't necessarily have to be separated for long, even under extenuating

---

[447] For explanation see footnote number 168 on Two-Thirds and Three-Fourths world missionaries.

[448] Ruth A. Tucker, *Bis an die Enden der Erde* (Metzingen: Franz, 1996), 7. Some say that the number of women from Western countries is decreasing. Paul Goring, *The Effective Missionary Communicator* (Wheaton: Billy Graham Center, 1991), x.

[449] One of the saddest stories indeed is that of Dorothy Carey, who neither shared her husband William's call nor wanted to go with him to India. She was pregnant with their fourth child when he presented her with the news and although she did go with him, she suffered many nervous breakdowns and had to be confined in the end. James R. Beck, *Dorothy Carey, The Tragic and Untold Story of Mrs. William Carey* (Grand Rapids: Baker, 1992). Countless biographies relate extended periods of separation of husband from family "for the sake of the gospel" but without regard to the familial duties of these fathers before God.

circumstances. Children are a natural inroad into a new culture. Helping them find their way in national schools, interacting with teachers and other parents, are profitable ways of making contacts which can lead to the communication of the gospel. Improved national schools, as well as the possibility of home schooling in pioneer areas, make it possible for parents and children to stay together. But even in a missionary children's boarding school situation, separation from the parents is rarely longer than four to six weeks at a time. A major emphasis on the family, particularly

> *Mission is increasingly seen as a partnership by the married couple, and the responsibility of the father and mother in the family is rightfully recognized as a "showcase" of Christian values.*

fathers taking responsibility for the care of their children, has freed up many mothers to invest their spiritual gifts in the missionary calling. Mission is increasingly seen as a partnership by the married couple, and the responsibility of father and mother in the family is rightfully recognized as a "showcase" of Christian values. Such emphases are a welcome relief especially for the majority of the missionary force: women.

And yet, for example, psychologist Raymond Chester's counseling experience and survey measuring tedium and burnout showed missionary wives rating higher than their spouses, regardless of the length of time married or on the field. His conclusion: "missionary wives are experiencing stress because of the 'role' into which they feel they must fit along with confinement (both cultural and social) that they experience in the home."[450] They are not appendages to their husbands; they are persons whom God has gifted and sent out as well. A way must be found to utilize the many gifts, resources and experiences of these wives, so they feel fulfilled and useful.

Missionary biographies are full of the struggles of women, single women in particular, suffering from loneliness on the mission field. In many cultures there is no single subculture; singleness is a non-entity and after a certain age, considered abnormal. A single woman expressed her frustrations: "I must think like a man, work like a horse, and act like a married woman." This contributes to the feeling of being a misfit in the new culture. In my research, this is especially true of younger singles. Older singles, if they have adapted well, have gained respect and feel included more as an aunt, mother or even grandmother figure. But loneliness is not an imagined state of the mind; it is a very real deficit with

---

[450] Raymond M. Chester, "Stress on Missionary Families Living in Other Culture Situations," K. and M. O'Donnell eds., *Helping Missionaries Grow*, (Pasadena: William Carey Library, 1988), 172.

which one has to contend. Although it is not exclusively the problem of women or singles, it is nevertheless a significant factor that single women deal with almost without exception and long beyond the period of initial adjustment. Loneliness is that hollow devastating feeling that one has to carry the weight of one's life alone, without being in a position to really share it with anyone special, with someone who really cares. There is little comfort for one caught in these feelings if there is not real empathy from other significant persons. And this is the challenge of the multicultural team. The forces of loneliness can sometimes be so overwhelming that the vision is lost. The single missionary is so engulfed by not having a counterpart to share her deepest needs, thoughts, ideas, and visions with that a part of her languishes and dies. This search for "significant people" may drive singles to leave the mission field to find this person, or to marry the one waiting at home who does not share her calling. Lottie Moon, Amy Carmichael, Helen Roseveare all share these needs frankly, but also talk of a certain "death" to these desires, a willingness to let Jesus fulfill them through other relationships - particularly with national colleagues of the same sex. Happy are those singles who find a partner who shares the same vision and joins them in their work. A missionary friend of mine was praying earnestly for a male colleague to join her in working with Middle-Easterners in Europe. God answered her prayer miraculously by giving her at age 45 a husband, a single pastor from her homeland who joined her in the mission work. There is great respect for her for not having compromised her calling and for him following his wife to a field new to him where he has to learn two languages and cultures at the outset! Missions can use other men of this quality and vision!

And yet for most single women, if the statistics of the past have relevance today, the future of many will involve a coming to grips with the reality of long-term singleness and finding good, creative solutions for overcoming loneliness. Finding good friends can make all the difference in staying psychologically healthy. Friendships within the team tend to be the most natural if the cultural barriers

> *Finding good friends can make all the difference in staying psychologically healthy.*

between team members are not too difficult to overcome. Again, what makes it hard for single women is that friendships with Christian women in the host culture, if not on the team, are sometimes viewed skeptically with the fear on the part of the colleagues that team secrets could be circulated or that other nationals might be envious because friendship with the missionary created advantages. For others the fear that lesbianism might be suspected makes them overly cautious about their friendships.[451] True, some lesbian relationships have come to the fore as a result of culture stress. Mission agencies need to be prepared to deal with the women involved, as a result of their personnel profiles and psychological tests, preferably preventatively. But one need not assume that women who prefer to live together are lesbian. This is culturally conditioned as well as a personal preference.

What is the responsibility of the multicultural team? An awareness of the deep need loneliness is and an understanding that the need must be met, is the starting point for the team. Jokes about them as spinsters should be stricken from the vocabulary. A single will be preoccupied with the deficit and paralyzed to be able to give herself fully to the Lord and to others in ministry if this need is not met. It bears underscoring that a deep personal relationship to the Lord Jesus and an ultimate trust in Him to meet her needs is the foundation for singles and married alike. But Jesus calls for the arms of other team members to hug and comfort, their mouths to compliment, encourage and pray, their minds to think creatively to include them in activities that will enrich their lives, and their ears to listen to their problems, fears and desires. I have observed that often those missionaries from stratified societies (Western societies in which only singles mingle with singles, marrieds with marrieds, and sometimes men only with men and women with women) have the tendency to stay within the stratum for social activities. Going beyond makes them feel uncomfortable and to relate to "unlike" sub-groups in another stratum and they tend to shift into a "duty" or "ministry" mode. No team member wants to be included just out of a sense of duty - but sometimes even that is better than nothing! Nor do they just want to be thought of when a babysitter is needed, although regular contact with children is healthy for all. If one finds, however, that a single team member has drawn back, one should initiate and include her, gently bringing her back into fulfilling relationships. This is especially true of singles from non-Western cultures who are not used to being alone or to verbally expressing their needs. The happiest singles are those who are also in a position to take the initiative and include others in their plans. They don't wait to be invited. With a variety of women from different cultural backgrounds in a multicultural team one cannot make generalizations about their desires or needs.

---

[451] Also observed in Elbers, *Protestantische Missionare aus Indonesien*, 131.

Non-Western Missionaries

Often the *Two-Thirds* world missionaries on a team have advantages over their Western colleagues. If they are serving in a non-Western country their identification with the people and their acceptance by the people comes more readily. They may share similar economic conditions; their normally simpler lifestyle doesn't create a barrier. The national struggle to free themselves from colonial powers gives them a common bond. Their country may be smaller and relatively "insignificant" on the landscape of the world map creating a kindred spirit with the host country. These missionaries are used to the so-called hardships of a developing country: slower modes of often irregular transportation, unpredictable bureaucracy, electrical brown-outs or black-outs.[452] These do not bother them as they do the technical-dependents of the West. Nor do the heat, the rains, the roads, or most foods. Some may possess an obvious affinity which gives them great advantage at the market place - the same color of skin; they are charged lower prices than whites. The chief of the village where the Indonesian missionary Lotje Peleau worked exclaimed she was one of them because she was dark skinned and she could "carry things on her head. The white man [woman] can't do that."[453]

There is no doubt that because of common hardships encountered, non-white, non-Western missionaries are sometimes more welcome in most parts of the world than Western missionaries.[454] An African mission team has been welcomed to China. Asian teams help to correct the mistaken notion that Christianity is a Western religion or that funds can be imported from the West. Non-Western missionaries identify more quickly on a social and economic level; the bond tends to be stronger. This is all the more reason to have well-adapted multicultural teams, whose credibility can be judged as a whole.

Because many non-Western missionaries come from more group-oriented cultures, they have many advantages. They are usually perceived as being more friendly and people-oriented. They experience less stress in being with people all the time and therefore require less private

---

[452] I am indebted to Veronika Elbers for her research with Indonesian missionaries, many of whom have served on multicultural teams, in *Protestantische Missionare aus Indonesien*. Her research validates to a great extent many observations and findings of my own research.

[453] Elbers, "Dritte Welt Missionarin," 48.

[454] Elbers, *Protestantische Missionare aus Indonesien*, 103.

space or personal time. They are good team members and follow the leader without the critical questionings of their Western colleagues.

The Indonesian missionaries Veronika Elbers described tend to be more flexible because they are not time-oriented. Their lives are governed by people, not plans or things. They are very hospitable and giving of their time and possessions. This is a natural inroad to identifying with most host cultures. In addition to this, they view the world as a composite whole, without separating humans from nature or the natural world from the spiritual world. Their faith is holistic and kindred to all but the Western world. There is no artificial separation between the sacred and the secular; they speak of God more readily than those in compartmentalized worlds. Religion is not a private issue. Many have

> The domination of one nationality puts pressure on the minority cultures to adapt in two directions. It may even produce a split deep within.

experience in relating to those of other faiths, especially Muslims. And when they serve in a Muslim country, they often have less difficulty getting visas.[455] Although all of these qualities cannot be generalized to include all non-Western missionaries, many do characterize them and thus give them advantages over western missionaries.

An area of concern, particularly for non-Western missionaries as a minority culture in a multinational team, is the domination of one nationality (other than that of the host country) which has become normative for the team. This puts undue pressure on them to adapt in two directions - toward the host culture, which is natural, and towards the majority culture in the team, which is unnatural. This is not only a disadvantage for them; it can even cause a splitting deep within. And it can indicate cultural imperialism on a team level. "No longer can one national entity dominate the decision-making process and control the agency with its secure advantage of power and prestige."[456] The same principle that applies to the agency applies to the team. It is no longer acceptable to allow Western cultural influence to dominate in a non-Western host culture. Nor is it appropriate to allow one non-host culture represented in the team to dominate another. This will, in the long run, have a detrimental affect on the involvement of minority cultures represented in the team. Eun Moo Lee, having worked in a multicultural situation, addresses misconception about the nature of missionary work. He feels the Western missionaries see it as being a one-way street, West to East. "Their [The

---

[455] Elbers, *Protestantische Missionare aus Indonesien*, 104.
[456] Peter Hamm, "Breaking the Power Habit: Imperatives for Multinational Mission," *Evangelical Missions Quarterly*, July, 1983, 180.

Westerners'] sense of superiority, escapism, and stubbornness of their own cultural ways, make it difficult to accept joining forces."[457] This is a sad commentary on the body of Christ. In most cases such dominance is just the force of habit, unconscious and non-malicious in intention. If this attitude of dominance is conscious, the cultural value of efficiency often causes the missionary to resist change. But such habits must be broken if all God's children are to be respected equally. Partnership in mission and in multicultural teams means, in reality, a division of power, healthy checks and balances against subtle nationalist and racist tendencies in us all. Even when the weighty resources of experience and finances would tend to tip the scales in one direction, true partnership tips them back. This need to control is perhaps only a camouflage of the missionary's underlying motivation or psychological need. A well-functioning multicultural team, in which feedback and corrections are encouraged, is a good safeguard against these tendencies. No one culture is allowed to wield influence and power unchecked.

> *No one culture is allowed to wield influence and power unchecked.*

In a parachurch mission, particularly in a pioneering situation, domination can also be exerted when a certain denomination is in the majority. The proliferation of denominationalism is an historical reflection of one avenue of church reform in the Western cultures, but increasingly from non-Western cultures, too. As dear as the traditions are to the missionaries, they do not represent the history of the church in the new land. Because many denominational practices arise out of historical settings, they, too, represent "cultural baggage," which needs to be carefully evaluated before it is passed on unfiltered, and certainly should not be communicated on the same level as biblical values. It is this historical syncretism which needs to be guarded against. "Such [denominational] divisions in mission an African church and for that matter, any other church, can ill afford because Christian missions are in stiff competition with other faiths and ideologies to win peoples."[458] Church splits, which have caused the formation of new denominations, cannot hold on to any bitterness that may have precipitated the split, if the gospel of hope is to be communicated to our world. (Many splits are due more to the charisma of personalities than to true theological issues.) The dialogue over theological differences can be a source of renewal for the church. Missionaries must be alert to the danger of transplanting *their* brands of de-

---

[457] Eun Moo Lee, "West and East Must Get Along - a Korean Missionary Speaks Out," *Evangelical Missions Quarterly*, July, 1983, 193.

[458] Pobee, "Christian Mission towards the Third Millennium," 9.

nominationalism, thereby overshadowing Christianity and Christ. Although there is a residue of some churches and mission agencies unwilling to work together, there is a "growing awareness among the churches today of the inextricable relationship between Christian unity and missionary calling, between ecumenism and evangelism."[459] On most mission fields where missionaries of different denominations work, the denominational barriers seem to fade in significance against the enormous needs to be met.

By comparison to their Western colleagues, the non-Western missionaries have disadvantages, too. Unfortunately - and this is a sad reflection of ethnocentrism in a team, they often bear most of the burden in adapting in team relations. Even if the missionary agency is Western in its origin, this inequality should not be so. It is unfair, yet it reflects a present reality. Bruce Nicholls has commented, "Third World missionaries . . . - need to understand at least four cultures: the Bible's, that of the Western missionary who first brought the gospel, their own and that of the people to whom they take the gospel."[460] If they are the only one on their team from their country, they also have the disadvantage of not having someone with whom to speak their own language or to check their cultural observations and perceptions. In the case of the Indonesian missionaries, it meant that they were unusually quiet in the team meetings, not due to their personalities, but rather because they didn't feel confident enough in English. They tended to learn the language of the host country more quickly, however. And as a consequence, they fought loneliness. Their teammates often had little knowledge of their home country and didn't know how to interpret their reactions. On the other hand, little knowledge is dangerous; some Western missionaries thought all Indonesians (for example) were this way, and Lotje Pelealu was hurt that they couldn't distinguish between her personality and her culture.[461]

> *The non-Western missionaries often bear most of the burden in adapting in team relations.*

---

[459] World Council of Churches, "Mission and Evangelism - An Ecumenical Affirmation," *International Bulletin of Missionary Research,* April, 1983, 65.

[460] Bruce J. Nicholls, *Contextualization: A Theology of Gospel and Culture* (Downers Grove: InterVarsity, 1979), 72.

[461] Elbers, "Die Dritte Welt Missionare," 47. In her dissertation, Veronika Elbers recommends that Indonesian missions should concentrate on a few fields of service to save resources of strength and money. This would also mean that there would be at least a substantial minority of Indonesian missionaries on teams of which they are a part, reducing the stress. Elbers, *Protestantische Missionare aus Indonesien,* 186.

Further, it is intimidating for most non-Western missionaries to be in a team with Western missionaries. They tend to see themselves as less confident or even less capable than their Western counterparts. This may be a carry-over from the national history of colonialism, or they may come from countries that have been oppressed by others for centuries. In both cases, there tends to be a lower self-concept that is sometimes compensated for by a greater nationalistic spirit.

Often the non-Western missionaries have to learn two languages simultaneously or in quick succession: English for their training and team, and the language of the host culture. Is it really necessary for them to learn English? Ideally, one would think that the team language would be the language of the host culture or country. But in reality, it is sometimes necessary to learn a language for official communication in the mission agency and among missionary colleagues beyond national borders. This is sometimes necessary for team communication initially, though eventually the national language should be used. The lack of being able to participate fully in the team as a result of lack of English language fluency contributed to the intensity of culture shock.[462] Most small countries or new sending countries cannot offer the missionary training, therefore English is needed for training in another country. Not knowing English can cause one to be excluded inadvertently in direct communication, in continental conferences, meetings, literature and communiqués. Knowing English is sometimes a very important prestige factor and an avenue for providing equal opportunities.

Conflicts or misunderstandings can easily be caused by such differences. For example, for holistic peoples (most non-Westerners) it seems artificial to separate work and leisure time. If the host culture (for example, Germany) is oriented to this and the team is strict about days off and accounting for vacation time, then proper provision should be made to be sure the non-Western missionaries also have plans for those times and also have the finances to afford them. Sometimes a holistic view of life may look like a lack of industriousness. One must be careful not to judge one another.

Related to a low self-concept, the lack of fluency in English and the lack of participation in meetings is the tendency to not want to upset the harmony in the team. This lack of analytical-critical thinking is a result of the group being viewed as more important than the individual. Serious "heated" discussions in the team may tend to disrupt their sense of harmony and should be explained. They will need time to be able to express their thoughts and feelings and eventually their own opinion. Until then

---

[462] Elbers, *Protestantische Missionare aus Indonesien*, 121-23.

it is incumbent on the other team members to read their non-verbal communication well to sense their approval or lack of it, their confusion or anger. Drawing them out will help them in the process of learning to dialogue. But this must be done without embarrassing them in the group. And indeed, for anyone speaking in his/her second or third language, finding the right words to communicate, without hurting someone or disrupting the harmony, is a challenge. Again, it's most helpful to meet on common ground, using the language of the host country.

A group-oriented culture is usually a shame-oriented culture, which means it will be difficult for non-Westerners to admit mistakes and ask for forgiveness. A high degree of vulnerability will be required for them to overcome the horrible sense of shame they feel. To learn to do so will require much love and acceptance from

> *Direct confrontation should be avoided with non-Westerners from a shame-oriented culture. A safe atmosphere of love and acceptance should be cultivated.*

the team so they don't feel like a failure as a missionary.[463] Direct confrontation, as such, should be avoided. Instead, a safe atmosphere of love and acceptance should be cultivated by Western missionaries as an example.

Due to the different lifestyles around them non-Western missionaries may be tempted by materialism to a greater degree than at home. Those who have grown up having to make choices of this nature can help them develop criteria for their purchasing. Many non-Westerners have had the strong pressure of a family/group at home to dictate or support their moral choices; in the absence of such strong controls they may be the enemy's prey. Older, more experienced missionaries can have strong fatherly or motherly influence on them in such vital areas. They need the team as a strong framework for their personal life and ministry.

Related to the values of saving face and prestige is the desire of some to take on more responsibility than they have training or gifts for.[464] Although opportunities for growth should be available at regular intervals, no missionaries should overestimate their own capacity at a given time, especially those who value saving face. The team leader and experienced missionaries should help all younger missionaries with such choices so they are more likely to succeed in their attempts. Job descriptions and the outlining of intermediate steps with supervision and guidance will help the younger missionary grow with minimal perceived loss of self-worth.

---

[463] Elbers, *Protestantische Missionare aus Indonesien*, 116.
[464] See Veronika Elbers, *Protestantische Missionare aus Indonesien*, 115-16, 120-21.

The Western missionaries should rejoice with their non-Western colleagues in their advantages and help them in their difficulties. And the non-Western missionaries can learn from the Western missionaries in areas where they are weak and help the Western missionaries in their areas of weakness. Mutual respect, with consideration and understanding of each other's difficulties, is crucial. At the outset, considerable explanation will be necessary. Nothing should be taken for granted. Misunderstandings should not be allowed to accumulate without the opportunity to discuss them. In the process, one filters out one's own cultural biases. The advice of the enemy of our souls to his underling, as fantasized by C. S. Lewis, shows the futility of ignoring feedback and demonstrates the law of diminishing returns:

> Let him [the Christian in his charge] do anything but act. . . . Active habits are strengthened by repetition but passive ones are weakened. The more often he feels without acting, the less he will be able ever to act, and, in the long run, the less he will be able to feel.[465]

Envying others, or comparing oneself to another, also gives the enemy a foothold to destroy the unity, not uniformity, that Jesus wants to preserve.[466] Respecting each other's spiritual experiences, as well as gifts, adds depth and breadth to team relationships. Refraining from reacting with suspicion or a critical attitude, just because something is unusual, communicates positively. For example, lack of spontaneity or emotion should not be judged as deadness and lack of spirituality. There is much we can learn from one another. To be sure, there are barriers and problems, but multicultural teams are worth it.

---

[465] C. S, Lewis, *Screwtape Letters* (Grand Rapids: Baker, 1969), 51.
[466] John 17:11.

5

SELECTION, TRAINING AND FORMATION OF

MULTICULTURAL TEAMS

Selection

The selection process of most established mission boards is far too complicated to comment on thoroughly in this context. References will be made to those qualities and qualifications necessary to evaluate for working in multicultural teams, in particular. Certain assumptions will be made regarding the general selection of missionaries for international service.

It is assumed that those applying for international missionary service have a vital relationship with the Lord Jesus Christ and that their faithful walk with Him has been observed by the local church and/or home mission agency. They should have had proven ministry experiences in their home culture (or be willing to acquire such experience before leaving for the field). Further, it is assumed that they have been called to communicate the gospel in another culture. Prior international experience, perhaps of a short-term nature, is helpful in determining adaptability. Written recommendations from the home church pastor, church or mission leaders, international project leaders, etc., supplement the information. A teachable attitude and a heart for God are indispensable.

In the initial interview, the mission becomes more acquainted with the person(s) and his/her/their call and desire for service. In the case of a couple, both partners apply and are interviewed separately. It need not be said how detrimental it is to missionary service if one of the partners is not whole-heartedly behind the idea or is, perhaps, not even qualified. A series of written evaluations, including psychological assessment, spiritual gift evaluation and personality tests, and a medical assessment, give a more complete picture, help determine suitability for the field, and point out possible potential problem areas that need to be resolved before raising support and going to the field.[467] A minimum of biblical training is necessary for all. Those in "non-vocational" ministry need proper theological training. The last phase of assessment in our mission, for example, is contingent upon completing an international training course with internship in a cross-cultural environment. Potential difficulties can then be detected through a closer, day-to-day interaction with the candidate.[468] "In my work with missionaries, I have become concerned at the degree of stress caused by unwise selection," says Dr. Marjory Foyle.[469] Many heartaches and personal failures on the part of candidates, and frustrations and griefs of team members could be avoided by careful selection and dealing with potential problems *before* the candidate reaches the field. Dr. Foyle specifically mentions the importance of sharing such test results with the candidates. In skilled hands, they are wonderful tools for growth.

> *Many heartaches and personal failures on the part of candidates, and frustrations and griefs of team members could be avoided by careful selection and dealing with potential problems before the candidate reaches the field.*

With this information available about a candidate, one looks for flexibility, the ability to cope with stress, the ability to work well with people and to assess themselves realistically, a healthy self-concept and humility. Niebuhr explained this mix in the character of Jesus well - He had proud humility and humble pride.

> The humility of Christ is not the moderation of keeping one's exact place in the scale of being, but rather that of absolute dependence on God and absolute trust in Him, with the consequent ability to remove mountains. The secret of the meekness and the gentleness of Christ lies in his relation to God.[470]

Certain personality types are not recommended for international service because the risk to the team, as well as to the individual, is too great - the immature personality structure, over-rigid types, hysterical or

---

[467] Esther Schubert, "Current Issues in Screening and Selection," Kelly O'Donnell, *Missionary Care,* (Pasadena: William Carey Library, 1992), 87.

[468] If this policy is adopted or practiced, this requirement should be very clear in the mission's application materials, even including the suggestion that those applying wait to officially terminate other employment until official acceptance has been given by the mission. It would be unfortunate if an applicant has terminated his other job, assuming he is accepted by the mission when this was not the case.

[469] Foyle, *Honourably Wounded,* 84.

[470] Niebuhr, *Christ and Culture,* 27.

histrionic personalities, overly-mystical types and overly-aggressive people.[471] These are extremes, personality disorders that would certainly present difficulties in a multicultural team. "People with personality disorders can consume hours of time every week, exhausting fellow team members, causing divisions, and monopolizing time of vulnerable fellow missionaries." [472]

Great and varied is the cultural and psychological baggage that missionaries carry with them to the field.

> Some have come onto the field having experienced childhood trauma (e.g., sexual, physical, emotional abuse) which has never been resolved. They may function at high levels for years before the symptoms of unresolved trauma begin to come forth in a way that can no longer be ignored.[473]

It is not uncommon for such unpleasant repressed memories to come to the conscious level of memory when under stress. In such situations, missionaries need help to process their past and may need to be removed from the stressful situation for a time. There seems to be a marked increase in the personal and psychological needs of candidates and missionaries. This mandates careful selection and training of candidates before they enter a stressful cross-cultural environment and a member care setup to help missionaries on the field and when they return for home leave.

> A few decades ago the average missionary candidate seemed better prepared to face the demands of cross-cultural service, in terms of spiritual, emotional, and interpersonal issues. The gap between what is required of missionaries *as persons*, and the skills they

---

[471] Foyle, *Honourably Wounded,* 92-93. Further detail on "immature personality structure" is in Foyle's book in chapter 8. Immature personality structure was mentioned earlier as those who have brought yesterday's problems to the field with them. In working through these problems on the field, they consume an inordinate amount of team resources, and the missionary may not have at his disposal the help he really needs. Over-rigid types are those who are unable to seek and use other's opinions. They find it impossible to work in teams and vice versa. Histrionic personalities tend to wear their emotions on their sleeves and that in exaggerated forms. They are self-centered, over-dramatic and exhausting for the team. Over-mystical types suddenly hear God's call and leave the work of the ministry to the others; they overburden the team. Finally, over-aggressive people are destructive to themselves and others, divisive and harmful.

[472] Esther Schubert, "Current Issues in Screening and Selection," 81. Schubert also describes various personality disorders, which would be unsuitable for cross-cultural missionary service.

[473] Karen Carr, "Trauma and Post-traumatic Stress Disorder Among Missionaries", *Evangelical Missions Quarterly*, July, 1994, 246.

bring to the challenge, seems to be growing. Widespread spiritual, emotional, and family deterioration in Western societies contributes substantially to this lack of personal preparedness.[474]

Almost all missions are wise enough to inquire about sensitive issues in a candidate's past, such as drug abuse, addictions, and different aspects of sexual behavior. It is generally agreed that if such problems have not been dealt with successfully prior to going to the field (or joining a multicultural team), the intensity of the cross-cultural environment and additional stresses will increase the chances of a relapse markedly.

In addition to jeopardizing the team, there may well be legal implications if mission policies are not clear on issues of extra-marital relations, and heterosexual and homosexual relationships of singles. Dr. Foyle cites as an example a recent survey of overseas church leaders on their willingness to receive homosexual missionaries as "a 100 percent negative response from the 80 percent of leaders who replied." She goes on to say that this view, plus clear mission policy, may help missions decide how to handle the issue. "What needs to be known is the present situation and personal belief of the person concerned."[475] All agree that it is better to deal with such issues in the home country than to expose a candidate to the stresses of a cross-cultural environment.

The qualities and qualifications mentioned all apply equally to expatriate and national candidates. All will be exposed to similar stress while working together. Whereas the national missionaries may be "exempt" from language learning stress per se, their ability to deal with the strains of a multicultural team in their homeland, learning non-verbal communication patterns of teammates, etc., will require as mature a person as the expatriate is required to be. One would be amiss to allow two different levels of qualifications for the sake of expediency. This would be to pre-program team problems detrimental to partnership.

> *The qualities and qualifications mentioned apply equally to expatriate and national candidates.*

Issues referred to before, such as a single missionary's attitude toward his singleness, the health of a couple's marriage relationship, as well as a divorcee's recovery and view of remarriage, are crucial in selection. Previous occult experience also must not be overlooked. Missionaries are "prime targets" in spiritual battle. In addition to being sound theologically on this issue, the processing of previous personal experiences is necessary.

---

[474] Kenneth Williams, "A Model for Mutual Care in Missions," 50.
[475] Foyle, *Honourably Wounded,* 95.

An overload due to a combination of "stress items"[476] prior to the additional stresses of training, support raising and moving, such as loss of a loved one, major financial or personal setbacks, would probably be reason enough to delay the move to the field. Close observation of the candidates during the training phase to determine how well they are dealing with their stress is imperative.

Mission leaders have observed that materialism has entrenched itself in many personal values. "It takes years to wean people off this culture," comments George Verwer. "The spiritual revolutionaries, the kind that Jesus talks about, really are on a head-on collision course with a lot that our 'all-American way' stands for." [477] Roger Greenway expands on this: "most of the missionaries sent out by Western churches have been enculturated since childhood to take for granted a very high level of physical comfort and an array of gadgets to entertain and make life easier."[478] Because the "need" for many possessions and the money to support a lifestyle, an almost insurmountable barrier is created on the field and within the multicultural team. Missions must look for people who are content with a simple lifestyle, who hold things loosely in their hands for God to evaluate and dispense as He pleases.

Another important criterion of an international missionary is the ability to train others. This "Barnabas" quality of enjoyment in seeing others grow and take responsibility, even eventually outshine the missionary-trainer and have responsibility over him/her, requires healthy humility and the perspective of what God wants to do in international

> *Another important criterion of an international missionary is the Barnabas quality, the ability to train others.*

missions. A commitment to serving with and under national leadership is indispensable.

In researching missionary profiles, Paul Goring discovered that 74 percent of his respondents were "SJ,"[479] people who seek order in their

---

[476] See the table "Stress Factors as a Result of Life Changes" in chapter 3.

[477] Jim Reapsome, "Recruiting: The Right Way and the Wrong Way," an interview with George Verwer, *Evangelical Missions Quarterly*, April, 1983, 141.

[478] Greenway, "Eighteen Barrels," 129-30.

[479] SJ and NF are personality types as defined by the Myers-Briggs Type Indicator (MBTI), a test developed by Isabel Myers and Katharine Briggs to test the personality of normal (as opposed to pathological) people, based on C.G. Jung's psychological types. Personalities are divided into four bipolar mentalities based on the way they view the world and make judgments or decisions about what is perceived. Isabel Myers and Mary MacCaulley, *A Guide to the Development*

environment and who dislike ambiguity, hardly the type to deal with the stresses of missionary life easily. Only 11 percent were "NF" personality types - people-persons, natural communicators, gentle, warm, understanding and tolerant.[480] This fact has implications for selection as well as team formation. It may also explain high attrition rates. Some estimate that 35-50 percent of first-termers don't return to the field.[481] Because of the time and money investment in training candidates for service, mission agencies will want to select people with endurance.

African leaders, such as Mukengeshay, Campus Crusade for Christ's Director in Zaire/Congo, want missionaries "who want to work with us, not just to come to do a particular job." They want those "who will invest their lives in people, who have servant hearts, and who will live as God wants them to live."[482] Nigerian Yemi Ladipo adds, "Missionaries are judged purely on an individual basis - often more on their *attitude* than on their *drive* to bring about rapid changes where they work."[483] He defines the quality of humility needed as not dwelling on sacrifice or having an exaggerated view of self, but being available to serve and willing to earn respect.[484]

Spiritual gifts in Western cultures are often seen very individually, rather than holistically and in the context of the whole body of Christ. It is the difference between asking, "Where do *I* fit in?" or "Where *could* I *fit in*?" The latter is a view towards cooperating with other teammates, on the one hand. There is often a real fear, on the other hand, that one will be "relegated" to a task that needs to be done, from which one will never be free. This is especially true of administrative tasks. As a medical doctor Helen Roseveare struggled with this when she found herself chained to a desk, filling out forms in her latter days of service in Zaire. Finally she realized that this was only possible because nationals, whom she had trained, were able to do the medical work but that the government required that she, a licensed physician, had to write and sign the reports - no one else could have done it. But spiritual gifts (and training) should not be overlooked for too long; unrest, even resentment could set in. It is unfair to consistently ignore gifts and training and assign certain

---

and Use of the Myers-Briggs Type Indicator (Palo Alto: Consulting Psychologists Press, 1985), 1.

[480] Paul Goring, *The Effective Missionary Communicator*, 8.

[481] Jim Chew, *When You Cross Cultures* (Singapore: The Navigators).

[482] Mukengeshay, "We Need People With a Heart to Serve," *Agape Impressions*, a publication of Campus Crusade for Christ (now Agape Europe), April, 1989.

[483] Yemi Ladipo, "Qualifications for Long Term Missionary Service in Africa," unpublished, n.d.

[484] See Appendix A for other highly rated qualities.

rather mundane tasks just to nationals (bureaucracy), for example, or to women (note-taking or refreshments). There is less tolerance of this in the younger generation of missionaries today. Samuel Rowan comments:

It is not sufficient to ask the missionary to be flexible. Flexibility which asks people to be less than what God has gifted them to be is no virtue - even if it seems to fill a needed slot in the mission machinery. Flexibility needs to be linked to creativity so that change opens up new vistas and opportunities for the use of the missionaries' gifts and knowledge.[485]

This is basic respect for the stewardship of God's gifts in one another. Whereas gifts of the Spirit are particularly important in team formation, the fruit of the Spirit is crucial for selection.

Methods and procedures in the selection, training and placement of missionaries is becoming more of an issue in North America. Local churches are playing a larger role in the selection and direct sending of missionaries. "They want a say in the screening of candidate papers from the sending bases, in the acceptance of probationers, in the orientation of new workers (especially in their cultural adjustment), and in their stationing. They also want to be involved in disciplinary matters which concern missionaries."[486] Churches and sending structures that are too independent tend to contribute to the transplanting of churches, structures and all (i.e., denominationalism), which indeed creates new problems. Except in true pioneer situations where no local church exists, when individual churches send, individual churches should receive.[487]

> *Under whose jurisdiction do the missionaries serve? Mission policy should be very clear on this issue.*

This means the expatriate missionaries of that church would work directly under the auspices of an already existing church, with the appropriate sensitivity to it. Mission policy should be very clear on this issue. Under whose direct jurisdiction do the missionaries serve? Many national church and mission leaders are upset, to say the least, at what they get. Clear communication between sending and receiving churches/countries is mandatory to minimize conflicts and to avoid jeopardizing the partnership. Conversely, a clear job description for the missionaries, without too much change after they ar-

---

[485] Samuel Rowen, "Doing Mission," *Evangelical Missions Quarterly*, July, 1983, 247-48.

[486] Alastair Kennedy, "The Other Side of Africa: How Churches and Missions Are Grappling with Issues," *Pulse,* Feb. 14, 1986, 4-5.

[487] Dr. Wagner handles this issue in the section on basic approaches to evangelism in his book of *North American Protestant Missions in Europe: A Critical Appraisal* (Bonn: Verlag für Kultur und Wissenschaft, 1993), 133-140.

rive, communicates honesty and respect. In our mission, the pre-selection is done in the home office but the receiving country makes the final selection after the candidate's file has been reviewed. These days, to eliminate some variables and gain a better picture, a trip to the field (for an internship or summer project) is made. From the psychologists who deal with missionary problems, however, comes the feedback that, in general, "the need is for a greater focus on the missionary's personal growth, with emphasis on spiritual, emotional, and interpersonal issues . . . beginning at the candidate stage, and continuing throughout missionaries' careers."[488]

In some countries, Germany, for example, employers, including mission agencies, are legally prohibited from using psychological testing as a part of their screening process. This is difficult because the only substitute is knowing the missionary candidate well, usually over a period of years and in various situations. The only solutions I know are to either make such testing voluntary and motivate the candidates to take the testing for their own good, or to withhold final selection until after the training period. This is a very difficult thing to do with today's tight job market and particularly if a whole family is involved. Not all the tools for testing are available in various languages, which makes it difficult for those not fluent in a major language. In most cases, sending missionaries is no little investment of time and money, both theirs, that of the mission agency of the sending country and the mission or church of the receiving country. Great care should be taken to minimize the risk involved that the missionary won't "make it" and will return home early and in disgrace. Serious personnel decisions have been made by ignoring the candidate evaluations of either the home country, the trainers or the receiving country in which the candidate has done an internship. One does neither the missionary nor the ministry a favor when one sends candidates who are not ready, i.e., not mature enough, or not suitable for the field. The chances of their maturing spiritually and psychologically is usually greater in their home country where the stress levels are lower (and the resources perhaps greater). But this is not to say that only perfect, mature missionaries will be sent to the field. And in some cases, problems will surface that may not have back home.

Careful, thorough selection is necessary to avoid missionary failure, which could well have been predicted and prevented. In addition to embarrassment due to failure which the missionaries themselves experience, drop-outs for the mission and national church are costly not only financially, but in their credibility in the host country.

---

[488] Kenneth Williams, "A Model for Mutual Care in Missions," 50.

Training

If, indeed, missionaries are being sent to work on multicultural teams, it is wise to conduct at least part of their training in a multicultural context. It is assumed that all missionaries, expatriate and national alike, should receive the same training. Not all sending countries are equipped yet to do the training, but there are missionary training centers available now on all continents.[489] It is a grave mistake to undertrain national missionaries. Again and again during the interviews I conducted, the national missionaries asked if it would be possible to receive the same cross-cultural training. And their colleagues echoed that it would indeed be of benefit to team and interpersonal relations.[490] And it is a mistake to undertrain any sub-group of the team; mothers and wives also are often not given training opportunities. It is a disservice to them and to the team as a whole. Selecting a location for the training (one location for each region that has sending countries) should involve a not-too-high cost of living area, without political risk, with cross-cultural ministry opportunities and livable for the trainers (who with their families live there all the time). This "reality training" helps the candidates keep uppermost in their mind that they are going to be working with such a conglomerate group, even if the future composition may be different. Learning sensitivity to teammates during training may help eliminate unpleasant surprises later. In addition to this, a language learning method is learned (LAMP) in a nearby country or subculture whose language most candidates don't speak. This is usually combined with a "sensitizing experience" in a poorer country. During the training process, candidates should decide which approach to language learning they plan to take upon arriving in the field, as well as their plan for "bonding" to the people of the new

> *It is assumed that all missionaries, expatriate and national alike, should receive the same training.*

---

[489] In conjunction with the Lausanne II Congress, the Missionary Consultation on Missionary Training met to discuss the training of *third-world* missionaries. Further coordination and networking of information in being done by Dr. William Taylor, including a publication "The Occasional Bulletin of the International Missionary Training Fellowship" as well as his book, *Internationalising Missionary Training: A Global Perspective* (Grand Rapids: Baker, 1991).

[490] Veronika Elbers' research confirmed this as well; missionaries in cross-cultural situations and in multicultural teams felt under pressure and burdened by not being able to deal with their stress. *Protestantische Missionare aus Indonesien,* 119.

culture. Field personnel can be asked to set up housing with nationals, if this is desired for their initial period of time in the new country.

These few months in preparation for many years of service are well-spent. I have observed cases where decisions were made to forego the cross-cultural training in the name of expediency. The sacrifice has been too great. Either the missionaries have had to struggle too much initially when jumping into their jobs to fill an urgent need and remaining ill-prepared for the cross-cultural move, or the team has had to take the brunt of the fatal decision of missionaries who insisted they were exceptions and didn't need the training. The excuses are legion: too costly, too hard on the family, the job is urgent. But in the end it is almost always more costly for all concerned if the training is neglected.

> *The excuses to be exempted from training are legion: too costly, too hard on the family, the job is urgent. But in the end it is always more costly for all concerned if the training is neglected.*

Other issues related to packing and shipping of goods must be considered. A previous trip might have provided insight in this area. If the candidates have begun to develop a conscience about their lifestyle in the new country, they will then ask themselves questions about the implications of their lifestyle on their future ministry. This will be helpful in considering practical issues on packing.[491] Families should be encouraged to take time to carefully discuss lifestyle issues at this juncture.

Most missions expect that the missionary will have completed some kind of biblical/theological training commensurate with the future assignment. In addition, some missions offer on-going biblical training courses. Missiologists recommend that biblical theology be given precedence over a systematic approach to theology, which tends to be more tied to the culture (and denomination) in which it was developed. If possible, the missionary should become acquainted with writings or courses from a theologian of the future host country (or at least a theologian who shares his/her form of logic). Learning to approach the application of Scripture with another cultural context in mind should be part of the training. Sometimes doing an internship with a multicultural team in a subculture (city, rural, youth, ethnic) in the home country offers this opportunity without learning language. Ideally, this is done concurrently with the more "theoretical" parts of cross-culture training.

There is a real tension in deciding what elements are *necessary* in the initial training phase. There are costs involved in centralized training

---

[491] The questions, as outlined in the section on finances in chapter 4, are helpful at this juncture for such decisions.

courses, families have to be moved, plus time is another important factor. There seems to be a trade-off between the time required for good, thorough training and an initial shorter period of orientation/training (with more training in context), which gets the candidates to the field while their motivation and energy levels are high (giving them a better chance to adapt). There is no one good solution. Experimenting with all the local factors to find the best solution for the trainers, candidates and field personnel involved will yield the answer. But sometimes mission agencies don't have that kind of personnel in the field to do the training. Sometimes the selection process is so tied to the training phase that it would be premature to send candidates. The ever-present demands of a field ministry usually imply that most of training be up-front. A number of factors need to be considered. Therefore, in our mission, theoretical training elements have, admittedly, been reduced to a minimum and put into a practical context.[492] The following training courses are offered over a ten to twelve week period:

I.   Culture and Language
II.   Personal Development
III.   Interpersonal Relationships
IV.   Biblical Perspectives for Mission
V.   Field Preparation

Included in these courses are area studies, exercises in language learning in a non-English speaking country, and non-Christian religions. Active learning is emphasized, and the team itself forms the basis for a case study. For example, they each analyze their country's values, as well as their own personal cultural values, and share these with one another. The candidates take the learning style inventory and do a personal profile test to learn as much as they can about themselves, their partners and their teammates.[493]

It is my experience, however, that a grasp of world history from a cultural perspective different from one's own is generally missing. As would be expected, in each country history is learned as it is related to that country, often woefully lacking a world perspective. Some history, particularly as it relates to the way one's home country is historically

---

[492] See Appendix D for Agape International Training. In William Taylor's *Internationalising Missionary Training*, 12 models of international missionary training are described. I have offered this model as the one I helped develop and which I teach.

[493] The Personal Profile System is published by Performax Systems International, Inc., U.S.A. and in Germany by Unternehmung Dieter Boy, Bonn. The Learning Style Profile can be obtained through Harvard Business School or Massachusetts Institute of Technology.

perceived by the host country, would be a vast enlightenment. "A willingness to criticize one's own cultural values and national policies in the light of global suffering and injustice," is recommended by Ramachandra.[494] This aspect could be included in their area studies project.

Training needs to continue on the field in the areas mentioned above in ministry-related and life-related training. It should never be suggested

> *Training needs to continue of the field; "member care" dare not be overlooked.*

that the training is "over," even when the initial training courses may have been successfully completed. But training, at this phase, should hardly be theoretical. In fact, it will be hard to separate it from such aspects of ministry, as such. The special emphasis in this "training phase" is soliciting feedback from nationals. Creating the atmosphere and channels for feedback is one of the first tasks upon arrival. The volume of feedback may diminish over the years, but these channels should always remain open and active. The In-Field Training Handbook[495] encourages the application of pre-field training (Agape International Training) after arrival in the host country. Field orientation, when at all possible, should be given by nationals. One factor, which most missions have become aware of, dare not be overlooked - namely, training and "pastoral care" (also called "member care," or "shepherding,"). It cannot be entirely delegated. Seminars may be offered, conferences held, experts invited to speak and counsel, but the leadership has the responsibility for the people, team members one for another, and each missionary for himself/herself. Responsibility cannot be abdicated at any level. Mission leaders, however, feel this lack of responsibility on the part of missionaries at times. There is a general feeling that missionaries of the new generation have the idealism of the pioneering missionaries, but lack their inner fortitude. "There are great expectations (often built by our society) of being a part of a loving community that will meet my needs. I fear that much of the interest in teaming arises from unspoken and yet real expectations of a safe group that will minister to me."[496] This could well be the result of the dysfunctional family situations in Western culture today.

Cross-cultural training cannot be dealt with here exhaustively, though it is of utmost importance. Such training for multicultural teams is a necessity for *all* team members. A combination of careful, prayerful selec-

---

[494] Ramachandra, "The Honor of Listening: Indispensable for Missionaries," 408.

[495] Roembke. See chapter 2 for a more complete description of in-field training.

[496] Frank M. Severn, "The Critical Context of Today's World Mission," *Evangelical Missions Quarterly*, April, 1992, 178.

tion and good training in a multicultural team context results in a positive prognosis for the longevity of service from joyful, growing missionaries.

Team Formation

There are many factors influencing the formation of teams that have the potential of functioning well together. My survey and interviews have shown that those missionaries who have worked on such teams are very positive about their own experiences, to the extent that they would almost always prefer the multicultural team over a single culture team. This, however, is not just based on their love of variety or on cognitive factors. It is based primarily on human factors, on the inner workings of the team as a whole. Much of what is good for a multicultural team is also good for a monocultural team. The neglect of taking such factors into consideration for a multicultural team carries graver consequences with it, however.

With the psychological and personality tests,[497] Learning Style Inventory,[498] and team tools available in major languages today, there is no good reason not to avail oneself of them in placement and team formation. For example, using the Learning Style Inventory I determined the best methods for my language learning. Because I am an AC-RO combination,[499] a structured environment was best for organizing the new language, also giving me a place to ask my questions after reflection. The LAMP method was chosen as a supplement to make sure the learning

---

[497] The Minnesota Multiphasic Personality Inventory (MMPI) is still considered the "gold standard" in basic psychological testing. It detects personality disorders and personality traits from bruised backgrounds. It will not detect sexual deviancy, which the Rorschach test can. All these tools must be used by trained personnel counselors. Other tests used by mission boards are the Millon Clinical Multiaxial Inventory (MCMI), which identifies personality disorders and is best used in a clinical setting; the Myers-Briggs (MBTI), the Sixteen Personality Factor (16PF), the Taylor-Johnson and the California Psychological Inventory (CPI) provide general personality descriptions but may not detect personality disorders or personality traits due to severe bruising. For this the MMPI is indispensable. The MMPI-II, while decreasing some ethnic bias, has not yet been normed for the missionary population. Esther Schubert, "Current Issues in Screening and Selection," *Missionary Care*, 85-87.

[498] This tool analyzes the preferred learning process and plots them in four categories or combinations thereof: **A**bstract **C**onceptualizer, **R**eflective **O**bserver, **A**ctive **E**xperimenter, and **C**oncrete **E**xperiencer.

[499] AC means abstract conceptualizer, RO reflective observer, two types of the Learning Style Inventory.

was practical and accent-free and to provide contact with people. For my learning style and personality type it was difficult to use, though none-theless, very profitable. The "Personal Profile System,"[500] for example, has a team building component, as do many other systems. Without ex-amining the details of each system, it is safe to say that these tools can predict, to a degree, personality types who will have difficulties with one another. Even if two missionaries are mature personalities and spiritual Christians, their working styles, for example, may be so different that they will be a constant "thorn in the flesh" to one another, causing them to perhaps spend an inordinate amount of time resolving conflicts instead of enjoying the team and getting on with the ministry. No one should ever expect a problem-free team situation, but if problems can be mini-mized the team will be in a better position to minister in the culture, as well as to one another. A rule of thumb to avoid unnecessary conflict, is not to place people of "too different" or "too similar" personality types together. Some degree of difference results in a complementary team; too much difference means they will inevitably be preoccupied with ironing out

> *A rule of thumb to avoid unnecessary conflict, is not to place people of "too different" or "too similar" personality types together.*

the tensions in the team, or the tensions will be ignored, with resultant implications for the missionaries (drop-out) and ministry (lack of credi-bility). Too much similarity may lead to competition. With too little similarity there may be boredom or lack of appreciation and cooperation. Homogeneity is not the goal. "There is a blessing in the broadness of being different. The unity in the body of Christ is not based upon Chris-tians being similar to one another, but their being different from each other . . . one body with different members."[501]

Although such tests are not fool-proof, they are good indicators. In a mission agency as large as Campus Crusade for Christ USA, it is not possible for all the candidates to come to the headquarters to be person-ally processed. The interviews are done by trained field staff, references are collected from reputable sources who know the applicant personally, the picture is completed with tests and all of this information is evaluated by the personnel department, which then makes a recommendation to the leadership. Sometimes, because of the great needs on the field, pressure will be exerted from field leadership to accept an applicant who does not

---

[500] The Personal Profile System examines work styles and the most beneficial environment for these types. It is useful in understanding different motivational environments. Further team tools are described in "Tools for Team Viability," by Kelly O'Donnell in *Missionary Care*, 184-201.

[501] Lehtinen, "Through the Prism," 13.

meet all of the qualifications, or by whom "questionable" areas have come to light. Almost always, when the opinion of the personnel or human resources department has not been followed by the leadership, a tragedy or major setback has resulted. Either the missionary returns before the term is up, he/she is sent home, no mutually satisfactory placement can be found for the missionary, or the stress in the team reaches a breaking point. The expertise of the leadership is mostly to be found in the area of vision and motivation for the task. They are usually good recruiters. For maximum benefit for the whole mission, including the co-workers on the field, however, the recommendation of the personnel department should be followed.

The tests results and the spiritual gifts alone don't paint the whole picture. Personal maturity and Christian growth are qualities that are desired by all team members in their teammates, since these qualities smooth the way in resolving conflicts. It is a great help to the team to have them all arrive in the host country and begin language learning and/or ministry at the same time. They all have the same starting point and are more or less equally motivated to become acquainted with each other as well as the host culture. Some teams have the advantage of having gone through training together. One such British-American team was to pioneer in the capital city in a Central Russian republic, with a large Muslim population. They got to know one another, thought, prayed and brainstormed together about the future as they were in their training course in a Muslim neighborhood in Birmingham, England.

Granted, it may be difficult if the team is too large, and there are not enough national missionaries on the team to balance them out. (1:1 is a good ratio, or having more nationals than expatriates.) Ideally, the team should have (or move toward having) a majority of nationals plus one, at the most two, expatriate culture(s), and be five to eight persons in size, not counting the children. (If the expatriate families are large, the adult team should be kept smaller, in order to have more time and energy to deal with the needs of the children.) I have interviewed some missionaries on large teams with eight to thirteen different nationalities; the cultural issues are overwhelming. A large team can be sub-divided to manageable sizes and reasonable complexities. This aids team dynamics and personal growth. In multicultural teams a problem is created if there are always new team members being added. It invariably creates the impression to the community and gives the feeling to the team members that the team is always floundering around in culture shock, sapping the energy and time of those (particularly nationals) in their second, third, fourth terms. The missionary "veterans" don't get the attention they deserve; they are continually forced to decide what's more important - team relations or ministry relations and responsibilities. This is a false dichotomy, to be sure, but the tensions are there. The feeling is like being in a large family with newborn twins demanding attention and ruling the family's routine initially, and with teens who have so much upheaval in their lives, who nevertheless hold back, waiting for a time to express themselves. With such high felt needs of the younger ones, necessary time for the teens doesn't come. But they are in desperate need of guidance and care too, just a different kind. Newcomers deserve care and orientation, therefore to have a constant flow of them is not advantageous either to them or the team. It is disruptive to a team as a whole, which is not big enough to spread the responsibility. It is recognized that not all situations are ideal, but if one can influence the decisions, the plans for the teams, it is well worth the effort to carefully consider these matters. It's not as if only newcomers need care. The ministry itself needs an outward orientation, as well, not just an inward concentration.

A majority of expatriates from one culture, with team leadership in its hands, is too great a concentration of power and influence, no matter how positive and benevolent that power may be. Only a national majority, or leadership in national hands, warrant such a concentration of power, but not without checks and balances that keep it sensitive to other cultures represented on the team. If the team is very large, such as the headquarters situation described earlier, it can be made more manageable by subdividing it (by departments or into home groups). A sociogram can be used with great benefit in such a context. Though I am not aware of any mission that follows this procedure, it would be interesting to see how teams would be formed through the use of a sociogram, in which each team member can (confidentially) choose individuals with whom they would prefer to work and/or associate with in a home group. An impartial person then takes these slips of paper with the preferences and forms groupings. Almost inevitably at least one or two of the person's choices can be respected. There is something to be said for the missionary having a voice in choosing persons with whom s/he would prefer to work closely. This fact should be respected with increasing tenure of service and age and as it becomes clearer to the missionaries themselves and the leadership of the mission who works best with whom. Experienced missionaries most often say that who they work with is as important, sometimes more important, than the exact job description itself.

> *A majority of expatriates from one culture, with team leadership in its hands, is too great a concentration of power and influence, no matter how positive and benevolent that power may be.*

Friendship provides mutual support on the field. If friendship sooner or later becomes the basis of the team, one has accomplished a lot. This is not to recommend that friends be added to a team in which others are strangers; it is recommended that in forming the team of different personalities, such potential for friendship is there. Sometimes this is only possible the second time around, after the initial term or job responsibility is finished. There is usually a greater commitment to work through problems and difficulties if one has been involved in the decision.

"In forming teams, the synergistic variable is important to *mix* the right combination of people together," says Harrison.[502] Synergy is "the simultaneous action of separate agencies which, together, have greater total effect than the sum of their individual effects."[503] This is team compatibility to the highest degree, in which each individual is able to function to the ultimate. This ideal situation presupposes personal maturity, spiritual vitality and willingness to overcome obstacles together. It means team members whose gifts complement one another, are placed together so they can work 60-70 percent of their time in an area of personal strength, but whose personalities, temperaments and leadership styles don't clash.

Although some missionaries indicated they would prefer people of the same age on their team (primarily assuming they would understand each other better and could play and pray together more naturally), others desired a mentoring situation with at least one more experienced missionary. Even if the team had all young missionaries, good relationships with experienced missionaries are enriching. Mentoring may be one of the most effective methods for personal development.[504] In urban mission situations, a variety of these needs can be met by interfacing the different teams. This can be accomplished if there are many teams in one location or in a larger city, though it can work against unity in the small team.

Teams might better be formed after the missionaries have reached a Level 2+[505] in the language and after the initial bonding period with peo-

---

[502] Harrison, *Developing Multinational Teams*, 162.

[503] *Webster's New World Dictionary of the American Language.*

[504] Harrison, *Developing Multinational Teams*, 162.

[505] See Brewsters' LAMP for "Self-rating Checklist of Speaking Proficiency" levels. Level 5 is "native speaker" *but* it is roughly estimated that each half level requires twice as much time as the previous level. For example, if from Level 0 to Level 0+ one week was required, from level 0+ to Level 1, then, two weeks would be required when working at the same intensity. At this rate, Level 2+ could potentially be reached in 19 weeks. Note: the Brewsters speak in terms of "units" rather than "weeks" because tougher languages demand more time and some people learn more quickly than others. The time can be estimated once

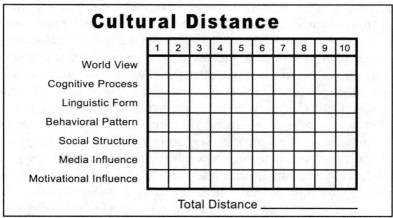

Figure 11: Cultural Distance (adapted from Hesselgrave, *Communicating Christ Cross-Culturally,* Zondervan: 1978, 102)

ple of the host culture, unless all missionaries are in the same phase of language learning and have no common language other than that of the host culture, or there is a national majority in the team to which the missionaries can bond. It also presupposes that the "pool" of missionaries is large enough to draw from at any given time, so as to form such compatible teams. This is, unfortunately, not the case, at least when each mission agency tries to do it alone.

In any case, whether the team is formed all together or little by little, each of the new members can be loved and accepted as he or she comes. Each represents a new person and culture to be approached with more than mere curiosity. The new missionaries need the wisdom and listening ear of the senior missionaries. This is really only possible in a team of manageable size.

Cultural distance among the expatriates seems to play a significant role in the team. In the stresses of a cross-cultural situation, some missionaries feel they have found "allies" or "kindred spirits" when they meet up with, not only those from the home culture, but those from close (M-2) cultures as well. Hesselgrave offers a grid for evaluating cultural divergence quantitatively. The higher the number assigned, the greater degree of divergence is perceived between the home culture and the host culture (or, in this case, the culture of the teammate). The higher the sum of these numbers, the greater difficulty one might expect to encounter in

---

language learning begins because, if the intensity of study is constant, the ratio remains the same.

communication.[506] When dealing with most international mission agencies, one usually expects a "Western orientation" to mission and missionary work. "I found that the Korean type of individualism made it hard to cooperate with Western missionaries," [507] comments Eun Moo Lee, who worked in Indonesia with Western missionaries. "Generally speaking, Korean missionaries want to develop their own style and own strategy in the mission field," he continues. In his case, a Western leadership style evidently won out, presumably because he, as a Korean with the Indonesian nationals were in the minority and had little influence. The superimposing of a leadership style on another culture might have been avoided if nationals had had more of a voice in the matter, or if an expatriate majority would not have been so overwhelming.

Placing culturally close expatriates together has been known to backfire, however, when the missionaries themselves prefer the more different and exotic culture. My coworker, a West German, once expressed that she felt the Americans were more appreciated in the ministry in East Germany (then a closed country) than the West Germans, in general, because they were less known, even forbidden, and more "exotic." This is sometimes an individual issue, however.

Even when cultures are similar, sometimes there may be animosities due to past wars and conflicts, which are nearly impossible to overcome in team formation. Although these relationships must be entered into cautiously, bridges can be built. The Japanese and the Koreans, the Russians and the Poles, the English and the Irish, the East Germans and the Russians, etc., have national, historical and political animosity, even though they are culturally closer to one another than to some other nations. Larry Poston adds from his experience:

> The bitterness between Korea and Japan is legendary. In India, there are deadly rivalries between Muslims, Hindus, and Sikhs. There are warring factions in the Philippines . . . and hatred between Cambodians and Vietnamese. In some Asian countries, Westerners are more welcome than certain other Asians.[508]

In some cases, hostility can be expected, which missionaries must be willing to endure if they want to work in that country. A multicultural team is a helpful backdrop in facing these hostilities. In such placement decisions, however, the missionaries affected should be consulted. Especially in cases where hostile attitudes exist, ethnocentrism is an aggravating characteristic. It is most aggravating in multicultural teams. "Na-

---

[506] Hesselgrave, *Communicating Christ Cross-Culturally,* 101-02.
[507] Eun Moo Lee, "West and East Must Get Along," 193.
[508] Larry Poston, "Should the West stop sending missionaries?" *Evangelical Missions Quarterly*, January, 1992, 61.

tional pride is valid, but a sense of national superiority in international mission is not."[509] Cheering for one's national team during the Olympics or World Cup is great fun - because it's a game, but partisan support in all other areas of life is looked upon critically. In fact, according to the missionaries surveyed, a bit more loyalty is expected from the missionary for the host country than for the home country. One must be careful not to act protectively of one's "own national identity," as if something valuable were being destroyed by adapting to the host culture.[510] Missionaries should be primarily representatives of Christ, not ambassadors for their country, whose actions are, more often than not, hard to defend in an international setting.

Whereas it would be difficult to say that there are impossible cultural combinations, it is clear that there are some very complementary combinations. These should be recognized and teamed up wherever possible.

Although Americans may be sometimes welcomed with open arms as exotic pieces of humanity, they are more often than not castigated as the "ugly Americans" because of their cultural baggage. Not wanting to add to the diatribe against Americans, I nevertheless realize that, as a highly visible world power and major source of missionary resources, something must be done to stem the tide that causes the American culture to produce so many "candidate flaws." Happily, there are wonderful exceptions to these examples. On the surveys I conducted, some American missionaries were actually mentioned by name as those with whom national missionaries wanted to work. What follows is neither a categorical judgment nor a call for a moratorium on American missionaries, as such. It can be taken, perhaps, as a warning to North American Christians, their families and churches, to evaluate their values,[511] to see them as the

---

[509] Butler, "Tensions," 417.

[510] Appendix A, items E.5 versus E.7, and C.14.

[511] Most enlightening is the list of American values that Ronald Iwasko offers that "all too often prevail unrecognized and unchallenged in our churches and in our schools:
1. Worth is determined by achievement.
2. Determination + persistence + knowledge + resources + time = success in just about everything.
3. *To know* and *to do* are the really important things; being is taken for granted.
4. Education is the key to success.
5. Role = individual worth.
6. Equality in everything is important.
7. Money can buy things that will achieve status that will bring us acceptance so that we can be happy.
8. Time is linear, proceeding toward a goal. Therefore, progress is paramount.
9. The individual is supreme."

non-Western world does and to begin to make important changes. Their children, as with Christians of their generation, will not just be needed to produce financial resources for missions. The world will still want to see the love of God in them, at home and abroad unencumbered by incredulous cultural baggage.

Francis Hsu points to a "triad" of weaknesses in Americans: "Self-reliance [which he does not equate with self-sufficiency], fear of dependence, and insecurity."[512] In the same article, Christopher Lasch's poignant inquiries are cited, "Have we Americans fallen in love with ourselves? Have we lost intimacy, joy, insight, and shared love in a frantic search for ourselves? And if the answers are affirmative, can dedicated mission candidates avoid such narcissism?"[513] Jennings pleads for a recognition of such enculturated flaws in order to begin overcoming them. Perhaps the American culture stands out in its flaws, perhaps the church has conformed too much to the world, or perhaps these characteristics are "just" flagrant in contrast to those of non-Western cultures. No doubt, other cultures have their heavy, offensive cultural baggage, though perhaps, not quite as noticeable because their numbers are smaller. If their idiosyncrasies are indeed barriers to the communication of the Gospel of our Lord Jesus Christ (and they are), the world begs for them to be filtered through the Word of God so God's love is clearly seen and felt in Christian compassion. And the multicultural team with non-Western missionaries usually carries this credibility.

> Can dedicated mission candidates avoid such narcissism?

If, after careful selection and good training, these factors are taken into consideration, the prognosis for teams, in which the members work well together and have an effective ministry in the host culture, is good.

Ronald Iwask, "A Personnel Director Speaks to Professors of Missions," a paper presented at the Annual Meeting of the Evangelical Society (New Orleans, November, 1990), as quoted in Jennings, "American Missionary Candidates - Out of these Worlds," *Missiology*, April, 1993, 208. (His emphasis)

[512] Francis L. K. Hsu, *Psychological Anthropology* (Homewood, IL: Dorsey, 1961), as quoted in George J. Jennings, "American Missionary Candidates," 219.

[513] Jennings, "American missionary candidates," 210-11, Christopher Lasch, *The Culture of Narcissism: American Life in an Age of Diminishing Expectations* (New York: Warner Books, 1979).

6

GUIDELINES FOR MULTICULTURAL MISSION

TEAMS AND CONFERENCES

The purpose of this chapter is to systematize practical steps in opening communication and preserving it between national and expatriate missionaries, among the team as a whole and between teams of various countries as they meet for international conferences.

Soliciting and Giving Feedback

One of the most difficult patterns of communication to establish in the multicultural team is personal dialogue aimed at correction. There are usually hurdles of perceived status to be overcome which would initially inhibit honest communication. The following guidelines attempt to open and keep open channels of communication between the expatriate and national.

Soliciting and Receiving Feedback: (For the Expatriate Missionary)

1. Nationals almost always view positively and want to cooperate when missionaries invite feedback and evaluation regarding the perception of their actions or words. This is because they are putting themselves in the role of a learner and people are most often inclined to help. This is not to say that the missionaries become overly-dependent on their national colleagues; one learns and moves on to other questions or issues. But giving the national a *carte blanche* to continue to give feedback on points previously discussed is helpful to both expatriate and national alike.

2.   The communication process may backfire, however, if the missionary approaches this as an academic exercise instead of as a means of building relationships. The national may quickly feel "used" only for the purposes of the expatriate.

3.   The expatriates' sincerity may well be questioned if they neglect to continually apply what they are learning. A barrier to further communication is then created.

4.   Validating the information they receive is necessary to avoid narrow or distorted applications. People within the culture vary in their perceptions, too. They are not to be played off against one another, but one needs to find the most reliable and articulate sources. Some have never reflected on their own culture. Some want to please and will not give critical feedback. If they don't have answers to all of one's questions, guarding against impatience is important.

5.   Therefore, for the expatriate to have one national as a primary "cultural guide," on the trust level of a friend, is good as an initial and final check point for all other observations and questions.

6.   Accepting the opinion of other expatriates, even experienced ones, as a final authority, is a risky thing. They, too, have processed their information through their cultural filters. It is not an affront to them to validate their impressions as well. It is a good idea to involve expatriates in one's discoveries to improve communication and help them.

7.   Expressing gratitude, not impatience or irritation, for feedback, even if it hurts to hear the truth, is important to encourage ongoing communication. Otherwise, one may lose the source of feedback very quickly. Thanking the person who gives feedback creates more openness for further feedback and deepens trust.

8.   It is often very difficult for most nationals to take the risk of giving feedback. This is especially true in cultures that value giving feedback indirectly rather than by confronting. One might want to include a good friend of the "cultural guide" in the circle of people offering feedback regularly in order to obtain information which the "cultural guide" is hesitant to express to you di-

rectly (e.g., situations in which you have directly offended him/her). Feedback from this third person is to be taken seriously.

9. The expatriate should continue to invite feedback actively until it becomes second nature to the national to offer it. One's perceived status may preclude it ever becoming second nature to the national, so continuing to ask indicates sincerity.

10. The expatriate should persist in soliciting feedback. One may grow confident in some areas, but there will always be surprising blind spots and new things to learn.

11. When one has a bad day and the tolerance for correction is low, one should admit this to the "cultural guide," with humor, if possible.

12. Expatriates may need to clear up the "mysteries" they may create by their behavior or speech with their national colleagues and explain what they were intending to say or do and how it works in their culture. The expatriate is probably the strangest person the national has ever tried to understand. Laughing at oneself is healthy medicine.

13. It is incumbent on expatriates, to be careful about creating stereotypes of the host culture or making them an object of humor with other expatriates. Their credibility sinks with each injuring remark.

14. Praying together for wisdom, and patience for the cultural guide, is important, as well as inviting God to participate in creating a bond between the missionaries.

Giving Feedback: (For the National Missionary, National Christian, National)

1. It is more comfortable and less risky to give feedback when it is invited. It's important to take the expatriates seriously when they invite one's opinion.

2.   Continuing to give feedback, even if the expatriates stop asking for it specifically, is crucial. If one is unsure, one can ask if feedback is still wanted.

3.   Correction is best done gently. The expatriates are very vulnerable because they are adults and are having to learn as children again. Being patient with them, even if they are not patient with themselves, is a very kind gesture.

4.   Hearing the reasons behind the correction, if you can verbalize them, helps them grow in their understanding of the context. Some of their questions will result in new insights into your own culture for you.

5.   The expatriate will appreciate being treated as a friend and partner; one's authoritative knowledge as a national should not be misused.

6.   Although giving unsolicited feedback does present a risk, they are your brothers and sisters in Christ. If they have done or said something that is offensive express the truth in love to them. They need to hear it and will appreciate it, if not right away, eventually.

7.   Part of the growth of the expatriates as persons, as well as the relevance and effectiveness of their ministry to your people, will depend upon how they are growing in understanding the nationals and the host culture. Withholding information from them that will help them hinders this process; the sooner they learn, the better for them and for the nationals.

8.   In matters of personal perception (as opposed to more absolute matters such as the correct use of grammar), one's perception can be expressed in terms of how one comprehends specific actions or words. It may be phrased as follows: "When you do that (describing the action or words), it makes me feel . . . (describing your feelings and thoughts)."

9.   Being as specific as one can in giving feedback, citing situations, words and actions, helps the missionary to learn the context and understand why something was not appropriate.

10.   Suggesting appropriate ways for them to improve what they were trying to say or do gives them alternatives to chose from. Assume that their motives are pure. If this is hard to assume, tell them how you perceive it.

11.   Especially if they are sensitive by nature, one should not laugh at them - first! If they laugh, one can laugh with them.

12.   It may be "cute" or humorous to imitate what they do incorrectly, especially language mistakes, but this may confuse or frustrate them and reinforce bad pronunciation habits. When the missionaries practice for months or even years to improve their pronunciation it does not help to imitate a mistake; it can be interpreted as a humiliating put down. This occurs primarily in situations in which the national missionary knows the mother tongue of the expatriate better than the missionary knows the host language.

13.   When the expatriates attempt to speak in your language, don't finish their sentences for them. It's demotivating and frustrating to them and they need the practice.

14.   Treating their mistakes confidentially will earn their respect. If they want to make them public, that's their choice. Levels of vulnerability differ from person to person. One should pray and move towards an openness in the relationship so the expatriates can feel free to laugh at themselves. It's a healthy sign.

15.   They need prayer support from the national missionaries in their learning process. They have a lot to learn and knowing they are supported in this way will encourage them.

These lists are not meant to be either exhaustive or authoritative. They are a summary of my gleanings over the years and are meant to aid communication and growth in relationships between nationals and expatriates. These principles apply equally to communicating with other teammates who don't represent the host culture. For goal-oriented people, there may be less conscious motivation to pursue such questions. But the process of interaction is nevertheless important for good team relations. Asking questions and seeking to understand teammates is a concrete way of showing *agape* love and well worth the effort. Of course, the size of the team plays a role in the depth one can go. One might, of necessity, have to be selective.

Team Talks

Composing a multicultural team properly and advantageously is a second important step after having selected qualified candidates. But that is not the end. A third, on-going step is necessary. The team must work together to become a well-oiled team, giving proper attention to team and individual needs without losing its focus on the missionary task. The following are suggested areas of discussion necessary for mutual under-standing in a well-functioning team. The order listed is not crucial, but some topics are better discussed initially (e.g., learning styles and lan-guage learning) and other topics after the team members know each other better and are inclined to be more vulnerable. It is important that *all* team members (including mothers) be present at such discussions as they have needs the team should be aware of, too. Part of the team growth occurs during the process of discussing these points together and becoming in-creasingly willing as a team, to listen and share, give and take. Special sensitivity to those who are not comfortable expressing themselves in the language, plus listening carefully and trying to understand, will make them feel they are a vital part of the team as well. Care should be taken that no one is overlooked and equal time is given to all.

1.   After an exercise in discovering *national cultural values* (per-haps already accomplished in pre-field training), each team member shares his/her *personal values*, in relation or contrast, to their national values. Each may share the top ten values in their order of importance. Allow enough time for discussion of the implications of potential harmony or conflict of values, as well as personal implications for change. The latter may not be able to be voiced if the team is newly formed. One may need to come back to this at a later date.

2.   Using the principle of the *concentric circles*,[514] have all team members assign their own values (from Team Talk 1) to the four concentric circles, circle D being the least likely values to change and circle A the easiest to change. All team members may share

---

[514] See "Values Categorized According to Concentric Circles" Figure 7.

their circle diagrams with the team and explain particularly
where they are now struggling and may need help in understanding themselves or the culture, or may need help in changing.

3.   *The leadership style*[515] of each member is determined through
testing and in discussing the results. Some background for tensions felt in the team already may become clear. This tends to
help the team cope better with the personality types, even laugh
at themselves and be more willing to change. The team may
want to try out several styles close to that of the host culture to
get a feel for them. As a team, try to come to a *consensus* about
which style of leadership would be most appropriate for the team
in its cultural context.

4.   After reviewing the section on *decision-making* in chapter 4, as a
team discuss and arrive at a conclusion for an appropriate
method for the team to make decisions in its given context.

5.   Discuss and decide on a method for *conflict resolution*[516] for the
team, giving careful attention to those from non-directive, non-
confrontational cultures and others who may tend to be more silent in the team. How much can and should be done in the team
as a whole? What decisions and with whom need to take place
prior to the team meetings?

6.   Discuss and agree on ground rules for *confidentiality*. If total
agreement cannot be reached, agree to respect the personal differences. For example, if one person shares something with other
team members and prefers they not share it with their spouses,
this should be stated and respected.

7.   Each member, with feedback from those who know him best,
analyzes his or her *spiritual gifts*, then shares with the team. Discuss how these gifts can be further developed and how they can
complement one another in the team and local church context.

---

[515] Chapter 4 discusses leadership styles. The DISC test determines the leadership style of the person and gives helpful tips about the benefits and difficulties
of such types.
[516] Two books were recommended in chapter 4 under "Authority, leadership
styles and decision-making" which could be read and summarized for the group.
Exercises in the book, which are applicable, could also be used.

8.   Take, then discuss, the *learning style inventory*. This is initially helpful when trying to put together a personal program for language learning. The closer the selected method of language learning fits to one's learning style, the more motivated the learner will be and enjoy the progress. Suggestions from the team may be very helpful to the individual. Discuss the possibilities of working together.

9.   Experiment with various *personality style tests*,[517] combining them with team exercises. They can be a good basis for seeing who might work best together on projects and where conflicts can be avoided.

10.   Using *Mayers' six pairs of values*,[518] each member can plot his and one other person's values. Talk in these pairs before discussing the implications for the team. Many more topics for discussion will result from this exercise, e.g., what is the host culture concept of time and how will the team function in this context? A great irritation in some teams involves the definition of "punctuality" related to starting team meetings! Once the host culture's concept of punctuality is explained, one's inner clock can be better adjusted.

11.   Do a *Bible study on 1 Corinthians 13, Ephesians 4:13* and related passages as a team and discuss how love would be expressed in the host culture. What are the personal implications for each team member in relation to the host culture? Allow each team member to express ways in which love can be communicated sincerely to him/her.

12.   Discuss expectations and *fears of being stereotyped*, categorized or misjudged due to national origin, gender or status. An alternative method, which is less threatening, but also a good listening exercise, is to discuss this in pairs in the team with each sharing the implications/desires/expectations of his/her partner in the larger group. What does Galatians 3:28 mean to you given your

---

[517] Tim LaHaye, *Transformed Temperaments,* (Wheaton: Tyndale, 1971), a popular version of variations on the choleric, melancholy, sanguine and phlegmatic to the 16 PF Test mentioned under psychological testing.
[518] Mayer's Six Pairs of Values are found in chapter 3 and the matrices in Appendix D.

cultural background? Where is the potential for repressing nationals, minorities, non-Westerners or women in our team? How can each member's gifts be used to the fullest without discriminating against status, gender and culture? The discussion may be theoretical in a newly formed team, but this topic should be taken up again after the team has worked together for a while. Care should be taken that each member expresses himself/herself on this issue. I am not aware of any marketed tool for discussing prejudices, but if any area of team life tends to repress one person or group of people, it needs to be brought to the surface and dealt with. The corporate team life will suffer greatly if such injustices - perceived or real - prevail.

13.   Discuss *team expectations*. What functions, activities, team atmosphere does each member expect from team life, as a whole? How often should the team meet and for what purposes? Is each team member satisfied with the present situation? How can it be improved? Is there anything you can/would like to add to our team life? What would each member like to contribute to our team? This may be especially important for minority cultures in the team who do not feel like they have anything to contribute to the team. A "significant" team responsibility in an area of their strength may help them feel appreciated and needed. For example, if language is a problem, playing the guitar for team worship may be a meaningful contribution. Does each member feel that his/her needs as a single/family are being respected? If not, what could be changed?

14.   Discuss *areas of entertainment* that the team can enjoy together. Are there things that one of the teammates feels are offensive? Why? What can be done about these things? (Study Romans 14 together for help on this issue.) What does "having a good time" consist of for you? What kinds of sports would be inclusive and fun for all? If mixed swimming is culturally offensive, what about hiking or picnicking together?

15.   Are there any *questionable practices or possessions* of team members or the team as a whole that you feel uncomfortable with in our team? For example, is the use of alcohol or tobacco, which some might consider as "non-negotiables" in their lifestyle or entertainment, etc., viewed differently by different team members' cultures? How is a computer or car as a personal pos-

session viewed? Are there conditions which would justify it from the team's perspective and the perspective of the host culture? (Sometimes the availability of the possession to others or just their involvement in the decision to purchase it can "defuse" an explosive situation.) Listen especially carefully to the nationals. If members are asked to rethink an area or activity, help them think through creative alternatives, dynamic equivalents to the activity acceptable in the host culture.

16.   Does each team member feel comfortable with the team's *non-verbal communication patterns*? (Such as shaking hands, touching, hugging, kissing, distance between persons in conversation, in meetings.) Does the gesture feel "too cool," lacking the warmth one feels in the host culture? Does it feel overbearing? Would you prefer to back off? Talk out the impressions and come to agreement among persons for team nonverbals, and for relations with the community. These forms of nonverbal communication may well remain different, yet they must not be offensive. Are there any gestures that are offensive and need to be changed? Is someone sending confusing signals which reflect non-congruence between verbal and nonverbal communication? For example, the hand gesture meaning "Ok! Top notch!" in North America happens to be a vulgar gesture in Nigeria.

17.   Referring back to the seven marks of *creative power*,[519] all team members evaluate themselves in relation to love, humility, self-limitation, joy, vulnerability, submission and freedom. Discuss these findings with feedback from other team members in regard to how creatively power is actually being used in the team.

Multinational Conference Planning

In addition to affecting person-to-person and team communication, cultural factors affect the atmosphere of retreats and conferences. When such missionary teams come together for refreshment and revitalization, they usually expect a relaxed environment in which they can "let down their hair." But this reversion of some expatriates to their home culture in

---

[519] Foster, *Money, Sex and Power*; see discussion in chapter 1, section "power - leadership."

such a context can bring negative reactions. Disregarding the cultural elements and different expectations and acting without sensitivity can produce a boomerang effect in what was planned as an uplifting and relaxing retreat for all.

The following are guidelines gleaned from 20 plus years of planning and running conferences, congresses and retreats for multicultural teams on a continental as well as local level. This list of guidelines is, of course, not exhaustive.

1. *The atmosphere* of a multicultural gathering should reflect the constituency - multicultural. As a general rule, no one culture should predominate. The possible exception to this would be that the culture of the country in which the conference is held. The host country may determine the flavor, but should not dominate. The missionaries from this country would then be the ones welcoming the other missionaries to their country, using their forms of greeting, music, dance, etc.

2. *The languages* used in the conference play an important role in an inclusive atmosphere. In most cases, several languages will be needed, with one or two being the shared conference language. For example, a retreat for the large staff team I described earlier required the use of two languages, spoken from the front, being sequentially translated. Both languages were also used in all written materials. Usually an international conference requires the use of the regional language (e.g., English, French, or Spanish) as the conference language. But, because it should not be a requirement for every missionary to learn a regional language, languages of all other participant missionaries from that area need to be included in translation. This means translation equipment, which is the easiest method for the translator, or people can sit in groups where whisper translation can take place. The most important written materials, whether schedules, lyrics to songs and hymns, or important new policies, announcements, or prayer requests must be translated and printed ahead of time. This communicates inclusiveness, forethought and unity and no one is left out. When this is overlooked, the missionaries affected feel second class. It's usually embarrassing for them, anyway, to have translation for personal conversations as well as for meetings, so this situation shouldn't be made more difficult than it already is. There need to be enough translators so they can trade off (four hours a day should be the maximum), realizing the

translators will hardly be able to personally interact with the message themselves. Language affects other areas as well.

3. *Small groups* within a large conference make the gathering more personal. If done well, they can be the heart of the conference. Group materials need to be translated and group leaders "recruited" ahead of time. It can be managed in an international setting, yet it is difficult to mix the languages in a small group, since translation is usually necessary. The group dynamic is affected - conversation doesn't flow as naturally. If this mix is desired, in spite of the difficulty, the majority of the group should be relatively fluent in the group language (not necessarily the conference language), with only one or two persons needing translation into a second language. One should be aware, however, that the translator becomes a "non-person" in the group, not having time nor energy to form his/her own thoughts and respond. Multilingual missionaries should not be expected to do this for every conference, even if they do volunteer. The group leaders need to be well trained and patient with the flow of the conversation. Group prayer is usually a highlight.

    The better alternative has usually been to let the missionaries choose their group, with language preference, e.g., some non-native English speakers enjoy testing their English and participating in an English-speaking group; others would prefer a group in their native tongue. Some language learners enjoy the freedom of using their mother tongue and others would prefer trying their hand at the new language. In any case, allowing the participants to choose their group language (even their group leader, for affinity's sake) has proven to be a good method to create a personal atmosphere in a group. There is nothing worse than forcing groups together.

4. More than almost anything else, *music* creates atmosphere. And almost more than in any other area, expectations tend to be very specific and culturally conditioned. Program coordinators should be sure to include a variety of styles, representative of the tastes and cultures of the missionaries, but particularly the area, region, or country. This is the easiest part of the task. The languages are the hardest. What has worked well has been to concentrate on using the two conference languages, primarily the regional language, if it is spoken by most, and simple lyrics which are repeated and not sung too quickly. (Singing all five verses of a

complicated text like "And Can It Be" is out!)[520] Having a conference theme song, which is repeated often, gives a sense of
unity and can be learned by all. Some of the basic praise songs
are translated into many languages and can be varied nicely -
first time through in English, the second time all sing simultaneously in their mother tongues, the third time, host language, etc.
New songs need to be introduced and the lyrics explained from
the front (so it goes through the translation) before they are sung.
It is usually better, as a rule, to repeat two verses than to sing all
four - too much of the meaning is lost. Most don't mind singing
"foreign" words if they know approximately what they are singing. Using a small instrumental and vocal group, composed of
missionaries from various countries, to lead the music from the
front, adds to the international flavor and gives a point of identity for many. Special music from a variety of participants in a
variety of languages (the message of which is introduced through
translation) adds to this positive atmosphere.

5.   *Prayer* is another integral part of the program and, if planned
correctly, can be a high point for each missionary. The prayers
from the front, not in the conference languages, should be translated sequentially, in order to include all. The program planners
need to respect the nature of the group. If it is inter-
denominational, there should be an appropriate balance between
liturgical and non-liturgical forms of prayer. There may be times
when the Korean style of prayer is used, each praying simultaneously in his/her own language. "Beehive" prayers (two to four
persons turning to their neighbors and praying together spontaneously) is also a good alternative. Language is not usually a
problem because people tend to sit next to at least one person
with whom they can talk in a common language. Having someone pray in a language other than the conference languages var-
ies the program but should be used rather sparingly as it requires
sequential translation. While the prayer is being translated into
the conference language and then into other national languages,
there is more time for the mind to wander. Each new method of
prayer needs to be properly introduced and practiced until it feels
natural. If prayer requests for countries or teams are given, such

---

[520] A sample of the first verse reads: "And can it be that I should gain an interest
in the Saviour's blood? Died He for me, who caused His pain? For me, who Him
to death pursued? Amazing love! How can it be that Thou, my God, shouldst die
for me?" Charles Wesley.

lists (translated, of course, into all the participants' languages) could be more complete and used later. Written translation requires a great deal of coordination but it's worth it, if all are to be included. The Lord's Prayer, and other prayers in the Bible, are already translated and, by just mentioning the reference, can be prayed in many languages simultaneously. Many songs are also prayers and could be sung as such.

6.   The *program leaders* need to be well-versed (i.e., feel fluent and free to express themselves) in the conference language. They should also be representatives from the continent or country, if possible. If not, this is something to train missionaries to do. The program leaders need not be the heads of the mission, who certainly should be involved in planning the conference and in speaking, but not necessarily in leading the program. The program leaders are missionaries with whom the other missionaries identify, a focus of identity. Some conferences have worked well with changing leaders from day to day during the conference, but if there are too many variables, the main thread will be missing. Particularly well-received in our experience has been a team consisting of a man and a woman from the host country, or two of different nationalities. This takes practice, though, to be effective. The "identity points" are multiplied. They need to be spontaneous in the conference language and have good skills in leading a large group, as well. They don't have to necessarily lead the music. They should give attention to including all "groups" in their thinking when speaking to their audience. Slang and insider jokes are out. They need to speak slowly and clearly, and still be spontaneous, remembering that some, if not the majority, are listening in a second language or through translation.

7.   *Speakers* for such conferences are hard to find. What applies to the program leaders also applies to chosen speakers as far as fluency in the conference language and rate of speed. In some rare cases, one will invite speakers who will speak in a language which is not a conference language, yet a language group represented at the conference, and be translated sequentially. This needs to be balanced out with other parts of the program, however, to avoid the "little vacations" that the mind can easily take during translation. It does, however, provide a welcome break for one language group to take off their head-sets! In addition,

the speaker should be well-respected by the group as a whole, or be likely to win their respect if previously unknown to them. (He or she should *not* be unknown to the program director and program committee!) If the speakers are noted for their language extremes, for example, using slang, superlatives, or other culturally inappropriate speech or behavior, this will not be appreciated and it could even discredit them with the audience. Someone else certainly should be chosen. The audience's level of toleration and ability to filter out extremes must be known. If there are animosities initially, they will work against them. A culturally close relationship to the audience, knowing the speaker understands them to a great degree, is helpful. In any case, outside speakers should be carefully briefed about their audience by someone from the program committee and given periodic feedback during the conference as to changes they might make to be still more effective. Most speakers are keen communicators, want to be sensitive to these issues and welcome feedback.

8.   The option of special interest *seminars* provides variety in the program, but are, admittedly, a big headache for translation. Because they are usually scheduled simultaneously, it sometimes means that some language groups are "assigned" to a particular seminar and have no choice because only one translator is available. Because of fatigue, some missionaries, who would otherwise listen through translation, don't attend. This is understandable. The amount of program should be scheduled accordingly, not as heavy as it could be with a monolingual group. Translation should be scheduled for the seminars, at least those seminars where the majority of those who signed up need translation. Preregistration for seminars helps in coordinating translation a great deal. What applies to main speakers and program leaders regarding language speed and fluency also applies to seminar speakers. In choosing seminar speakers, it is good to lean more towards allowing missionaries from the region or young missionaries to gain experience in this area, or ask them to co-lead with an expatriate who has lots of experience. Both should be known for their practical expertise, however, or credibility will be sacrificed.

9.   *Facilities* for international conferences have been the object of much criticism. I, too, prefer modest accommodations, simple meals and non-ostentatious meeting rooms. As long as the con-

ference group is small, this is possible. But the fact is, for a large group, the host country probably has few alternatives to offer if one needs translation equipment, childcare facilities (that will ensure adequate hygiene), food services and accommodations, meeting rooms and seminar rooms for a large number of people. Often the best hotels offer cut-rate prices off-season, providing a good opportunity for large conferences. Expediency should not be the highest value - health may be, though. If children are sick at a conference, the parents will profit little from coming and it will remain a bad memory. One can arrange to have simple, uncomplicated meals that foster fellowship, but are not so drawn out as to irritate hungry, sleepy children. In general, at least three of the four required facilities - namely, food service, meeting rooms, childcare, and sleeping facilities - should be located together so as not to unnecessarily tire out the missionaries or lose time in the program. The fourth should be no further than a ten minute walk away.

10. Conferences and retreats that serve such a multicultural group will provide a learning process for all involved. If the conference organizers themselves are not representatives of this multicultural group, they will miss many unwritten elements that have become important over the years that the missionaries have met together. The *missionaries from the area or country* (depending on the scope of the conference) should be *included in the planning committee* as soon as possible to begin gaining experience on an international level.

11. *Evaluations*, written and verbal, are a must. The evaluation should assess how close one has come to reaching the goals of the conference, as well as how suitable individual parts of the program and facilities were. And all the missionaries should be allowed to write in their own languages to insure candid impressions. For this reason it is important to arrange for translation or use a form that is easy to evaluate statistically with fewer open-ended questions. Evaluations reveal to the planners what is offensive, what is appreciated and desired to be included again and what should be changed. As a final note, in evaluating the evaluations one needs cultural sensitivity as well. The superlatives of the Americans and the understatements of the British, for example might be saying the same thing!

7

CONCLUSIONS

The harmonious operation of multicultural mission teams is an integral issue in theology. Communicating the love of God is mission, is what motivated God to visit humankind; it is the sending force behind missionary activity as well as the motivation in team relationships. To summarize this thesis in one all-encompassing guideline, a multicultural mission team could begin by completing the following sentence, "In this culture, *agape* love is . . ." "This culture" would, of necessity, refer to, on the one hand, the host culture and, on the other hand, to each culture represented by all the team members. But the primary focus or direction of adaptation should not be overshadowed by the pull of another cultural majority or the culture of the team leadership; the team as a whole and each team member is adapting foremostly to the host culture. And this adaptation can not be just an intellectual exercise; it assumes appropriate responses, based also on *agape* love. Behind this statement, however, is a myriad of assumptions which need to be brought into conscious thinking: What *does* express the love of an almighty God who became a human being and died for us in order that we might know Him? Love could then be . . . learning to express oneself in the other person's language. Or . . . being sensitive to and correcting those factors in one's lifestyle that are offensive. Or . . . renouncing the use of power over others. In essence, love means a *willingness* to adapt, a desire to remove barriers for the credible communication of the gospel. This is not mindless conformity, but a filtering of one's cultural values through timeless biblical values (in contrast to the cultural values of biblical times) and adapting to those values of the host culture that are not in contradiction. But that may even be a step too far. Adaptation is, in light of biblical values, being willing to part with one's own cultural baggage, insofar as it is a barrier to communicating the Gospel in the host culture. And this is done out of love - out of love for God, love for the people with whom the missionary now lives and love for the teammates with whom one serves. This process is not as easy as it may sound because cultural values are so ingrained that they often blind one from seeing one's offensiveness in a new cultural context. That's why the multicultural team, so uniquely constituted, challenges the missionaries, at almost every turn, to hold their cultures up to the light of God's values.

In this complex structure of a multicultural team, neither the leader's culture, nor that of the majority of the team, nor the international mission's mother culture should usurp the place of the host culture (that, of course, being filtered through biblical values) as the norm for the team. Although all teams members, in a sense, are adapting to one another, they are adapting together primarily in the direction of the host culture and their national teammates. *We/they* (the expatriates/the nationals) *polarizations*, then, which make fun of, or inappropriately criticize, the host culture are hurtful for the national missionary and unacceptable. Feedback is helpful to all team members to evaluate how they are being perceived by the host culture and by their teammates. Feedback, after being validated, should be turned into action.

Ignorance is easier to correct than unwillingness; one dare not harden one's conscience. There need be no fear of losing one's personal identity. "Identification with" does not mean "identical to." Identification means the real me plus what Christ wants to continue accomplishing in me. If resistance to adaptation is felt, one should discover why this is the case. There may be personal insecurities blocking the forming of new relationships. Change is not to be forced, but change is natural in the context of friendship, in which one party does not want to hurt the other. Lack of sensitivity to this may be forcing others to change *de facto* by the mere, perhaps unconscious, pressure of an expatriate majority. Identification is, rather, an attitude of compassion that removes the barriers to one's expressing and another's receiving God's love. The willingness to be involved in a learning process, to listen and heed, is valued greatly. Teams formed to avoid any given expatriate cultural plurality which include nationals (forming a plurality, if possible), all other selection factors being equal, are most likely to succeed. A team made up of five to eight members, who are neither too different nor too similar, is an optimal combination.

The selection of missionaries who are personally and spiritually mature, who have had a proven ministry in their home culture, who are flexible and sensitive, and who love people, are imperatives for multicultural teams. Such teams need thoughtful, well-trained leadership and on-going care: Weekly meetings (or more frequent, depending on logistics) for team sharing, praying, studying the Bible in light of their new cultural context, worshipping as well as relaxing together, are integral to team life. And these should be heavily sprinkled with sincere appreciation and encouragement. Is this not the essence of the second greatest commandment, which is like the first, "Love your neighbor as your-self"?[521] In addition, each team member needs access to an impartial third party for counsel and conflict resolution.

Are multicultural teams worth it? To some it may sound, and some-times feel, like walking on eggs. But for most, becoming aware and be-ing sensitive have become second nature, a result of their desire to have others experience the love of God in a very personal way. Cultural ad-aptation multiplied by the number of cultures represented in the team may give some feeling of being restricted, not being free to be oneself. It is indeed quite the opposite; it is freedom. This kind of adaptation out of love gives a new sense of freedom to move within the culture and inter-act with the team because one is not burdened down by wondering if one is communicating or behaving in the right way. This freedom of fellow-ship among team members, supported by the love that genuinely wants the best for the other, leads to change; it doesn't force it. In addition to the rich spiritual interchange possible, multicultural teams have the po-tential of being an important primary filter, refining and fine-tuning the message of the gospel for communication in the host culture. Purified from barriers offensive to communication and from the cultural baggage brought from "strange cultures," the missionaries and the message they bear gain a much more credible hearing with the people. Such a team presents a challenge to rethink one's presuppositions, lifestyle and use of resources. A well-functioning team, with members from different cul-tures, is a good opportunity for growth and a foretaste of heaven.

---

[521] Matthew 22:39.

APPENDIX A

CREDIBILITY FACTORS IN COMMUNICATING THE GOSPEL IN A CROSS-CULTURAL SETTING WITH A MULTICULTURAL TEAM

Please read through the survey the first time and mark in the LEFT column 1, 2, 3, 4, or 5, the description you think best applies to the statement. YOUR ADDITIONAL COMMENTS ARE MOST WELCOME!
The second time you read through use the RIGHT column to indicate the number of expatriates (foreign workers) in your team who fit into EACH category.
The total number of expatriates on your team is _____.

1 = necessary for credibility
2 = adds to credibility
3 = neutral
4 = tends to hinder communication of the Gospel in a credible way
5 = communicates negatively, lacks credibility
↓
? = cannot really evaluate

		++	+	0	-	- -	?
	A.1. knows and uses Bible well						
	A.2. is growing in Bible knowledge						
	A.3. lives as best as s/he can according to what s/he knows of the Bible						
	A.4. has vital personal prayer life						
	A.5. is spiritually accountable to someone						
	A.6. fruit of the Spirit seen in his/her life						
	A.7. trusts the Lord in spiritual battles						
	B.1. is compassionate						
	B.2. initiates conversations on spiritual matters						
	B.3. leads a small group and is well rec'd						
	B.4. speaks publicly and is well received						
	B.5. is able to discern real spiritual issues (and not confuse a cultural reaction)						
	C.1. doesn't emphasize what s/he misses from home						
	C.2. appreciates new things in host culture						
	C.3. eats (cooks) national foods						
	C.4. learned language well						
	C.5. has "fun" the way national staff do						
	C.6. continues to grow in language ability						
	C.7. has adopted manners of host culture						
	C.8. sensitive to culturally appropriate dress						
	C.9. wise use of money						

C.10. culturally appropriate standard of living						
C.11. is aware of culturally offensive things + tries to change						
C.12. avoids overgeneralizing characteristics of nationals or culture						
C.13. growing in cultural awareness						
C. 14. does not try to protect own national identity						
C.15. respects local customs						
D.1. has a good understanding of history of host country						
D.2. understands uniqueness of province in which s/he lives						
D.3. keeps current on news events						
D.4. knows national heroes/heroines						
D.5. appreciates important local historical settings						
D.6. is growing in historical understanding						
E.1. knows names of national leaders						
E.2. aware of national political issues						
E.3. sees connections between faith and political action						
E.34. speaks out against injustices						
E.5. loyal to his/her home country						
E.6. is growing in political consciousness						
E.7. loyal to his/her host country						
F.1. takes initiative in getting to know others						
F.2. is faithful						
F.3. not superficial						
F.4. enjoys being with nationals						
F.5. knows what it means to be a friend in host culture						
F.6. is forgiving						
F.7. is generous						
F.8. respects authority						
F.9. respects people from all classes equally						
F.10. is respectful of opposite sex						
F.11. values family life						
F.12. values the individual						
F.13. values group interaction						
F.14. has a cultural guide (friend) and listens to feedback						
G.1. shows personal maturity						
G.2. friendly						
G.3. not defensive						
G.4. racially unprejudiced						

G.5. time conscious							
G.6. person-oriented							
G.7. result-oriented							
G.8. informal							
G.9. goal-oriented							
G.10. not boastful or proud							
G.11. hardworking							
G.12. has a strong sense of "mission"							
G.13. has a healthy self-concept							
G.14. is open, vulnerable							
G.15. resilient, bounces back from failure or setbacks quickly							
G.16. is tactful							
G.18. handles ambiguity (lack of clarity) well							
G.19. has a sense of humor							
G.20. profits from own mistakes							
(other qualities . . .)_____							

The second time you go through the survey, please remember to put the <u>number</u> of expatriates on your team into the categories which apply to them on the RIGHT side of the page.

Your own evaluations/recommendations:

I feel a missions team composed of people from different cultures . . .

If I could choose my team members I would choose those who . . .

__ I have worked in my homeland (name of country)_____ for ___ years.
__ I have been an expatriate in _____ for ____years.

____ single   ____ married   ___number of children

__age 20-29   __age 30-39   __age 40-49   __age 50-59 __age 60+

total number of years served in full-time ministry___
MINISTRY AREA: (check only one, please)
__ field   __ vocational   __ administration
__ leadership   __ traveling team   __ other_____

Please return the survey in the addressed envelope as soon as possible.

All the information will be kept confidential. If you wish to have information of the results of this survey and research, please give me your name and address:
Thank you!   Lianne Roembke

% ALL SURVEYED

CREDIBILITY FACTORS IN COMMUNICATING THE GOSPEL IN A CROSS-CULTURAL SETTING WITH A MULTICULTURAL TEAM

Please read through the survey the first time and mark in the LEFT column 1, 2, 3, 4, or 5, the description you think best applies to the statement. YOUR ADDITIONAL COMMENTS ARE MOST WELCOME!
The second time you read through use the RIGHT column to indicate the number of expatriates (foreign workers) in your team who fit into EACH category.
The total number of expatriates on your team is _____.

1 = necessary for credibility
2 = adds to credibility
3 = neutral
4 = tends to hinder communication of the Gospel in a credible way
5 = communicates negatively, lacks credibility
        ↓

? = cannot really evaluate

	1	2	3	4	5	?
A.1. knows and uses Bible well	56	42	2			0
A.2. is growing in Bible knowledge	39	49	8	2		2
A.3. lives as best as s/he can according to what s/he knows of the Bible	74	23	1			2
A.4. has vital personal prayer life	51	40	8			1
A.5. is spiritually accountable to someone	18	53	28	1		1
A.6. fruit of the Spirit seen in his/her life	84	15	1			0
A.7. trusts the Lord in spiritual battles	63	31	5			1
B.1. is compassionate	40	57	2			1
B.2. initiates conversations on spiritual matters	26	58	16			0
B.3. leads a small group and is well rec'd	16	60	22			2
B.4. speaks publicly and is well received	6	60	34			0
B.5. is able to discern real spiritual issues (and not confuse a cultural reaction)	41	56	2			1
C.1. doesn't emphasize what s/he misses from home	13	63	20	2	1	1
C.2. appreciates new things in host culture	29	64	6			1
C.3. eats (cooks) national foods	10	62	25			2
C.4. learned language well	31	63	4	1		1
C.5. has "fun" the way national staff do	6	70	22	1		1
C.6. continues to grow in language ability	25	67	7			1
C.7. has adopted manners of host culture	18	68	12			3
C.8. sensitive to culturally appropriate dress	39	56	6			0
C.9. wise use of money	23	63	13			1
C.10. culturally appropriate standard of living	30	56	12			3
C.11. is aware of culturally offensive things + tries to change	53	45	1			1

C.12. avoids overgeneralizing characteristics of nationals or culture	41	52	5			3
C.13. growing in cultural awareness	36	61	1			2
C. 14. does not try to protect own national identity	10	46	36	4	1	3
C.15. respects local customs	41	54	3	1		2
D.1. has a good understanding of history of host country	6	76	16			2
D.2. understands uniqueness of province in which s/he lives	8	73	17			2
D.3. keeps current on news events	8	63	26			3
D.4. knows national heroes/heroines	5	61	32			2
D.5. appreciates important local historical settings	1	66	31			2
D.6. is growing in historical understanding	2	69	28			1
E.1. knows names of national leaders	18	71	9			2
E.2. aware of national political issues	13	70	16			1
E.3. sees connections between faith and political action	10	39	36	5	2	8
E.34. speaks out against injustices	4	41	34	14	6	2
E.5. loyal to his/her home country	7	22	56	6	2	6
E.6. is growing in political consciousness	4	38	49	6		4
E.7. loyal to his/her host country	16	62	16	4		3
F.1. takes initiative in getting to know others	46	47	4			3
F.2. is faithful	71	24	3			2
F.3. not superficial	50	45	1			4
F.4. enjoys being with nationals	34	37	15	1		13
F.5. knows what it means to be a friend in host culture	51	46	1			2
F.6. is forgiving	70	26	2			2
F.7. is generous	28	51	15	4		3
F.8. respects authority	44	48	4	2	1	2
F.9. respects people from all classes equally	32	30	10	6	1	2
F.10. is respectful of opposite sex	43	46	7			4
F.11. values family life	50	43	7			
F.12. values the individual	56	39	4	1		1
F.13. values group interaction	28	51	19			2
F.14. has a cultural guide (friend) and listens to feedback	47	44	6	1		1
G.1. shows personal maturity	50	47	1	1		1
G.2. friendly	44	53	3			1
G.3. not defensive	37	56	4			3
G.4. racially unprejudiced	61	36	1			2
G.5. time conscious	3	34	27	17	1	19
G.6. person-oriented	42	61	5			2
G.7. result-oriented	3	19	27	43	4	6
G.8. informal	5	44	47	2		3
G.9. goal-oriented	6	37	34	18	2	3

G.10. not boastful or proud	36	56	6	1		2
G.11. hardworking	28	58	13			1
G.12. has a strong sense of "mission"	32	33	14	7	1	12
G.13. has a healthy self-concept	34	52	11	1		2
G.14. is open, vulnerable	17	63	12	6		3
G.15. resilient, bounces back from failure or setbacks quickly	28	50	7	5	4	7
G.16. is tactful	38	54	4	3		2
G.18. handles ambiguity (lack of clarity) well	31	56	8			6
G.19. has a sense of humor	35	54	11			0
G.20. profits from own mistakes	39	54	6	1		1
(other qualities . . .)_____						

The second time you go through the survey, please remember to put the <u>number</u> of expatriates on your team into the categories which apply to them on the RIGHT side of the page.

Your own evaluations/recommendations:

I feel a missions team composed of people from different cultures . . .

If I could choose my team members I would choose those who . . .

__ I have worked in my homeland (name of country) _____ for ____ years.
__ I have been an expatriate in _____ for _____years.

__single   ___married   ___number of children

__age 20-29   __age 30-39   __age 40-49   __age 50-59 __age 60+

total number of years served in full-time ministry___
MINISTRY AREA: (check only one, please)
__ field   __ vocational   __ administration
__ leadership   __ traveling team   __ other_____
Please return the survey in the addressed envelope as soon as possible.

All the information will be kept confidential. If you wish to have information of the results of this survey and research, please give me your name and address:
Thank you!   Lianne Roembke

% NATIONAL MISSIONARIES SURVEYED

CREDIBILITY FACTORS IN COMMUNICATING THE GOSPEL IN A CROSS-CULTURAL SETTING WITH A MULTICULTURAL TEAM

Please read through the survey the first time and mark in the LEFT column 1, 2, 3, 4, or 5, the description you think best applies to the statement. YOUR ADDITIONAL COMMENTS ARE MOST WELCOME!
The second time you read through use the RIGHT column to indicate the number of expatriates (foreign workers) in your team who fit into EACH category.
The total number of expatriates on your team is _____.

1 = necessary for credibility
2 = adds to credibility
3 = neutral
4 = tends to hinder communication of the Gospel in a credible way
5 = communicates negatively, lacks credibility
↓
                          ? = cannot really evaluate

		1	2	3	4	5	?
	A.1. knows and uses Bible well	63	38				
	A.2. is growing in Bible knowledge	33	54	4	8		
	A.3. lives as best as s/he can according to what s/he knows of the Bible	71	29				
	A.4. has vital personal prayer life	71	25	4			
	A.5. is spiritually accountable to someone	38	46	13	4		
	A.6. fruit of the Spirit seen in his/her life	79	21				
	A.7. trusts the Lord in spiritual battles	67	25	8			
	B.1. is compassionate	46	50	4			
	B.2. initiates conversations on spiritual matters	29	58	13			
	B.3. leads a small group and is well rec'd	25	63	13			
	B.4. speaks publicly and is well received	13	63	25			
	B.5. is able to discern real spiritual issues (and not confuse a cultural reaction)	63	33	4			
	C.1. doesn't emphasize what s/he misses from home	8	54	29	8		
	C.2. appreciates new things in host culture	25	63	13			
	C.3. eats (cooks) national foods	0	50	46	4		
	C.4. learned language well	42	46	8	4		
	C.5. has "fun" the way national staff do	8	54	33	4		
	C.6. continues to grow in language ability	33	54	13			
	C.7. has adopted manners of host culture	21	58	17			
	C.8. sensitive to culturally appropriate dress	25	54	21			
	C.9. wise use of money	38	50	13			

C.10. culturally appropriate standard of living	29	46	25			
C.11. is aware of culturally offensive things + tries to change	42	54	4			
C.12. avoids overgeneralizing characteristics of nationals or culture	42	42	8			8
C.13. growing in cultural awareness	25	71				4
C. 14. does not try to protect own national identity	25	42	21	4		8
C.15. respects local customs	38	50	4	4		4
D.1. has a good understanding of history of host country	25	46	25			4
D.2. understands uniqueness of province in which s/he lives	13	58	25			4
D.3. keeps current on news events	17	54	21			8
D.4. knows national heroes/heroines	13	33	50			4
D.5. appreciates important local historical settings	4	46	46			4
D.6. is growing in historical understanding		63	33			4
E.1. knows names of national leaders	8	67	21			4
E.2. aware of national political issues	21	58	17			4
E.3. sees connections between faith and political action	25	33	29			13
E.34. speaks out against injustices	8	50	33	4	4	0
E.5. loyal to his/her home country	21	25	25	21		8
E.6. is growing in political consciousness	4	21	63	4		8
E.7. loyal to his/her host country	29	58	4	4		4
F.1. takes initiative in getting to know others	50	42	4			4
F.2. is faithful	75	21				4
F.3. not superficial	42	38	4			17
F.4. enjoys being with nationals	46	46	4			4
F.5. knows what it means to be a friend in host culture	46	46	4			4
F.6. is forgiving	71	25				4
F.7. is generous	17	54	17			13
F.8. respects authority	46	42	4			8
F.9. respects people from all classes equally	17	54	13	8		8
F.10. is respectful of opposite sex	50	42	4			4
F.11. values family life	75	25				
F.12. values the individual	54	42		4		
F.13. values group interaction	29	50	21			
F.14. has a cultural guide (friend) and listens to feedback	46	42	8	4		
G.1. shows personal maturity	54	42		4		
G.2. friendly	54	46				
G.3. not defensive	29	54	4			4
G.4. racially unprejudiced	50	42	4			4
G.5. time conscious	8	50	25	13		4

G.6. person-oriented	33	50	13			4
G.7. result-oriented	13	21	25	33		8
G.8. informal	8	63	25			4
G.9. goal-oriented	29	50	17	4		
G.10. not boastful or proud	46	42	8			4
G.11. hardworking	33	54	13			
G.12. has a strong sense of "mission"	46	21	25	4		4
G.13. has a healthy self-concept	38	38	17	4		4
G.14. is open, vulnerable	38	42	8	4		8
G.15. resilient, bounces back from failure or setbacks quickly	17	46	4	13		21
G.16. is tactful	46	38	4	8		4
G.18. handles ambiguity (lack of clarity) well	21	50	8			21
G.19. has a sense of humor	21	50	29			
G.20. profits from own mistakes	29	54	8	4		4
(other qualities . . .)						

The second time you go through the survey, please remember to put the <u>number</u> of expatriates on your team into the categories which apply to them on the RIGHT side of the page.

Your own evaluations/recommendations:

I feel a missions team composed of people from different cultures . . .

If I could choose my team members I would choose those who . . .

__ I have worked in my homeland (name of country) _____ for _____ years.
__ I have been an expatriate in _____ for _____ years.

__single   ___married   ___number of children

__age 20-29   __age 30-39   __age 40-49   __age 50-59 __age 60+

total number of years served in full-time ministry___
MINISTRY AREA: (check only one, please)
__ field   __ vocational   __ administration
__ leadership   __ traveling team   __ other _____

Please return the survey in the addressed envelope as soon as possible.

All the information will be kept confidential. If you wish to have information of the results of this survey and research, please give me your name and address:
Thank you!   Lianne Roembke

% EXPATRIATES SURVEYED

CREDIBILITY FACTORS IN COMMUNICATING THE GOSPEL IN A CROSS-CULTURAL SETTING WITH A MULTICULTURAL TEAM

Please read through the survey the first time and mark in the LEFT column 1, 2, 3, 4, or 5, the description you think best applies to the statement. YOUR ADDITIONAL COMMENTS ARE MOST WELCOME!
The second time you read through use the RIGHT column to indicate the number of expatriates (foreign workers) in your team who fit into EACH category.
The total number of expatriates on your team is _____.

1 = necessary for credibility
2 = adds to credibility
3 = neutral
4 = tends to hinder communication of the Gospel in a credible way
5 = communicates negatively, lacks credibility
↓
                                 ? = cannot really evaluate

		1	2	3	4	5	?
	A.1. knows and uses Bible well	55	43	2			
	A.2. is growing in Bible knowledge	43	48	10			2
	A.3. lives as best as s/he can according to what s/he knows of the Bible	75	21	1			2
	A.4. has vital personal prayer life	45	44	10			1
	A.5. is spiritually accountable to someone	12	55	32			1
	A.6. fruit of the Spirit seen in his/her life	86	13	1			
	A.7. trusts the Lord in spiritual battles	62	33	4			1
	B.1. is compassionate	38	60	1			1
	B.2. initiates conversations on spiritual matters	25	58	17			
	B.3. leads a small group and is well rec'd	13	60	25			2
	B.4. speaks publicly and is well received	4	60	37			
	B.5. is able to discern real spiritual issues (and not confuse a cultural reaction)	35	63	1			1
	C.1. doesn't emphasize what s/he misses from home	14	65	18		1	1
	C.2. appreciates new things in host culture	29	64	5			1
	C.3. eats (cooks) national foods	13	65	19			2
	C.4. learned language well	29	68	2			1
	C.5. has "fun" the way national staff do	5	75	19			1
	C.6. continues to grow in language ability	23	70	6			1
	C.7. has adopted manners of host culture	17	70	11			2
	C.8. sensitive to culturally appropriate dress	43	54	1			
	C.9. wise use of money	19	67	13			1

C.10. culturally appropriate standard of living	30	58	8			4
C.11. is aware of culturally offensive things + tries to change	56	43				1
C.12. avoids overgeneralizing characteristics of nationals or culture	40	55	4			1
C.13. growing in cultural awareness	39	58	1			1
C. 14. does not try to protect own national identity	6	48	40	4	1	1
C.15. respects local customs	42	55	2			1
D.1. has a good understanding of history of host country	1	85	13			1
D.2. understands uniqueness of province in which s/he lives	7	77	14			1
D.3. keeps current on news events	6	65	27			1
D.4. knows national heroes/heroines	2	69	27			1
D.5. appreciates important local historical settings	0	71	27			1
D.6. is growing in historical understanding	2	71	26			0
E.1. knows names of national leaders	20	73	6			1
E.2. aware of national political issues	11	74	15			0
E.3. sees connections between faith and political action	6	40	38	6	2	7
E.34. speaks out against injustices	2	38	35	17	6	2
E.5. loyal to his/her home country	4	21	64	2	2	6
E.6. is growing in political consciousness	4	43	45	6		2
E.7. loyal to his/her host country	12	63	19	4		2
F.1. takes initiative in getting to know others	45	49	4			2
F.2. is faithful	70	25	4			1
F.3. not superficial	52	48	0			0
F.4. enjoys being with nationals	31	35	18	1		15
F.5. knows what it means to be a friend in host culture	52	46				1
F.6. is forgiving	70	26	2			1
F.7. is generous	31	50	14	5		0
F.8. respects authority	43	50	4	2	1	0
F.9. respects people from all classes equally	37	46	10	6	1	0
F.10. is respectful of opposite sex	40	48	8			4
F.11. values family life	45	47	8			0
F.12. values the individual	56	38	5			1
F.13. values group interaction	27	51	19			2
F.14. has a cultural guide (friend) and listens to feedback	48	45	6			1
G.1. shows personal maturity	49	49	1			1
G.2. friendly	40	55	4			1
G.3. not defensive	39	57	2			1
G.4. racially unprejudiced	64	35				1
G.5. time conscious	1	30	27	18	1	23

G.6. person-oriented	44	52	2			1
G.7. result-oriented	1	18	27	45	5	5
G.8. informal	4	38	54	2		2
G.9. goal-oriented	0	33	39	21	2	4
G.10. not boastful or proud	33	60	5	1		1
G.11. hardworking	26	60	13			1
G.12. has a strong sense of "mission"	29	37	11	8	1	14
G.13. has a healthy self-concept	33	56	10			1
G.14. is open, vulnerable	11	69	13	6		1
G.15. resilient, bounces back from failure or setbacks quickly	31	51	8	2	5	2
G.16. is tactful	36	58	4	1		1
G.18. handles ambiguity (lack of clarity) well	33	57	8			1
G.19. has a sense of humor	39	55	6			0
G.20. profits from own mistakes	42	54	5			
(other qualities . . .) *tactful, flexible*	63	38				

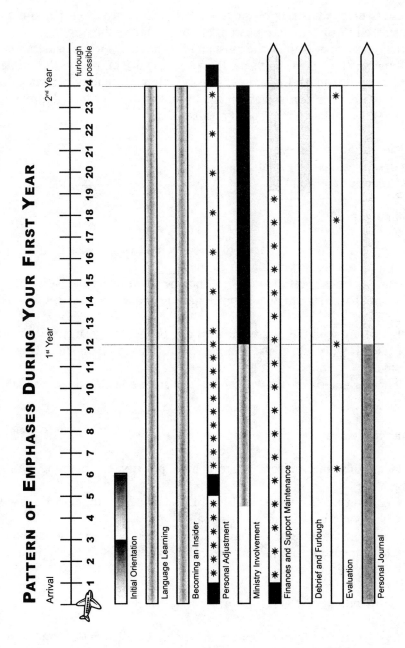

PATTERN OF EMPHASES DURING YOUR FIRST YEAR

Arrival

1ˢᵗ Year   2ⁿᵈ Year

1 2 3 4 5 6 7 8 9 10 11 12 13 14 15 16 17 18 19 20 21 22 23 24

furlough possible

Initial Orientation

Language Learning

Becoming an Insider

Personal Adjustment

Ministry Involvement

Finances and Support Maintenance

Debrief and Furlough

Evaluation

Personal Journal

Basic Values

These twelve categories of thought are not the only ones that could be considered in such a classification of values, but in the ongoing study of society these appear to be the most significant values for consideration of difference. If s/he grasps these, the analyst can then derive the primary motivational values of a society. Possibly eighty to ninety percent of behavior within a given society opens to understanding once the relationship of these values to the society is discovered.

0 = doesn't describe me
1 = describes me somewhat
2 = describes me well

Time-oriented

a) Time-oriented persons tend to be concerned with the element of time in relationship to what they are doing._____
b) Time-oriented persons will be concerned with the punctuality of any event. There should be a definite starting and stopping point for every activity._____
c) In dealing with the future, the next day or the next year, time-oriented persons will set goals. Setting goals makes them feel comfortable._____
d) Time-oriented persons will tend to feel stressed when their schedule is upset._____

Goal-conscious

a) Goal-conscious persons place a high priority on attaining definite goals. _____
b) Goal-conscious persons will tend to sacrifice or cut short time spent with people in order to reach a goal._____
c) Goal-conscious persons may tend to choose as their friends people whose goals are similar to theirs. They will not let friendship stand in the way of their goals._____

Event-oriented

a) Event-oriented persons tend to downplay the element of time in relationship to what they are doing._____

b) Event-oriented persons are more concerned with the event itself that with any time considerations attached to it. They will stay with something/someone until it is done._____

c) Event-oriented persons do not concern themselves much about the future but live in the present._____

d) Event-oriented persons can easily adjust their "schedule" to allow for unforeseen delays or opportunities. _____

Interaction-conscious

a) Interaction-conscious persons will place a high priority on interacting with people. _____

b) Interaction-conscious persons will tend to sacrifice a goal for the sake of spending time with people._____

c) Interaction-conscious persons would not use "goal-consciousness" as a criterion for choosing friends. For them security comes in getting to know people and being involved with them. _____

Dichotomizing

a) Dichotomizing persons will tend to polarize life in terms of black/white, here/there, themselves/others, right/wrong. _____

b) It is relatively easy for dichotomizing persons to evaluate a person, program or idea on the basis of such dichotomies. _____

c) Dichotomizing persons need to feel they are right, that they are doing the right things and thinking the right thoughts in order to feel satisfied with themselves._____

d) Dichotomizers gain a sense of security when they understand where they "fit in" and where others "fit in." _____

Declarative

a) Declarative persons will seek the advice of an expert when a decision needs to be made. _____

b) Declarative persons find security in having an authority to which they can refer to again and again. They will seek out the "best" authorities as a basis for their decision-making. _____

c) Declarative persons tend to put their problems in historical perspective. Other people have faced similar problems and their insights and solutions can guide them in solving theirs. _____

d) Declarative persons place a lot of emphasis on comprehending their teachers and on being able to reverbalize what they have been taught. They feel comfortable with the lecture method. _____

Holistic

a) Holistic persons will tend to see life as a whole, with all the parts functioning interrelatedly within the whole. _____
b) It is frustrating for holistic persons to evaluate anything apart from the context in which it occurs. A part does not have meaning outside of the whole. _____
c) Holistic persons derive their satisfaction through being able to integrate their thoughts and life, whether it occurs naturally or through planning. _____
d) Holistic persons tend to fell insecure whenever placed in a category. _____

Interrogative

a) Faced with making a decision, interrogative persons need to be able to choose an answer from among various alternatives. _____
b) Interrogative persons find security in having a variety of alternatives from which they may choose an answer. They want to make their own decision. _____
c) Interrogative persons tend to approach a problem as though it were unique and therefore deserving of a fresh and unique solution. _____
d) Interrogative persons tend to be frustrated in a situation where an expert lectures on a subject. They would want to voice their own opinions and insights. _____

Prestige Achieved
a) Such persons feel that prestige is earned and it is a result of one's effort or skill rather than one's position in society. _____
b) Such persons tend to ignore formal credentials. _____
c) They will pay more attention to what a person means to them than to that person's formal rank. _____
d) They will work hard to achieve prestige in their own eyes rather than to gain a status role in society. _____

Vulnerability as a Weakness

a) Persons who see vulnerability as a weakness hate admitting mistakes._____
b) They will take every necessary step to avoid making an error, double-checking everything they do, being methodical and organized._____
c) They will find it difficult to expose their weaknesses or tell stories about their mistakes. _____
d) They avoid being involved in things that are new and experimental._____

Prestige Ascribed

a) These persons see prestige as the result of social class and/or rank or position within society. _____
b) They respect formal credentials and view them as important._____
c) They tend to associate most with those of their own rank, class or prestige group. _____
d) They work hard to achieve the rank and prestige in society that they deserve. _____

Vulnerability as a Strength

a) Persons who see vulnerability as a strength do not find it difficult to admit mistakes._____
b) They find it easy to tell stories about themselves, which expose their weaknesses. _____
c) They are willing to be involved in new experiments. _____

Adapted from: Marvin K. Mayers, chapter 11, "The Group: Value," *Christianity Confronts Culture, Grand Rapids: Zondervan, 1974.*

APPENDIX D

AGAPE INTERNATIONAL TRAINING CURRICULUM

Weeks 1-5
  Servant Mentality in Ministry
  Cultural Analysis Tools
  Field Ministry Orientation
  Becoming a Learner
  Cross-Cultural Communication
  Philosophy of Language Learning
  Stress Management

Weeks 6-7
  Personal Values
  Cultural Values
  Cross-Cultural Ministry
  Cross-Cultural Evangelism
  Cross-Cultural Discipleship

Weeks 8-9
  Basis of Interpersonal Relationships
  Self-Concept
  Listening Skills
  Communication Skills
  Problem Solving and Conflict Resolution

Weeks 10-11
  Cultural Adjustment
  Spiritual Warfare
  Preventative Health
  Spiritual Leadership
  Cross-Cultural Teamwork
  Reentry
  Mission Strategy
  Missionary Role

Weeks 1-11 (throughout the training time)
  Teamwork
  Spiritual Development and Growth
  Ministry Training

APPENDIX E

ROOMMATE RELATIONSHIPS

Part I: A Personal Bible Study

Many conflicts with our roommates/housemates result from our not observing proper scriptural guidelines on which to establish our relationships. This study will help you discover some Biblical principles for relating to one another.

Find a place where you can be alone and uninterrupted for about an hour in order to do the following Bible study. Pray that God will speak to your specific roommate situation through His Word.

Using the following worksheet, look up the scripture references and determine the general principle implied in each. Make applications of the general principles to your living situation. Be specific. Think about things like: What is my attitude now? What does it need to be? Who is affected and how? What am I going to do about it?

Verse	General principle implied	Application
Example: Mark 12:31-33	"Love others as yourself"	Means being selfless being as concerned about my roommate's wants and needs as my own. That's tough . . . only God can give me that perspective. Just to start I'm going to ask Jim and Mike if I can do their laundry for them next time I do mine.
Philippians 2: 1-8		
Hebrews 10:4		

Verse	General principle implied	Application
Galatians 6:1-3; 10		
Matthew 7:12		
Matthew 18:15		
Romans 13:10; 15:2		
2 Corinthians 2:10-11		
Proverbs 10:12		
Proverbs 17:9, 14		
Proverbs 19:11, 22		
Proverbs 22:9		

Proverbs 25:9-12		
Ephesians 4:15-16		
John 13:35		
John 15:5		

Conclusions:

Part II: Getting to Know Your Roommate

Many conflicts between roommates develop from a lack of understanding of each other's likes and dislikes, temperaments and habits. We are not always sure how to communicate when areas of conflict arise.

This questionnaire is designed to help you learn to communicate with your roommates in potential problem areas, and to help you establish communication with them. When you are able to come to mutual understandings, or to agree to disagree on some things, it is easier to appreciate and adjust to each other's differences. This will enhance a harmonious home.

Beginning with prayer, discuss the following questions with all of your roommates. This will be a special and rewarding time for you. Discuss each question thoroughly. Feel free to talk about other related areas as well. Be sure everyone is given an opportunity to comment on each question.

Jot down your thoughts about what you learn about your roommates and your planned action in response to this new knowledge.

Questions for Discussion	Thoughts and Planned Actions
1. Do you tend to be introspective or outgoing and aggressive?	

2. Do you like to spend a lot of time alone, or are you more comfortable if there are people around to talk to?	
3. Are you a patient person? If you are impatient, how does this manifest itself in your life? Do you keep it inside? Blow up? Or verbalize your feelings?	
4. If something bothers you, what do you do about it?	
5. If something bothers me about you, would you rather I subtly confront you with the situation or should I come right out and say it?	
6. What types of things irritate you? What are some of your pet peeves?	
7. If I notice that you seem to be upset about something, or hurting inside, how do you want me to respond?	
8. Do you like things fairly structured and organized, or do you generally like things unplanned and spontaneous?	
9. Do you like to spend a lot of time with your roommates in outside activities, i.e., church, parties, shopping, or would you rather do things on your own?	

Managing Our Home

This part of the questionnaire is designed to help you and your roommates discuss how to set up your household so that it is creative, efficient, and a home in which you and others feel comfortable. Happy living arrangements and a home where guests are welcome contribute toward a more fruitful ministry.

Again, use these questions as a basis for your prayerful discussion.

Questions for Discussion	Thoughts and Planned Actions
1. Do you have strong opinions about household management, or do you think you are quite flexible?	
2. Do we want to cook and eat individually or all together?	
3. Do we want to cook some meals	

together and some separately?	
4. If we cook together, talk about: cooking and shopping schedule, cooking budget, eating habits, schedule, clean up, guests, diets etc. Should the budget include special items of food that an individual wants, or should the persons buy those themselves?	
5. If we cook individually, talk about: cupboard and refrigerator space paying for common household items eating schedules	
6. How will we divide the household duties and how often will they be done?	
7. How will you feel toward me if I don't get my household job for the week done? Or if I leave my dishes stacked in the kitchen all day?	
8. How should we pay the bills for our home (electricity, gas, water, rent, telephone)?	
9. Do you have things, e.g., dishes, candles, cookware that you prefer to be used only on special occasions?	
10. Discuss phone policies: Does each have their own line or length of time on the phone? How or where are phone messages left? Whose name will the phone be under?	
11. How do we deal with a situation when someone has violated a household policy?	
12. Do you feel that we need to set a specific time to discuss household decisions and/or conflict areas?	
13. Are you a heavy or a light sleeper?	
14. What kinds of things keep you awake at night?	
15. Do you like to sleep late?	
16. Are you quiet or talkative in the morning?	
17. Do you like to stay up late?	

18. How much time do you need in the bathroom in the morning and evening?	
19. How often do you prefer to take a shower or a bath? In the morning or evening?	
20. Do you have a set routine in the morning? How can we work together so we can all be ready on time?	
21. What do you feel is an acceptable form of modesty with your room-mates?	
22. Do you feel that your bedroom is private? Should someone come in only if invited?	

Part III: Personal Habits

Questions for Discussion	Thoughts and Planned Actions
1. What do you feel is your greatest area of weakness in communicating?	
2. Do you think that people are usually sensitive to your personal needs and desires? Explain.	
3. Would you like to have a specific time of prayer and devotions together? When?	
4. Do you like to have parties? What kind?	
5. Should I expect to be included when your guests come over, or should I wait to be invited?	
6. Would it make you feel awkward or inconvenienced if my boyfriend/girl-friend were over a lot of the time? Why? How can we make it less awkward for you?	
7. How would you feel about discussing your dates with your roommates or having them share about the men or women in their lives?	
8. How would you feel if your room-mate wanted to entertain a guest alone in the living room? Do you think they should leave if they want to be alone?	

9. How do you feel about having overnight guests – male and female?	
10. Do you mind having things lying around or do you like everything to be picked up?	
11. What do you think about trying new methods of housekeeping and cooking?	
12. Do you have any strong opinions about how our home should be decorated?	
13. How should we go about decorating our home?	
14. How do we want to work out buying furniture, dishes, appliances or any other large items that are common to all of us?	
15. How do you feel about loaning your car or bike?	
16. How should we share car expenses if a roommate doesn't have a car?	
17. How do you feel about borrowing or loaning money?	
18. How do you feel about borrowing or loaning clothes or cosmetics?	
19. Do you mind if I read your books? Listen to your cds or cassettes?	
20. How much should we keep each other informed of our schedules?	
21. How warm or how cool do you like the temperature set in our home?	
22. What do you feel about use of TV, radio and recorders? (hours, type, volume etc.)	
23. How do you feel about having pets?	

Conclusions:

Part IV: HOW TO LIVE IN HARMONY WITH YOUR ROOMMATE(S)

The following are some thoughts and suggestions for relationship with your roommates. They cover seven areas of potential problems. Remember, problems are opportunities for us to trust God and grow in grace.

These few pages will not guarantee a perfect relationship with the ones God has chosen to live with, but they will prayerfully help in creating harmony so that God can use that person in your life.

Individualities: How to Appreciate Another's Differences

Don't squeeze your roommate into your mold.

Accept from the beginning that you are all different with different backgrounds. This will affect the way you view and do things. "Different" does not mean "wrong" – just different.

Allow for individuality while seeking to help sharpen one another in love for each other, in organization, use of time, good habits, etc.

Be graciously honest with each other. Discuss your likes and dislikes. Agree to disagree. No two people will ever agree on everything. Accept that in each other.

Be considerate of your roommate's desires, personal needs, etc. (For example, if she is a tidy housekeeper, keep your things picked up in the common areas.

Consideration: How to Demonstrate Love in a Practical Manner

Express appreciation! This is the best in-service training for marriage you will ever have.

Ask God to give you a genuine love and concern for your roommate.

Seek to serve one another by offering to run errands for each other, cover each other's household chores.

Eat at least one meal together daily. This is a great way to get to know one another.

Take time to listen to your roommate's interests, needs, problems.

Look for little ways to surprise each other.

Be aware of the other's need to be alone and be quiet.

Be considerate of your roommate when inviting friends over.

Take time to do fun things together.

Together, as a project, entertain people, students, other missionaries, church people, neighbors, and acquaintances, in your home. This builds closeness.

Communication: How to Create an Open Atmosphere

Practice a "roof off, walls down" policy. Develop an attitude of openness: "Nothing between us and God, Nothing between ourselves and other Christians."

Do not give the impression that you do not care or are not bothered about something when you really are. Share your disapproval "speaking the truth in love," after praying about it.

Do not ignore inconsistencies in your roommate's life. You are not being a friend when you do not help that person see him-/herself as others see them. Be careful not to "pounce" on every detail, but help each other in love, preferring one another. Take the "beam out of your own eye" first. (Matt. 5:7) There may be occasional conflicts and irritations that God will use to strengthen and humble us if we accept them in the right spirit. Don't be afraid of them.

When two people are not compatible no matter how hard they try, invite the help of a wise counselor.

Belongings: How to Deal with One Another's Personal Possessions

Be cautious about borrowing from other people. (Exodus 3:22; Deuteronomy 15:6; 28:12)

Respect one another's personal belongings. Do not assume all things are held in common; ask before borrowing.

Be prepared to replace or repair borrowed things that break or are damaged while you had them in your possession.

Neatness: How to Maintain a Comfortable Living Arrangement

Be tidy as an act of love for your roommate. A mess may not bother you, but don't force your roommate to live with it.

Make your bed before you leave the house; then half the room is already straightened up.

Clean up immediately after you cook.

Put away toilet articles right after you use them.

Pick up clothes and shoes.

When you are the one serving guests in the home, clean up the dishes, kitchen, etc., after them.

Dividing Responsibilities: How to Share the Workload

Establish a weekly house meeting to discuss duties, complaints, plans, etc. You may not think you need it, but time will come when you wish you had this established. Small things build into a mountain.

Sit down within the first several days of living together and plan, discussing likes and dislikes, dividing household duties, (make a chart), creating an atmosphere in which you are free to discuss problems as they arise.

Train yourself to see things that need doing and do them without being asked.

Spiritual Life: How to Maintain Spiritual Vitality in Your Relationship

Pray together daily. This makes even the most unbearable situation workable. Pray for each other daily. This draws you together in Christ and helps you love each other.

Have a weekly Bible study together with mutual sharing. You may want to have a brief daily devotional (3-4 minutes) at meals you eat together.

BIBLIOGRAPHY

Allen, Roland. *Missionary Methods St. Paul's of Ours?* Grand Rapids: Eerdmans, 1995. (First published 1912).

Bacon, Daniel W. *From Faith to Faith: The Influence of Hudson Taylor on the Faith Missions Movement.* (D Miss Deerfield, 1983), Singapore, 1984.

Barrett, David B. "Annual Statistical Table on Global Mission: 1996." *International Bulletin of Missionary Research,* January, 1996.

Beals, A. and Hoijer, H. *An Introduction to Anthropology.* New York: Macmillian, 1959.

Beck, James R. *Dorothy Carey, the Tragic and Untold Story of Mrs. William Carey.* Grand Rapids: Baker, 1992.

Bilezikian, Gilbert. *Beyond Sex Roles.* Grand Rapids: Baker, 1985.

Bonhoeffer, Dietrich. *Sanctorum Communio.* Munich: Kaiser, 1954. (Dissertation, 1930).

Bonhoeffer, Dietrich. *Widerstand und Ergebung.* Hamburg: Siebenstern, 1951.

Bonhoeffer, Dietrich. *The Cost of Discipleship,* (*Nachfolge.* Munich: Kaiser, 1937, trans. R.H. Fuller). New York: Macmillian, 1963.

Bonk, Jonathan J. "Missions and Mammon: Six Theses." *International Bulletin of Missionary Research,* October, 1989.

Bonk, Jonathan J. *Missions and Money.* Maryknoll: Orbis, 1991.

Booth, Catherine. "Female Ministry: Woman's Right to Preach the Gospel." New York: The Salvation Army Supplies, 1975 (First printed, London, 1859).

Bosch, David J. *Transforming Mission: Paradigm Shifts in Theology of Mission.* Maryknoll: Orbis, 1991.

Brewster, Elizabeth and Brewster, Thomas. "Dynamic Equivalence . . . To Communicate Effectively." Arrowhead Springs, CA: Lectures at Agape International Training, 1974.

Brewster, Elizabeth and Brewster, Thomas. *Language Acquisition Made Practical.* Colorado Springs: Lingua House, 1976.

Brewster, Elizabeth and Brewster, Thomas. *Bonding and the Missionary Task.* Dallas: Lingua House, 1982.

Bruce, F.F. *The Pauline Circle.* Grand Rapids: Eerdmans, 1985.

Buber, Martin. *Begegnung, Autobiographische Fragmente.* Gerlingen: Lambert Schneider, n.d.

Bühlmann, Walbert. *The Search for God.* Maryknoll: Orbis, 1980.

Bühlmann, Walbert. *God's Chosen Peoples.* Maryknoll: Orbis, 1982.

Burgess, Alan. *Daylight Must Come, the Story of Dr. Helen Roseveare.* London: Pan Books, 1975.

Butler, Brian. "Tensions in an International Mission." *Evangelical Missions Quarterly,* October, 1993.

Carr, Karen. "Trauma and Post-traumatic Stress Disorder Among Missionaries." *Evangelical Missions Quarterly,* July, 1994.

Castro, Emilio. *Sent Free: Mission and Unity in the Perspective of the Kingdom.* Grand Rapids: Eerdmans, 1985.

Chester, Raymond M. "Stress on Missionary Families Living in Other Cultures." K. and M. O'Donnell, eds. *Helping Missionaries Grow.* Pasadena: William Carey Library, 1988.

Chew, Jim. *When You Cross Cultures.* Singapore: The Navigators.

Clinebell, Howard J., Jr. *Growth Counseling Hope-Centered Methods for Actualizing Human Wholeness.* Nashville: Abingdon, 1979.

Cloud, Henry and Townsend, John. *Boundaries.* Grand Rapids: Zondervan, 1992.

Conn, Harvie M. *Eternal Word and Changing Worlds.* Grand Rapids: Zondervan, 1983.

Conrad, Christa. "Die ledige Missionarin und ihr Dienst." *Evangelikale Missiologie,* 2/1992.

Costas, Orlando E. *Christ outside the Gate.* Maryknoll: Orbis, 1982.

Dammann, E. "Sprache." Müller, Karl and Sundermeier, Theo, eds. *Lexikon Missionarische Grundbegriffe.* Berlin: Dietrich Reimer, 1987.

Danielson, Edward. *Missionary Kid.* Pasadena: William Carey Library, 1984.

Dayton, Edward R. and Fraser, David A. *Planning Strategies for World Evangelization.* Grand Rapids: Eerdmans, 1980.

Dayton, Edward R. and Wilson, Samuel, ed. *The Future of World Evangelization.* Monrovia: MARC, 1984.

Demarest, Bruce. "The Quest for God in African Ways." *Evangelical Missions Quarterly,* April, 1982.

Elbers, Veronika. "Die Dritte Welt Missionare - Ein Interview mit Lotje Pelealu, Indonesische Missionsgesellschaft." *Evangelikale Missiologie,* 2/1992.

Elbers, Veronika. "Protestantische Missionare aus Indonesien." (ThD Heverlee/Leuven, Belgium, 1995) Unpublished.

Elmer, Duane. *Cross-Cultural Conflict.* Downers Grove: InterVarsity, 1993.

Fiedler, Klaus. "Wo sind die 20 000? - Eine kritische Analyse von Lawrence E. Keyes' Konzept der 'transkulturellen Drittweltmissionare' und der ihm zugrundeliegenden Daten." *Evangelikale Missiologie* 3/1989.

Fiedler, Klaus. *Ganz auf Vertrauen: Geschichte und Kirchenverständnis der Glaubensmission.* Giessen/Basel: Brunnen, 1992.

Fiedler, Klaus. *Christentum und afrikanische Kultur: Konservative deutsche Missionare in Tanzania, 1900 bis 1940.* Bonn: Verlag für Kultur und Wissenschaft, 1993. (*Christianity and African Culture: Conservative German Protestant Missionaries in Tanzania, 1900-1940.* Leiden, New York, Köln: Brill, 1996)

Foyle, Marjory F. *Honourably Wounded.* Bromley, Kent: MARC Europe, 1987. (Also published under the name of: *Overcoming Missionary Stress,* Wheaton: EMIS.)

Flournoy, Richard; Hawkins, Don; Meier, Paul and Minirth, Frank. *How to Beat Burnout.* Chicago: Moody, 1986.

Forman, Charles W. "The Study of Pacific Island Christianity." *International Bulletin of Missionary Research,* July, 1994.

Forster, Roger T. and Marsten, V. Paul. *God's Strategy in Human History.* Wheaton: Tyndale, 1973.

Foster, Richard J. *Money, Sex and Power: The Challenge of a Disciplined Life.* San Francisco: Harper and Row, 1985.

Freytag, Walter ed. *Theologische Besinnung. Mission zwischen Gestern und Morgen.* Stuttgart: Evangelischer Missionsverlag, 1952.

Gates, Bill. *Der Weg nach Vorn.* Hamburg: Hoffmann und Campe, 1995.

Gensichen, Hans-Werner. *Glaube für die Welt: Theologische Aspekte der Mission.* Gütersloh: Gerd Mohn, 1971.

Glaser, Arthur and McGavran, Donald A. *Contemporary Theologies of Mission.* Grand Rapids: Baker, 1983.

Goring, Paul. *The Effective Missionary Communicator.* Wheaton: Billy Graham Center, 1991.

Greenway, Roger S. "Eighteen Barrels and Two Big Crates." *Evangelical Missions Quarterly,* April, 1992.

Gundry, Patricia. *Woman Be Free!* Grand Rapids: Zondervan, 1977.

Gundry, Patricia. *Neither Slave nor Free.* San Francisco: Harper and Row, 1987.

Hall, Edward T. *The Silent Language.* Greenwich: Fawcett, 1985.

Hamm, Peter. "Breaking the Power Habit: Imperatives for Multinational Mission." *Evangelical Missions Quarterly,* July, 1983.

Harrison, Myron S. *Developing Multinational Teams.* Singapore: Overseas Missionary Fellowship, 1984.

Hesselgrave, David J. *Communicating Christ Cross-Culturally.* Grand Rapids: Zondervan, 1978.

Hesselgrave, David J. *Counseling Cross-Culturally.* Grand Rapids: Baker, 1984.

Hiebert, Paul G. *Cultural Anthropology.* Philadelphia: Lippincott, 1976.

Hiebert, Paul G. *Anthropological Insights for Missionaries.* Grand Rapids: Baker, 1985.

Hiebert, Paul G. "Critical Contextualization." *Missiology XII.*

Hiebert, Paul G. "Introduction: Mission and Anthropology." *Readings in Missionary Anthropology II.* Smalley, William A., ed. Pasadena: William Carey Library, 1978.

Hill, Harriet. "Incarnational Ministry: a Critical Examination." *Evangelical Missions Quarterly,* April, 1990.

Hill, Harriet. "Lifting the Fog on Incarnational Ministry." *Evangelical Missions Quarterly,* July, 1993.

Holy Bible. The New International Version: Inclusive Language Edition. London: Hodder & Stoughton, 1998.

Hsu, Francis L.K. *Psychological Anthropology.* Homewood, IL: Dorsey, 1961.

Jennings, George J. "American Missionary Candidates - Out of These Worlds." *Missiology,* April, 1993.

Johnson, David. *Reaching Out: Interpersonal Effectiveness and Self-Actualization.* Englewood Cliffs: Prentice-Hall, 1972.

Johnston, LeRoy. "Core Issues in Missionary Life." *Missionary Care.* O'Donnell, Kelly, ed. Pasadena: William Carey Library, 1992.

Josuttis, Manfred. *Petrus, die Kirche und die verdammte Macht.* Stuttgart: Kreuz , 1993.

Kähler, Martin. *Schriften zur Christologie und Mission.* Munich: Kaiser, 1971.

Kelly, D. P. *Destroying the Barriers.* Pasadena: William Carey Library, 1982.

Kennedy, Alastair. "The Other Side of Africa: How Churches and Missions are Grappling with Issues." *Pulse,* Feb. 14, 1986

Keyes, Lawrence E. *The Last Age of Missions.* Pasadena: William Carey Library, 1978.

Keyes, Lawrence E. "Third World Missionaries: the More and Better." *Evangelical Missions Quarterly,* October, 1982.

Keyes, Larry E. and Larry D. Pate. "Two-Thirds World Missions: The Next 100 Years." *Missiology,* Vol. 21.

Kinsler, F. Ross. *The Extension Movement in Theological Education.* Pasadena: William Carey Library, 1978.

Kobobel, Janet, *But Can She Type?* Downers Grove: InterVarsity, 1986.

Kohls, L. Robert. *Survival Kit for Overseas Living.* Chicago: Intercultural Network/System, 1979.

Kraemer, Hendrik. *The Christian Witness in a Non-Christian World.* London: Edinburgh House, 1938.

Kraft, Charles H. *Christianity and Culture.* Maryknoll: Orbis, 1979.

Kraft, Charles H. *Communicating the Gospel God's Way.* Pasadena: William Carey Library, 1985.

Kraft, Charles H. and Wisley, Tom N. *Readings in Dynamic Indigeneity.* Pasadena: William Carey Library, 1979.

Ladipo, Yemi. "Qualifications for Long Term Missionary Service in Africa." unpublished. n.d.

LaHaye, Tim. *Transformed Temperaments.* Wheaton: Tyndale, 1971.

Lang, Joseph R. and Motte, Mary, eds. *Mission in Dialogue.* Maryknoll: Orbis, 1982.

Langley, Myrtle. *Equal Woman.* Hants, UK: Marshall Morgan and Scott, 1983.

Larson, Donald N. "The Viable Missionary: Learner, Trader, Storyteller" *Missiology.* Vol 6, No. 2., April, 1978.

Lausanne "Manila Manifesto," *Proclaiming Christ Until He Comes.* Minneapolis: Worldwide, 1990.

LeBar, Lois E. *Focus on People in Church Education.* Westwood: Revell, 1968.

Lee, Eun Moo. "West and East Must Get Along - a Korean Missionary Speaks Out." *Evangelical Missions Quarterly,* July, 1983.

Leeuven, Mary Stewart Van. *Gender and Grace.* Downers Grove: InterVarsity, 1990.

Lehtinen, Kalevi. "Through the Prism." Unpublished. n.d.

Lewis, C. S. *Screwtape Letters.* Grand Rapids: Baker, 1969.

Liefeld, Walter L. and Tucker, Ruth A. *Daughters of the Church.* Grand Rapids: Zondervan, 1987.

Lingenfelter, Sherwood G. and Mayers, Marvin K. *Ministering Cross-Culturally.* Grand Rapids: Baker, 1986.

Lochman, Jan Milic und Moltmann, Jürgen. *Gottes Recht und Menschenrechte.* Neukirchener, 1976.

Loewen, Jacob A. "Roles: Relating to an Alien Social Structure." *Missiology.* Vol. IV, No. 2, April, 1976.

Luzbetak, Louis J. *The Church and Cultures.* Maryknoll: Orbis, 1988.

McCann, Dennis P. *Christian Realism and Liberation Theology: Practical Theologies in Creative Conflict.* Maryknoll: Orbis, 1981.

McDowell, Josh. *His Image My Image.* San Bernardino: Here's Life, 1984.

McDowell, Josh and Stewart, Don. *Handbook of Today's Religions.* San Bernardino: Here's Life, 1983.

McGavran, Donald A. *The Bridges of God.* New York: Friendship, 1955.

McKinney, Lois. "Why Renewal is Needed in Theological Education." *Evangelical Missions Quarterly,* April, 1982.

McQuilkin, Robertson. "Six Inflamatory Questions - Part 2." *Evangelical Missions Quarterly.* Vol. 30. No. 3.

Madeira, Eugene. "Roots of Bad Feelings: What the Locals Say." *Evangelical Missions Quarterly,* April, 1983.

Malcolm, Kari Torjesen. *Women at the Crossroads: A Path beyond Feminism and Traditionalism.* Downers Grove: InterVarsity, 1982.

Maslach, Christina. *Burnout-The Cost of Caring.* Englewood: Prentice Hall, 1982.

Maslow, Abraham H. *Motivation and Personality.* New York: Harper and Row, 1970.

Mayers, Marvin K. *Christianity Confronts Culture.* Grand Rapids: Zondervan, 1974.

Mead, Margaret. *Anthropology: A Human Science.* Princeton: Van Nostrand, 1964.

Mickelson, Alvera, ed. *Women, Authority and the Bible.* Downers Grove: InterVarsity, 1986.

Moltmann, Jürgen. *The Crucified God.* SCM. 1974. Harper Collins, 1991. Minneapolis: Fortress, 1993.

Moran, Robert. *International Management.* March 1988.

Morgan, June. Unpublished lectures 1983.

Müller, Karl and Sundermeier, Theo, ed. *Lexikon Missionstheologische Begriffe.* Berlin: Dietrich Reimer, 1987.

Müller, Klaus. "Elenktik: Gewissen im Kontext." Kasdorf, Müller, eds. *Festschrift zum 80. Geburtstag von George W. Peters.* Lahr: Johannis VLM, 1988.

Myers, Isabel and Maccaulley, Mary. *A Guide to the Development and Use of the Myers-Briggs Type Indicator.* Palo Alto: Counseling Psychologists Press, 1985.

Nelson, Martin. *Readings in Third World Missions.* Pasadena: William Carey Library, 1976.

Newbigin, Lesslie. *The Gospel in a Pluralist Society*. Grand Rapids: Eerdmans, 1989

Newbigin, Lesslie. *A Word in Season: Perspectives on Christian World Missions*. Grand Rapids: Eerdmans, 1994.

Nicholls, Bruce J. *Contextualization: A Theology of Gospel and Culture*. Downers Grove: InterVarsity, 1979.

Nida, Eugene A. *Customs and Culture*. New York: Harper and Row, 1954.

Nida, Eugene A. *Message and Mission*. Pasadena: William Carey Library, 1960.

Nida, Eugene, A. *Religion Across Cultures*. Pasadena: William Carey Library, 1968.

Niebuhr, H. Richard. *Christ and Culture*. N.Y.: Harper and Row, 1951.

O'Donnell, Kelly, ed. *Missionary Care: Counting the Cost for World Evangelism*. Pasadena: William Carey Library, 1992.

Ornsby, Ron. "How to be Downwardly Mobile." *Evangelical Missions Quarterly,* October, 1993.

Palmer, Donald. *Managing Conflict Creatively: A Guide for Missionaries and Christian Workers*. Pasadena: William Carey Library, 1990.

Pobee, John S. "Christian Mission Towards the Third Millennium: The Gospel of Hope." Missions Studies, IAMS, Vol. V-1, 1988.

Poland, Larry. "Serve or Minister?" in *Expressions,* Vol., 4, No. 8, 1987.

Pluedemann, James E. "Beyond Independence to Responsible Maturity." *Evangelical Missions Quarterly,* January, 1983.

Poston, Larry. "Should the West Stop Sending Missionaries?" *Evangelical Missions Quarterly,* January, 1992.

Priest, Robert J. "Missionary Elenctics: Conscience and Culture." *Missiology.* Vol. XXII. No. 3, July, 1994.

Ramachandra, Vinoth. "The Honor of Listening: Indispensable for Missionaries." *Evangelical Missions Quarterly,* October, 1994.

Reapsome, Jim. "Does Short-term Expedience Spell Long-term Disaster?" *Evangelical Missions Quarterly,* April, 1982.

Reapsome, Jim. "Recruiting: the Right Way and the Wrong Way: Interview with George Verwer." *Evangelical Missions Quarterly,* April, 1983.

Reapsome, Jim. "Of Trials and Towels: the Causes and Cure of Spiritual Imperialism." *Evangelical Missions Quarterly,* July, 1983.

Reapsome, Jim. "He Got a Second Chance: Interview with Wilbert H. Norton." *Evangelical Missions Quarterly,* April, 1984.

Reed, Lyman E. *Preparing Missionaries for Inter-Cultural Communication*. Pasadena: William Carey Library, 1985.

Regez, Peter. "We Need People With a Heart to Serve: An Interview with Mukengeshey." *Agape Impressions*, Auggen, Germany 1989.

Reichenbach, Bruce R. "The Captivity of Third World Churches." *Evangelical Missions Quarterly,* July, 1982.

Rennstich, Karl W. *Mission und Wirtschaftliche Entwicklung*. München: Kaiser, 1978.

Rennstich, Karl W. *Handwerker-Theologen und Industrie-Brüder als Botschafter des Friedens*. Stuttgart: Evangelischer Missionsverlag, 1985.

Rennstich, Karl W. *Die zwei Symbole des Kreuzes: Handel und Mission in China und Südostasien.* Stuttgart: Quell, 1988.

Rennstich, Karl W. *Korruption: Eine Herausforderung für Gesellschaft und Kirche.* Stuttgart: Quell, 1990.

Rennstich, Karl W. "Mission und Geld. Einführungsvortrag zum Missionstheologischen Symposium Mission und Geld." Unpublished, April 18, 1995.

Rennstich, Karl W. "Vom Ältestenamt über Ordination und Priesteramt zur Theologie des Laientums." Unpublished, 1996.

Rennstich, Karl W. "Geld and Macht in ökumenischen Beziehungen." Unpublished, 1996.

Rennstich, Karl W. "Mission und Kulturen" in *Der ferne Nächste: Bilder der Mission und Mission der Bilder 1860 -1920.* Ludwigsburg: Katalog zur Ausstellung im Landeskirchlichen Museum, 25. May - 10. Nov. 1996.

Rennstich, Karl W. "Missionarische Ethik." Unpulbished, 1996

Rennstich, Karl W. "Streit und Konflikte." Unpublished, 1996.

Rennstich, Karl W. "Mission nach dem Neuen Testament." Unpublished, n.d.

Rennstich, Karl W. "Paulus als Geschäftsmann." Unpublished. n.d.

Rennstich, Karl W. "Die soziale Verantwortung der Christen heute." Unpublished, n.d.

Richardson, Don. *Peace Child.* Ventura: Regal, 1974.

Richardson, Don. *Eternity in Their Hearts.* Ventura: Regal, 1981.

Roembke, Lianne. *International Representatives In-Field Training,* Unpublished 1981.

Roembke, Lianne. "Die Frau aus biblischer Perspektive." Unpublished, 1987.

Roembke, Lianne. "Using the N/O/P/E Cycle in Developing Staff Training." Unpublished. n.d.

Roembke, Lianne. "Interpersonal Relationships and Problem Solving." Unpublished. n.d.

Roseveare, Helen. *He Gave Us a Valley.* Leicester: InterVarsity, 1976.

Roundhill, Ken S. "The Two Shall Become One." *Evangelical Missions Quarterly,* July, 1983.

Rowen, Samuel. "Doing Mission." *Evangelical Missions Quaterly,* July, 1983.

Sauer, Anna-Maria. "Die 'soziale Gerechtigkeit' in der Lausanner Bewegung 1974-1989." (Akzessarbeit im Fach Ethik für die Universität Basel, 11. Dec. 1992.)

Schattschneider, David A. "Pioneers in Missions: Zinzendorf and the Moravians." *International Bulletin of Missionary Research,* Vol. 8, No. 2.

Schubert, Esther. "Current Issues in Screening and Selection." *Missionary Care.* Pasadena: William Carey Library, 1992.

Senior, Donald and Stuhlmueller, Carroll. *Biblical Foundations for Mission.* Maryknoll: Orbis.

Severn, Frank M. "The Critical Context of Today's World Mission." *Evangelical Missions Quarterly,* April, 1992.

Smalley, William A. "Respect and Ethnocentrism." Smalley, William, ed. *Readings in Missionary Anthropology II.* Pasadena: William Carey Library, 1978.

Smalley, William A., "Missionary Language Learning in a World Hierarchy." *Missiology*, October, 1994.

Spencer, Aída Besançon. *Beyond the Curse: Women Called to Ministry*. Nashville: Thomas Nelson, 1985.

Spickelmeier, Jim. "Invest in Only the Best." *Evangelical Missions Quarterly*, April, 1984.

Stafford, Tim. *The Friendship Gap*. Downers Grove: InterVarsity, 1984.

Steuernagel, Valdir Raul. "The Theology of Mission in its Relation to Social Responsibility within the Lausanne Movement." (Chicago: ThD, 1988.)

Stott, John R.W. *Christian Mission in the Modern World*. London: Falcon, 1975.

Stott, John R.W. *The Cross of Christ*. Leicester: InterVarsity, 1986.

Stott, John R.W. *The Contemporary Christian*. Leicester: InterVarsity, 1992.

Strunk, Reiner. *Vertrauen: Grundzüge einer Theologie des Gemeindeaufbaus*. Stuttgart: Quell, 1985.

Taylor, Robert B. *Introduction to Cultural Anthropology*. Boston: Allyn and Bacon, 1973.

Taylor, William. *International Missionary Training: A Global Perspective*. Grand Rapids: Baker, 1991.

Thompson, Phyllis. *A Transparent Woman: The Compelling Story of Gladys Aylward*. Grand Rapids: Zondervan, 1971.

Tournier, Paul. *The Gift of Feeling*. London:SCM, 1982.

Troutman, Charles. "Ten Commandments for Nationals from the Standpoint of Missionaries." *Evangelical Missions Quarterly*, April, 1982.

Troutman, Charles. "Steps to Mature Servanthood Overseas." *Evangelical Missions Quarterly*, January, 1983.

Tucker, Ruth A. and Rennstich, Karl, ed. *Bis an die Enden der Erde*. Metzingen: Franz, 1996.

Verkuyl, Johannes. *Contemporary Missiology*. Grand Rapids: Eerdmans, 1978. (translated from the Dutch edition, 1975)

Verwer, George. "Recruiting: the Right Way and the Wrong Way." An Interview by Jim Reapsome. *Evangelical Missions Quarterly*, April, 1983.

Vine, W.E. *An Expository Dictionary of New Testament Words*. Old Tappan: Revell, 1966.

Wagner, C. Peter. *On the Crest of the Wave*. Ventura: Regal, 1983.

Wagner, Maurice. *The Sensation of Being Somebody*. Grand Rapids: Zondervan, 1975.

Wagner, William Lyle. *North American Protestant Missionaries in Western Europe: A Critical Appraisal*. Bonn: Verlag für Kultur und Wissenschaft, 1993.

Walz, Brad. "The Hard Road to Missions Vision in National Churches." *Evangelical Missions Quarterly*, October, 1994.

Ward, Ted. *Living Overseas*. New York: Free Press, 1984.

Whiteman, Darrell L. "Effective Communication of the Gospel Amid Cultural Diversity" *Evangelical Missions Quarterly*, July, 1984.

Wietzke, Joachim. "Introduction." *Missions Studies*. International Association of Missions Studies, Vol. V-1, 1988.

Williams, Kenneth. "A Model for Mutual Care in Missions." *Missionary Care*. Pasadena: William Carey Library, 1992.

Williamson, Mabel. *Have We No Rights?* Chicago: Moody, 1957.

The Willowbank Report of the Lausanne Committee for World Evangelization 1978. Winter, Ralph D. and Hawthorne, Steven C., eds. *Perspectives on the World Christian Movement*. Pasadena: William Carey Library, 1981.

Winter, Ralph D. and Hawthorne, Steven C., eds. *Perspectives on the World Christian Movement*. Pasadena: William Carey Library, 1981.

World Council of Churches. "Mission and Evangelism - An Ecumenical Affirmation." *International Bulletin of Missionary Research*, April, 1983.

G

H

M

N

O

P

T

Y

Z

About the author:

Dr. Lianne Roembke is an instructor in intercultural studies and an educational and member care consultant. She has served with Campus Crusade for Christ since 1970, at first in the USA, her home country, and since 1975 in Germany. She has lived in Magdeburg since the Fall of the Berlin Wall.

Presently Dr. Roembke offers seminars and workshops for mission leaders, HR personnel, workers, psychologists and therapists on the topic: "*The New Reality: Working in Multicultural Teams and Partnerships*". She is also a speaker and consultant for various mission agencies and international churches worldwide. As guest professor she offers block courses at Columbia International University/Korntal Campus, Fuller School of World Missions and Wheaton Graduate School of Theology.

For more information about her courses, contact the university of interest mentioned above.
For information about times and locations about various seminars and workshops, contact:
Middle East Member Care Team - www.memct.org
tim@memct

For seminars in German contact: smf@aem.de

For other workshop or consultation inquiries contact:
LRoembke@aol.com